Musings gives the reader an enthralling less[...] history, culture, traditions, philosophy, religi[...] His musings reflect a brilliant and intellectual mind, always curious and inquisitive. This is the George Yeo I know and admired as a colleague in the Singapore Armed Forces, a boss in the Ministry of Foreign Affairs and a good friend. A man destined for bigger things. Though not written as a biography, it gives a fascinating insight into his life, especially his Teochew identity and his strong attachment to his ancestral home in China. This book has something for everyone and is a must-read for every Singaporean.

Winston Choo
Former Chief of Defence Force and Diplomat

George Yeo is a distinguished public figure of international stature. He is a widely respected thinker with a deep understanding of history. He has a great zest for life. This monumental work is a treasure trove. He shares the rich experiences of his life's journey and discusses a wide range of matters relating to our times and the human condition. His observations are wise and perceptive. His insights are profound and illuminating. Readers will find *Musings* thought provoking and enriching and will learn a great deal from it.

The Honourable **Andrew Li Kwok-nang**
First Chief Justice of the Hong Kong SAR of the
People's Republic of China

George Yeo is widely read, widely travelled and widely admired, as you will find from this book. I have met few people like him who live and enjoy every moment of life with unflagging intellectual curiosity and interest. His abiding love for China, because of his roots, is understandable but his love affair with India led me to remark once that in his previous birth he must have been an Indian!

P Chidambaram
Member of Parliament, Former Finance Minister of India

George Yeo writes from both the head and the heart. He is sympathetic with human vulnerability but also champions what the human spirit can achieve. I have known George since I was the Foreign Minister of the Republic of Korea and the Secretary General of the UN and seen how he has always tried to bring East and West together. His *"Musings"* are those of a cultural envoy and a peacemaker.

Ban Ki-moon
Former United Nations Secretary-General

George Yeo is brilliant. Singaporeans know this. Now, through this delicate mingling of personal stories, insightful anecdotes and deep historical and philosophical reflections, George Yeo allows the soul of Singapore to shine through in these pages. The exceptional economic success story of Singapore is well known. George Yeo has done his fellow Singaporeans and the world a great service by sharing this extraordinary rich Singapore soul. Like Lee Kuan Yew's memoirs, these musings will be read and reflected on for generations. An absolute must read. And, amazingly, a very easy read, accessible to all.

Kishore Mahbubani
Distinguished Fellow at the Asia Research Institute,
National University of Singapore, author of *Has China Won?*

By sharing intimate thoughts about his world, George Yeo shows us how plural a "Singaporean" can be. He relates every connection in life that he finds memorable — whether at work, at home, or at play — and a complex diversity shines through. The simple strokes he makes on this canvas illustrate an exceptional Chinese Singaporean as but one intriguing part of a multi-coloured national mural. Reading his musings reminds us how much more there is to tell about this new island state.

Wang Gungwu
University Professor

We live in a complex world and a turbulent era. Mere analyses do not seem to offer us much certainty. We need wisdom that is grounded in real-world experience. George Yeo's diverse Musings are woven into a masterpiece of insights so relevant to our world today. Myriad contradictions — in cultures, identities, history and realities — are treated with sensitivity and thoughtfulness. What one gains from the series are not references and models, but a deep sense of understanding that would be very useful when we navigate our unpredictable future.

Eric Li
Shanghai Venture Capitalist and Political Scientist

A vivid remembrance by a visionary statesman of the search for his Chinese heritage and his impassioned exploration of Asian connections that bind Southeast Asia with both South and East Asia. George Yeo's evocative *Musings* provide an intellectual foundation and a moral compass for politics in our time, showing how scholars and statesmen can celebrate diversity and strive together for an Asian renaissance.

Sugata Bose
Gardiner Professor of Oceanic History and Affairs,
Harvard University

Musings is an easy, entertaining, and yet educational book. Especially for people like myself who live in the generally homogeneous society of mainland China, Singapore's diversity, as richly presented by George Yeo, serves as an epitome of mankind. For students of international affairs, George Yeo in this pictorial volume teaches us how to integrate strategic vision, intercultural knowledge, and diplomatic skills to contribute to his own country and indeed the whole world.

Wang Jisi
President, Institute of International and Strategic Studies,
Peking University

George Yeo's beautifully written memoir is both highly informative about the world (not least about India and Singapore) and fun to read. Yeo's variety of experiences as a military officer, leading statesman and public thinker are all striking, but in addition he shows an exceptional ability to recount past events entertainingly and also explain why the recounted events may be important.

One of the intellectual developments on which Yeo throws exceptional light concerns the attempted revival of the oldest university in the world, Nalanda, established under Buddhist leadership in the fifth century.

Yeo was, from the beginning of the efforts in reviving Nalanda, a member of the mentor group and played a powerful role. Yeo's account of the political events which led to his resignation as second Chancellor cannot be read without a sad realization of what India lost as a result.

Amartya Sen
Thomas W. Lamont University Professor at Harvard University

SERIES ONE

GEORGE YEO

Musings

with

Woon Tai Ho

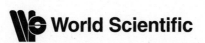
World Scientific

NEW JERSEY · LONDON · SINGAPORE · BEIJING · SHANGHAI · HONG KONG · TAIPEI · CHENNAI · TOKYO

Published by

World Scientific Publishing Co. Pte. Ltd.

5 Toh Tuck Link, Singapore 596224

USA office: 27 Warren Street, Suite 401-402, Hackensack, NJ 07601

UK office: 57 Shelton Street, Covent Garden, London WC2H 9HE

British Library Cataloguing-in-Publication Data
A catalogue record for this book is available from the British Library.

GEORGE YEO: MUSINGS
Series One

ISBN 978-981-125-969-2 (hardcover)
ISBN 978-981-126-128-2 (paperback)
ISBN 978-981-125-970-8 (ebook for institutions)
ISBN 978-981-125-971-5 (ebook for individuals)

For any available supplementary material, please visit
https://www.worldscientific.com/worldscibooks/10.1142/12931#t=suppl

Editorial Team:
Keith Yap

World Scientific:
Chua Hong Koon, Jimmy Low, Nicole Ong, Lai Ann

Printed in Singapore

Series One is dedicated to the memory of:

My parents
Yeo Eng Song *and* Kan Lee Hoon

My eldest brother
Joseph Yeo Han Pio

My only sister
Nellie Yeo Seow Eng

My third auntie
Polly Yeo Seow Gek

Foreword

In March 2021, Woon Tai Ho suggested a series of interviews with me which could be compiled into a book. He had discussed the idea with Chua Hong Koon of World Scientific. As it seemed like a project which would not require too much effort, I agreed. I knew Tai Ho from my days as Minister for Information and the Arts and thought well of him. He was then Head of News and Current Affairs for the Television Corporation of Singapore, the precursor to MediaCorp. Separately, Keith Yap, a graduate from Yale-NUS College and the Lee Kuan Yew School of Public Policy, emailed me in April recommending that I create a website to make my speeches and writings more accessible to young Singaporeans and offering his assistance. I put him in touch with Tai Ho, who agreed that Keith could help us as a research assistant for the book project. He ended up doing much more than that.

I found my thoughts too scattered during the first few interviews and decided to write down what I intended to say before each interview, which took 10 to 12 hours each time. For six months, we met every Monday for an interview of about two hours. The book grew and took shape gradually. We then decided that it should be broken up into three parts as putting all the musings into one volume would make it too heavy. After the interviews were concluded, Hong Koon went through the draft chapters and felt they were too long. He recommended I break them up into smaller ones. This involved considerable re-writing. For each series, I had to look for old pictures which was time-consuming. Some were in hard copies scattered in different boxes. Others were buried deep in old computers. As I always took care to have the content of each old computer nested in a new one, digging out old photographs was laborious and a bit of a treasure hunt. Choosing the photographs to include was itself an exercise which involved much mental and nervous energy. I also sought the help of a few friends. We had access to photographs from the Singapore Press Holdings (SPH) archives since *Lianhe Zaobao*, which is part of the SPH Group, is responsible for producing the Chinese version of *Musings*.

Musings is split into three series. They do not constitute a biography or memoir. There is no clear structure. I have no theory to propound. There is history, but not from the perspective of a historian. There are recurrent themes, but only tentative conclusions. The photographs are integral, but not essential to *Musings*. The publisher thought there were too many at first, but relented when I said that he should look at them like pictures in a scrapbook. These are not pictures you find in a textbook or a history book. I hope they make reading easier and more interesting, and are not a distraction. For me, they evoke emotions.

If I had known at the beginning the amount of time and work involved in putting together these musings and the accompanying pictures, I would surely not have embarked on this journey. But that, I suppose, is life. Life's journey is never smooth. One needs faith. Innocence and ignorance also help. Covid-19 helped too as I could not travel and was forced to spend much time at home. Tai Ho and Keith were encouraging and constructive. They were fellow travellers who kept my spirit up, for which I am most grateful. I thank Hong Koon and his colleagues in World Scientific, Nicole Ong, Lai Ann and Jimmy Low, for their assistance, patience and understanding.

George Yeo

Acknowledgements

I am grateful to the following individuals for running through my drafts and making helpful suggestions — Kishore Mahbubani, Adithya Venkatadri Hulagadri, K. Kesavapany, Wang Gungwu, Gopa Sabharwal, Umej Bhatia, Vanu Gopala Menon, Anandakumar Chinnaiya, Tansen Sen, Choo Lian Liang, Lee Huay Leng, Lim Jim Koon, Chin Harn Tong, Tan Siah Kwee, Jacky Foo, Foo Teow Lee, Chin Siat-Yoon, Raymond Mak, Gary Wong, Ker Sin Tze, Ervin Yeo, Ken Siah, Lien We King, Martino Tan and Terence Ho.

And to Bill Chua, Michael Lim, Kishore Mahbubani, Edmund Chin, Quek Swee Kuan, Seah Kia Ger, Mun Chor Seng, Singapore Press Holdings and National Archives Singapore for supplying some of the photographs.

Contents

Introduction

A former colleague once whispered in my ear, "I can listen to George Yeo all day." We were attending one of George Yeo's monthly lunch meetings when he was the Minister of Information and the Arts. I was the Head of News and Current Affairs back in the days of Television Corporation of Singapore. The colleague echoed my feeling and probably the feelings of all the other editors from the various media platforms. To engage in a discourse with the minister was to enter into the vastness of an intellectual mind, a mind that was, and is, relentlessly curious, and one that is interested in all aspects of the human condition, from the most mundane to the highly spiritual.

When I left MediaCorp, and when he retired from politics, we kept in touch over the years; we even met up in Yangon for a meal while I was running a TV channel there. He bought me a welcome-back lunch when I ended my stint in Yangon, and I broached the idea of a book, in the form of a conversation. That was the beginning of what eventually became *Musings*. For a good part of 2021, research assistant Keith Yap and I spent two to three-hour sessions with him every Monday and mused over a wide range of topics. They were usually followed by lunch. Those Monday sessions harked back to the days of the Ministry of Information and the Arts lunch meetings, inspiring, immersive, vivid, even picturesque, because of his visual language.

The title, *Musings*, was chosen by George Yeo early, and it instructed and guided how the book was written, conversationally, anecdotally. The book is being released in three series, Series One at the end of August 2022, Series Two in December 2022 and Series Three in the first quarter of 2023. A relentless consumer and thinker of news and current affairs, he is a great believer that to move intelligently forward, we must take heed of and understand our collective past. With the developments in Russia and Ukraine, the consolidation of ties between Europe and the United States (US) and further strain in US–China relations, George Yeo has grown increasingly cautious of the popular western press. He takes pain to seek alternative viewpoints. This three-part series confirms the George Yeo we all know, but for me, it also surprises.

Every reader will take away something from the three series. For me it is in these two words: *identity* and *diversity*; they recur and underline the narrative of the entire series. It is important to know who we are, feel comfortable in our own skin. If we do not know our own identity, we cannot respect the identities of others. If we are not secure about our own identity, we become uncomfortable with the strength of another person's identity. Projected onto the national and international fronts, is his concept of Big Singapore. Here George Yeo talks of the importance of seeing Singapore's diversity as integral. It requires Singaporeans to have big hearts and minds so that we accept those who are different from us as also being a part of us. In embracing diversity, it is not enough to "tolerate" diversity. There has to be genuine respect for the other and an appreciation of their strength and goodness. And it is this respect that George Yeo brings with him when he talks of his "passages" to India; his involvement with the revival of what was possibly the world's first university, Nalanda; his fascination with the homogeneity of China and the role he played in Singapore's relations with these two Asian giants.

Much of what is said in the three series is not new. What is new is how they are presented as part of his life journey and the personal descriptive details that come with them. Our eyes open and we are surprised by the accompanying joy and pathos. Series One sets the tone with a vivid and intimate look at himself through *Identity*. Personal details are usually set against a larger political backdrop, giving the events a sense of history and time. An example: his parents were married in China. One month after their marriage, Japan invaded China and his parents hurried back to Singapore. For more than 40 years, his mother was not able to return to China. When she finally did, she knelt before her parents to seek forgiveness for her prolonged absence. She had left as a young bride and returned a grandmother.

A special salute to diversity is his closeness to the Eurasian community, less than 1% of Singapore's population and once subsumed under "Others". If we use the metaphor rojak to describe Singapore (we are a mix of many races), the Eurasians are the prawn paste; they pull the other races together. Without the Eurasians, he thinks Singapore would be a harsher place. And they make an outsized contribution to Singapore, E.W. Barker drafted Singapore's constitution, which established our beginning as an independent nation, and Joseph Schooling won Singapore's first Olympic gold medal. All great countries are judged by how they treat the smallest among them, so when Singapore affirms Eurasians as a distinct fourth community, we affirm that all communities in Singapore are respected in their separate identities, whatever their size or contribution. The morning Joseph won the gold in 100m butterfly, George Yeo and his wife "jumped out of bed to sing Majulah Singapura." A precious and touching image.

The minds of many readers will be on his 2011 election defeat and his relationship with Lee Kuan Yew. These are mulled over throughout the three series, but it is in the chapter associated with identity that his relationship with Lee Kuan Yew comes into early focus. In his application to join the People's Action Party, he stated that his values were Chinese and Christian. Before he became Health Minister, Lee Kuan Yew asked for his views on the government's plan to introduce legislation on the Advanced Medical Directive and abortion regulations. His answer, that he would not do anything that he was not prepared to defend in church, probably did not go down well with Lee Kuan Yew.

In 1996, someone complained to Lee Kuan Yew that George Yeo had been unduly influenced to favour one hospital over another. Then Permanent Secretary Kwa Soon Bee was questioned by Lee, and in confidence, Lee Kuan Yew expressed two concerns about George Yeo, that he was Teochew and Catholic. While it was an episode that profoundly troubled George Yeo, I am also reminded of what he said: "Identity centres our entire being."

Series Two and Three will cover Europe and a period of western ascendancy, the American experience, the US–China protracted struggle, his time in the various ministries, the Singapore Armed Forces, his interest in calligraphy and *taijigong,* religion and God.

When I talk to people about George Yeo, they are almost always enthusiastic, whether they have known him through school or higher learning, in the army, in politics, through religion or his stint in Hong Kong, they are all taken by his depth and eloquence. But I doubt if they are aware of the way he has thought about so many areas of life, or the full spectrum of his interests. *Musings* offers all that under one book title, this interdisciplinary brilliance, supported by photographs he has meticulously culled from his own archives over the years.

Woon Tai Ho

Ora et Labora

CHAPTER 1

❖

Identity

In Chapters 1 and 2, George Yeo discusses his identity as a
Teochew Chinese, a Roman Catholic and a native Singaporean.

Q: You relate well to different communities. How do you describe your own identity?

When I applied to join the People's Action Party (PAP) after resigning
from the Singapore Armed Forces (SAF) in 1988, I described my values
as Chinese and Christian.

My identity came from my family. My paternal grandfather came to
the Nanyang region from Wenli (文里) Village in the town of Anbu (庵埠).
He owned rubber plantations along the Johor River, only accessible by
boat, and became a man of means. With the money he made, he came
to own substantial farmland back in Anbu Town and built a big house
in the village. He attained a certain social status when he returned to
China and was called Ah Ye (阿爷). My father was born in Johor in 1916
on a rubber plantation but had his birth registered in Singapore.

When my grandfather died, my father, then aged 21, went to China
in 1937 for the funeral. Under local custom, he could marry within 100
days or observe mourning for three years. Relatives advised him to find
a wife. With the help of intermediaries, he married my mother, who was
from the nearby village of Xianxi (仙溪), also in Anbu Town. She was
born in 1919 and was 19 years old then. The bridal chamber with the
old bridal bed are still in the old Yeo house in Wenli Village.

1986, with my wife at my parents' bridal chamber at the Yeo ancestral home

My parents' marriage certificate in Anbu Town, 1937

A month after their marriage, the Marco Polo Bridge Incident happened, marking the beginning of Japan's invasion of China proper. My parents hurried back to Singapore. For over 40 years, my mother was not able to return to China. When she finally did in 1978, she knelt before her parents to seek forgiveness for her prolonged absence. She had left as a young bride and returned as a grandmother.

Being the eldest in her family, my mother always felt a strong sense of responsibility for her parents and siblings in China. No matter our family's circumstances, she would try to eke out some money to send home every month. During difficult famine years, she and her relatives in Singapore would pack salted pork lard in kerosene tins and ship them to China. Those kept entire families alive.

In my secondary school days, I did the remittances for her at the Bank of China Katong branch. I still remember handing $40 or $50 over the counter and being given little receipts made of thin paper, which tore easily if written too hard on. Inside the bank, I was in a different world. Chinese Communist propaganda posters hung on the walls and leaflets were freely available on side tables. I knew such material was either banned or frowned upon in Singapore but took some regardless.

I treasured a little calendar card with a picture of the first bridge erected across the Yangtze River in Nanjing in 1968. Naturally, China was very proud of that achievement. After Soviet advisors pulled out from China, they had to bootstrap themselves and overcome many challenges. Today, the bridges across the Yangtze River are too many to count.

As a young Chinese boy, I felt an affinity to China and was proud of its achievements, including the first atomic bomb in 1964 and the first hydrogen bomb in 1967. As I grew older, I came to realise that this was partly the result of my mother's influence. She kept up constant correspondence with her relatives, the content of which kept clear of politics. As her youngest child, I probably spent more time with her than my older siblings. She would show me pictures of her parents, siblings and my cousins, and tell me stories about them. I only communicated with her in Teochew.

Q: Tell us about your first trip to China.

In 1983, I decided to follow my parents to China. After 1978, visiting China became an annual pilgrimage for them. I was then 29 and a Lieutenant Colonel in the Air Force. At that time, our passports did not allow for travel to China, Cuba and North Korea. I had to apply for special permission to travel to China.

The Internal Security Department (ISD) called me down for a one-hour interview. They were polite and offered me coffee. The rules in those days allowed older Singaporeans to visit China, but younger ones needed a good reason to make the trip. However, the Singapore government was gradually relaxing its controls because China was changing under Deng Xiaoping. It was only because of China's change of policy that my parents had been able to visit China in 1978 with one of my older brothers, who is an American citizen. Singapore was reviewing its position and the ISD wanted to know about my reaction to China. They requested that I inform them upon my return to Singapore and be interviewed again.

As I did not inform the ISD immediately upon coming back to Singapore, they called me instead. I spent another hour with them giving my impressions and drank another cup of coffee. Being from the SAF, I understood full well why I was given special attention: the Singapore government did not want me, an SAF scholar, to somehow be captured by communist China. For this reason, when Malay friends complain about the special security consideration they receive in the SAF, I tell them my own story, which gives comfort to some of them. There is nothing personal and it is certainly not racist.

During Sukarno's *Konfrontasi*, all those with Indonesian connections came under security interest. Security classifications varied with the security situation. For example, an old friend of mine, Mohamed Rahmat, affectionately known as Tok Mat, the former Information Minister of Malaysia, told me how he had been denied a scholarship by the Malaysian government in the 1960s because he was Javanese.

Looking back, it is amusing how my two encounters with the ISD bookended my first visit to China. Since then, the world has changed dramatically and China has become very important for Singapore's future. Today, if you are a new migrant to Singapore with strong mainland Chinese connections, you will naturally come under interest to the security services. It is the ISD's responsibility to ensure that foreign powers do not make use of their connections in Singapore to groom agents of influence. We can only have good relations with them if the ISD does its work.

My first visit to China was eye-opening. We first spent a couple of days in Hong Kong. At the hotel, my father wanted to call my mother's brother in Anbu Town. We waited hours in the hotel room for the call to be put through. That was the state of connectivity with China then.

We took a slow boat to China from Hong Kong. It was an old German ship bought by China named Dinghu (鼎湖). The moment we boarded, we were in a different world. Rousing mainland songs were being played on the public address system. All payments were in foreign exchange certificates, or *waihui juan* (外汇卷). My parents and I had bought tickets for a cabin with six seats.

Boarding the ship in Hong Kong   *Arrival in Shantou*

When we entered the cabin, we saw a man sitting across from us whose right hand looked as if it had melted. Our immediate thought was that he might have leprosy. My father and I looked at each other. Without saying a word, we quickly left the cabin and decided to sleep on deck. My parents found benches. I slept beneath a staircase.

The following morning, we arrived in Shantou (汕头). I felt great excitement arriving at my ancestral home. Everyone was wearing blue, grey or black. We had to collect our bags from a shed. A young girl helped us with the luggage. My mother wanted to tip her for her service but she refused. My mother persisted and chased her around the corner until, out of sight of others, she accepted the money. My mother understood what was in her mind.

We were enthusiastically received by my relatives. One of my uncles, who was an official, provided a van to send us to the village. As a youth, he was in the Communist underground and only surfaced after the Cultural Revolution to become part of the new local leadership. From Shantou to Anbu Town, we trundled for an hour on a bad road. During

At my maternal grandparent's house in 1983

Accompanying father to the Yeo House

the Japanese occupation, there had been a railroad running from Shantou to Chaozhou City. The rails have since been removed, but the road is still referred to as the railroad, or *huo che lu* (火车路).

For a week, I stayed at my maternal grandparents' house. We did not have close relatives on my father's side. The Yeo family had been classified as rich farmers in 1949 and their properties expropriated. After 1978, the Yeo ancestral home was legally returned to the family but not the farmland. It is now being looked after by a distant relative who rents it out for various uses.

In contrast, my maternal grandfather had been adjudged to be a good man at a mass gathering following the capture of power by the Communist Party of China. His house was therefore never taken away from him. He worked in a pharmacy.

Q: What were living conditions like?

They were not good at all. It was a tough adjustment for me. For 30 years, the part of China facing Taiwan was in a potential war zone and deliberately under-developed. That included all of Fujian and eastern Guangdong province, where the majority of Chinese Singaporeans came from originally.

Anbu Town was backward. Without sewer lines, the smell of dung and night soil was everywhere. Everywhere we went, beggars would come up to my parents. Once, to rid himself of one, my father tossed him a 5 RMB note which caused our relatives to protest.

I immediately recognised my maternal grandparents' house from the pictures I had seen in Singapore. Plastered on the wall, in multi-coloured mosaic which had seen better days, were the characters "高举毛泽东思想伟大红旗" (Hold high the great red flag of the Mao Zedong Thought). It had been some years since the end of the Cultural Revolution. Even though pieces of mosaic had fallen off, Mao's legacy was obviously still there for everyone to see.

I was not used to outdoor toilets and had to learn how to scoop water from a well. I stayed in a room so damp that a book left on the floor at night became soft and wet the next morning. Beds were raised from the floor. I slept under a mosquito net. The trick was making sure that there were no mosquitoes inside the net before sealing it.

Outdoor toilets. My wife posing with a child. At the back, my father on the right and my cousin on the left doing their business, while a water buffalo stood watching.

The house did not have a refrigerator. There was not enough electricity, and the sole lightbulb in the house turned brown in the evening. Leftover food was brought to a boil and kept covered in cabinets, which had footings surrounded by little saucers of water to keep ants out.

Despite what seemed to me primitive conditions, hygiene standards were high. Water was always boiled. Teochew tea (功夫茶) was drunk everywhere, late into the night. People fussed over their food, which was consistently good and fresh.

Q: What were your impressions of your grandparents?

Both my grandparents were in their 90s. My grandmother was suffering from dementia. She repeatedly mistook me for my elder brother, who is a medical doctor, and kept asking me to help her. In contrast, my slightly-built grandfather was spry and lucid.

One of the rooms had a ladder which led to an attic. Curious, I asked my grandfather what was kept up there. He told me that they used to keep old documents there but burned them all during the Cultural Revolution. It was now empty. During the Cultural Revolution, those caught with documents of the past were accused of harboring hopes to reclaim old properties, which was seen as evidence of reactionary intent.

A hundred years ago, the Communist Party of China (CPC) was formed. In 1949, the People's Republic of China was established. This was followed by land reform, but many people still nursed the wish to recover their old possessions. The creation of communes during the Great Leap Forward contributed to the severity of the subsequent famine affecting large parts of China. Mao was criticised and retreated to the second line. Some policies were reversed. Mao saw his revolution subverted and launched the Cultural Revolution. When it went out of control, the People's Liberation Army (PLA) was called in to re-establish order. Mao was too much of a romantic and made serious mistakes in his later years. In his youth, he was adamant that cadres conduct thorough social investigations before formulating policies. In his later years, he was too cut off from ground reality and became subjective.

For all the cruelty and harm done by the Cultural Revolution, this tragic period of Chinese history marked the final clearing of the land before a new China under Deng Xiaoping could make a fresh start. Unjust distribution of land had led to the Communist Revolution. One of its most important achievements was bringing land under collective control. The collectivisation of land after 1949 made China's remarkable progress after 1978 possible. Today, one can invest in Chinese properties as a foreigner and choose where to live, but only on a leasehold basis. This collective control of land enabled China to urbanise rapidly and build infrastructure on a scale that astonished the world.

In his life, my maternal grandfather never travelled beyond the Chaoshan (潮汕) region. Yet, when I spoke to him, he had a good under-standing of China's geography and history. He leafed through some of the material I brought on China from Singapore and showed familiarity with the information contained in them. I don't think he was an exception. Chinese students study China and are thus familiar with a

Maternal grandparents in 1983

big canvas. Despite living in the same village his whole life, he knew China's mountains and rivers, its resources and history.

If I were to ask a young Singaporean today where Palembang or Kuala Lipis is, he would struggle to give me the answer. We do not teach our students enough about the region we live in. This is a great deficiency. In my school days, we learned about Malaya from old British textbooks. Our historical links then were with Malaya. Then, we merged with Malaya to form the new Malaysia. Indonesia was however largely *terra incognita*. One day, when I was in St Patrick's Primary School, we were standing on the beach by the sea when my teacher pointed to the land on the horizon and said that that was Indonesia. Indonesia seemed so mysterious then, made worse by newspaper and radio reports of Sukarno's shrill attack on the Malaysian proposal.

When I joined the Air Force, I was acutely aware of my lack of knowledge of Indonesia and resolved to put this to rights. I went on a Nam Ho tour to Sumatra and Java, armed with a travel book called the Indonesian Handbook. It was my first visit to Indonesia. The tour guide was more interested in taking us shopping. For the single men who were interested, he brought them to catch chickens at night.

I became the tour guide for those with intellectual interests. The Indonesian Handbook, which was a treasure trove of information, was banned in Indonesia because it described the corruption of the First Lady and others. Some years later, over lunch, I was greatly amused when the Indonesian Ambassador to Singapore made a request to Eddie Teo, our Director of Security and Intelligence, to have the book banned. In my office, I pinned up Air Force maps covering the entire Nusantara, from Aceh to Papua. In my free time, I committed key features like towns, volcanoes, airbases and military districts to memory.

The point I am making is this. If you are Chinese, Indonesian, American or European, you are likely to have a big mental map because, like my grandfather, you are required to know your own country and region. In Singapore, we are too focused on ourselves and neglect the region around us. In fact, we have a tendency to look down on our region, thinking that we are an advanced country. This lack of knowledge about the larger environment in which we live in can be serious weakness.

Q: What about your other relatives in China? What was your general impression of the Chaoshan region?

They saw us as rich relatives then. Not so now. For years, we were their lifeline, for which they were penalised in China. None of my immediate cousins went to university for this reason.

One day, one of my cousins decided to try my Heads and Shoulders shampoo and washed his hair beside the well with visible delight. That picture of him with a full head of lather would have made a great shampoo advertisement. On another day, I found bits of hair on my Gillette razor, which someone else must have decided to try on his whiskers.

On the day we left Shantou for Guangzhou, one of my cousins asked if I could give him my old Olympus camera as he knew that I had a new one. I happily handed it over to him and saw how he immediately tinkered with his new possession. He had no difficulty mastering the functions at all. Young Chinese did not lack education. What they needed was opportunity. Their desire to learn and improve was palpable.

In 1986, when I brought my wife to Chaoshan and to China for the first time, an uncle who was a professor at the new Shantou University (汕头大学) brought us on a campus tour. The university was founded and endowed by Li Ka-shing. He was born in Chaozhou City and, like many Chinese businessmen who made good overseas, he never forgot his roots. The spanking new campus stood out in stark contrast to the dilapidation of the surrounding area, like an oasis in the desert. As we wandered around the modern facilities, I saw female students dancing to the tune of Michael Jackson's music. It felt surreal. China was opening an exciting new chapter in its history. Shantou University has since achieved a certain reputation because it is seen as Li Ka-shing's university. Mr Li told me once how when he launched a condominium project in

Shantou University in 1986

Undergraduates doing aerobics to Michael Jackson's music

Shantou, he decided at the spur of the moment to donate the entire project, without debt, as an endowment to the university.

As a child, my mother would talk to me about the relationship of the village to the town, and of the town to the city. We were from Wenli Village, which, as part of Anbu Town, came under the jurisdiction of Chao'an (府城). Guangzhou was far away from the provincial capital (省城). Since then, there have been a number of administrative changes, but the same names are re-used. Chao'an is now Chaozhou City. Chao'an has been retained as the name of a district and Anbu Town has become its capital city. In the Confucianist world, hierarchy is important.

The first Yeos migrated from Fujian Province to Anbu Town during the Southern Sung Dynasty. My ancestral village produced two Yeo brothers who were high scholar-mandarins, or *jinshi* (进士) serving Ming Emperor Zhengde. Wenli was the name given by the Emperor to honour them. Till today, the majority of the families in Wenli Village carry the surname Yeo.

History of Wen Li

Yi'an (义安), as in Ngee Ann Kongsi, was an old name of the Chaoshan region. For a long time, the Chaoshan region had eight major districts, and was hence known as Bayi (八邑). Today there are three major cities, Shantou, Chaozhou and Jieyang. The famous Singaporean artist, Chen Wen Hsi, was from Jieyang. The Singaporean tycoon, Goh Cheng Liang, came from Chaozhou (like Li Ka-shing). The best goose for braising comes from Chenghai (澄海). Many famous Teochew businessmen are from Chaoyang (潮阳). Both Chenghai and Chaoyang are now part of Shantou City.

Among Teochews, these sub-divisions are sometimes made much of. My regular *bak kut teh* coffeeshop in Tiong Bahru is run by people from Chao'an, which makes me feel strangely at home there. According to a programme I watched on CGTN, the Chaoshan region gives the most attention to ancestral temples in all of China. This is intriguing and perhaps a reason why the Teochews are sometimes thought of as being clannish.

The Teochew people were blessed to have the great scholar-mandarin Han Yu (韩愈) spend some months in Chaozhou during the Tang Dynasty. It was the good fortune of the Teochew people that Han Yu was exiled by Emperor Xianzong for his memorial opposing the excessive veneration of a Buddha relic. During the Ming Dynasty, of the top eight scholars of the Tang and Sung listed, Han Yu was ranked number one.

In Chaozhou, he got rid of crocodiles which infested a swampy estuary. Apparently, to propitiate them, the local people sometimes sacrificed young girls. He wrote a famous memorial to the crocodiles giving them ample warning to go away or face the consequences. Han Yu could have killed the crocodiles from the beginning but knew that he needed to rid the Teochew people of the thinking that the crocodiles were deities. The intention of the memorial was to exorcise their minds. I decided to write a few characters from this famous memorial in my calligraphy class: 潮之州，大海在其南，鲸鹏之大，虾蟹之细 (roughly translated as 'In the region of the tides, where the vast sea is to the south, the whales and rocs are large while the prawns and crabs are delicate.'). I found the prawn and crab references particularly interesting. When I first visited the temple across the river in Chaozhou City, which is named after him, it had been damaged during the Cultural Revolution. His statue was disfigured. Since then, it has been restored, renovated, and enlarged. Chinese leaders visiting Chaozhou City pay their respects to him at the temple. The main river in Chaoshan is also named after Han Yu.

In the past, I visited Chaoshan every two to three years, always with my wife, sometimes with my children. When I worked in Hong Kong, my wife and I found it most convenient to take the fast train from West Kowloon. We might go twice a year, principally to enjoy the food. Over time, the older relatives gradually passed away, leaving just my cousins and their children on my mother's side. On the Yeo side, a deep sense of kinship remains even though there are no close relatives.

As a minister or former minister, I would always lead a ceremony to pay respects to our ancestors, which takes place two weeks before Chinese New Year, at the branch ancestral temple whenever I am present.

At Han Yu's temple 韩文公

With family, relatives and friends before the statue of Han Yu

潮之州大海在其南鯨
鵬之大蝦蟹之細無不
歸容以生以食鰐魚朝
發而夕至也
韓文公句
榮文

My attempt at calligraphy of a passage from Han Yu's famous Memorial to the Crocodiles written in Chaozhou

Han River named after Han Yu. My father and mum's brother resting below a tree on the river dyke.

There are two levels of ancestral temples in the Yeo clan, the branch and the main. The ancestral worship ceremony takes place at the branch temple, while the main Yeo temple has a history going back to the Southern Sung period. When it was renovated, they asked my brothers and I to make a major donation, which was not a lot of money. Many businessmen would have been happy to donate much more but, as a Singapore minister, they wanted my name inscribed on the pillars.

At some time during the Kangxi era, three sub-temples were established for three sons. My family belongs to the *er fang* (二房) branch temple, which is the one I visit regularly. It was shut

At the main Yeo temple when it was refurbished

down for many years and only revived in 1994. I am happy to see my sons also showing some interest. Daughters are traditionally excluded from the registry because their place is supposed to be with their husbands.

The ceremony to pay respect to ancestors is held a fortnight before Chinese New Year. It lasts two to three hours. The smell of incense fills the courtyard, and those participating wear traditional robes. It is a formal ceremony. A pig and a goat are disembowelled beautifully, their organs neatly arranged in basins placed below the carcasses. Offerings of fish, fowl and fruit are also laid out on long tables.

We have to kneel, make offerings, stand, process and pour libations of wine repeatedly before the ancestral tablets. At the end of the ceremony, pieces of paper with the names of prominent ancestors are read out and burned, including those of my parents and grandparents.

重修闲云杨公宗祠暨晋升为二房公祠庆典大会

新加坡宗亲杨荣文部长为庆典致辞

Officiating the opening of the Yeo branch temple

At the Yeo Branch Ancestral Temple

With two of my sons at Yeo branch ancestral temple. Wife and daughter standing behind.

At the the Yeo branch temple before ancestral tablets. My second son and I holding the tablets of my father and grandfather.

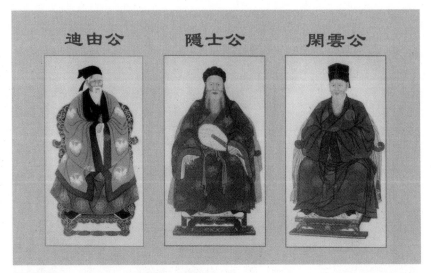

Yeo forebears

One cousin once commented that I seemed to have no difficulty kneeling for long stretches. I told her I am Catholic and used to kneeling.

On one of our earlier visits, one of my sons asked if I was allowed to hold joss sticks as a Catholic. Should I not bring candles instead? It was a funny suggestion. I told him that joss sticks and candles are the same. In Singapore, I do not normally use joss sticks because of tradition. As a politician, I never held joss sticks so that I would not be seen as an opportunist.

In China, conforming to traditional rites is important. This issue of Chinese rites was debated within the Catholic Church for centuries. The Jesuits argued that ancestral worship was a mark of respect, not idolatry, while the Dominicans and Franciscans disagreed. The debate was intense and went all the way to the Vatican. Historically, it was called the 'Rites Controversy'.

Among Protestants, some still see ancestral worship as idolatry or superstition. This has created divisions within families when some children refuse to take part in ceremonies honouring deceased parents. When I attend such ceremonies in Wenli Village, I usually say Catholic prayers in my heart silently.

＊

CHAPTER 2

Early Formation

Q: How much of your identity came from your parents?

Probably more than I am conscious of. My memory of my mother is inseparable from her origin in China. Being the eldest in her family and a pillar of support for them for many years, she had an honoured place in Xianxi, her home village. She was always provided with a chamber pot so that she did not have to use the outdoor latrine. She  also often had a basin of warm water to wash her feet after a long day walking on dusty roads. Sometimes I thought she felt more at home in her old house than back in Singapore.

Language was a major handicap for her in Singapore. She never learned Mandarin or English. She could speak Cantonese which was commonly used by the extended Yeo clan in Singapore and a smattering of market Malay. I often heard her complain that the government only sends you letters in Chinese when they want money from you. As our signages and documents became increasingly written in English only, her alienation grew. Because of this, from a young age, I empathised with the grievances felt by older generations of Singaporeans against the government's language policy.

Relatives in China told me that my mother had been a top student in the Xianxi primary school. She did not go beyond primary school because her father believed that girls should not be over-educated. I don't know why she did not learn Mandarin or English when she came

My mother's old primary school

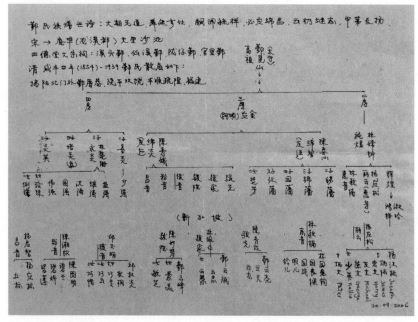

My mother's family tree

to Singapore. Not everyone is good at languages. However, my mother was wise in matters of human relations and took a lively interest in international politics, which she followed in the former *Nanyang Siang Pau* newspaper. She always felt that the English-educated lacked subtlety of understanding. One of her most biting criticisms of her children was to say that we behaved like *babas* (male Peranakans), with a straight alimentary canal from the mouth to the other end.

During the Tiananmen Incident, when international media reported that people were being slaughtered mercilessly with tanks rolling over demonstrators in Tiananmen Square, she cautioned me against believing the news. I only learned much later that she was right and many of those reports were wildly exaggerated and some were false. She was sceptical from the outset and, despite newspaper reports, expressed little sympathy for the demonstrators. When she saw the Goddess of Democracy, which looked like a replica of the Statue of Liberty, on television, she immediately saw American and Taiwanese hands behind the protests.

On one occasion, after reading of Yang Shangkun's involvement in the crackdown, I lamented that he brought shame to the Yeo name. My mother reminded me that I did not know what was really going on and admonished me not to talk like that. She stopped me dead in my tracks. Looking back, I am glad she did.

In January 1992, not long after the Tiananmen Incident, Yang Shangkun visited Singapore and met Lee Kuan Yew. As a note-taker during the meeting, I had the privilege of watching Lee Kuan Yew interacting with Yang at close range. Yang was a big man, but displayed no trace of defensiveness even when Lee Kuan Yew proffered difficult advice.

I got to know Yang's son, Yang Shaoming, who was a photographer. He came to Singapore a few times. When he did a pictorial spread on Singapore, my Ministry provided some assistance. Each time he came to see me, he would present me with a thoughtful gift of little objects bought from small shops or street vendors wrapped in newspaper. I still keep some of them. Before the return of Hong Kong to China in 1997, he presented me with a photographic pastiche of an image of Deng Xiaoping superimposed on a photograph of the Hong Kong Convention Centre which was the site of the handover ceremony on 1 July. I declared the picture for tax purposes and paid $50 plus 3% GST for it. I brought it to Hong Kong and hung it in my apartment to show to friends, including Leung Cheung-Ying after he retired as Chief Executive of Hong Kong.

During the Second World War, my mother lost her second son who was then only an infant. Because it was wartime, there was no burial, no grave. After the war, her third son died in my father's arms, also from febrile convulsion. Before he died, my father was moved to baptise him.

My father was then a lapsed Catholic. He himself had been baptised when he studied at St Joseph's Institution (SJI) in the 1930s. He had boarded at SJI's housing facility, which is now the site of St Patrick's School. When he married my mother in Anbu, the wedding ceremony was traditional. Under Catholic teaching, anyone, even a non-Christian, can baptise an individual in an emergency so long as it is done in the name of the Father, Son and Holy Spirit.

In their grief, my parents decided that the family should become Catholic. My mother learned her catechism in Teochew at the Sacred Heart Church at Tank Road where all of us were baptised. I was a cradle Catholic and was not given a Chinese name when I was born. My mother thought that to break the spell of untimely deaths, we should only be given Christian names and not Chinese ones. She was a devout Catholic and often prayed the rosary.

After she died, I found a small envelope which contained the birth certificates of my second and third brothers. On it was written in Chinese: birth certificates, Yeo Cheng Pio, Yeo Joo Pio, dead sons (报生子，杨清标，杨裕标，亡子). The envelope also had their vaccination certificates. Mothers never stop grieving when their children die.

Mother kept this envelope till she died

Family portrait with me carried by my father

> A
>
> Name and Baptism Name ...George Yeo...
> Date of Birth ...13 - Sept - 1954...
> Date of Baptism ...16 . Oct . 1954...
> Father's Name ...Yeo Eng Song & Mary Kan Lee Hoon...
> Mother's Maiden Name ......
> Church of Baptism ...Sacred Heart Church, Tank Rd....
> Home Address ...29 . River Valley Rd....
>
> P. Chin.

My baptism certificate without a Chinese name

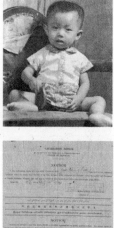

My second brother's birth certificate when Singapore was Syonan-to

My second brother's vaccination certificate

My third brother's birth certificate when Singapore was Syonan-to

My third brother's vaccination certificate

Our Catholic inculturation ran deep. We observed the Catholic calendar and learned all the prayers. In the early 1960, Mass was said in both English and Latin. Our Sunday Missal carried both languages. We fasted before receiving Holy Communion. On Maundy Thursday, my father made a point of taking us to all the Catholic Churches in Singapore in order to recall Jesus asking his apostles to pray with him at the Garden of Gethsemane before his crucifixion. It was quite an effort which ended after midnight. The high point was dinner at the Hainanese restaurant, Mooi Chin, at Purvis Street.

Latin, being a language I heard in my childhood, has a certain resonance for me. During the Covid-19 pandemic, I decided to learn a little Latin from Duolingo, principally so that I can better understand Catholic prayers said or sung in Latin. My mother had to wear a black veil over her head every time she went to church. These practices were abolished soon after the Second Vatican Council. Muslim women wearing tudung is unremarkable to Catholics, as Catholic nuns wear tudung too.

In the late 1950s, my mother decided that her children not having Chinese names was wrong and had to be rectified. I vaguely recall accompanying her to meet an old man who wore glasses, poring over a book in a dark room to find names for us. The names up to my fourth brother ended with 标 (biao). From my fifth brother onwards, our names ended with 文 (wen). The bridge was between my fourth and fifth brothers' names, which carried a common first character 炳 (bing).

When I entered Primary One, my mother decided that I should take Malay as my second language. All my older siblings had taken Chinese. If I could roll back the clock, I would have preferred to have studied Chinese too. Learning Chinese as an adult, as what I did, is much more difficult. My mother sensed the political tides changing. The People's Action Party (PAP) government was preparing Singaporeans for merger with Malaysia. The popular jingo then was "Malaysia, as sure as the sun rises". Alas, the sun also sets.

I only started learning Chinese seriously as an undergraduate in Cambridge. I bought books from Guanghwa book shop in London's

Primary Five Malay teacher Tengku Bedah. I was standing at the back next to her.

Me with a front tooth missing   *Malay Cultural Month*

Chinatown which came with audio cassettes. It is one of my regrets in life not to be proficient in Chinese. The Malay language, which I am also not proficient in, did however expose me to a different cultural universe. It gave me an appreciation of the Malay community in Singapore. My wife also took Malay as a second language, though her

Malay is better than mine. She is quite able to give instructions in Bahasa to the workmen looking after our vacation house in Johor.

I had an enthusiastic Malay teacher in Primary Six, Tengku Bedah, who enrolled me in *pantun* competitions for which I wore baju, sarong and songkok. I even managed to win some prizes. I knew she was dating an officer from the Malaysian Army because his officer's cap was at the back of her car. One competition organised by 4PM, the Malay youth literary association, was held in Kampong Ubi at a time when the entire area was a vast Malay settlement. I felt I was entering a different world. I still remember the lines of a *sha'ir*, which expressed the sad lament of a blind orphan.

Aku buta	*I am blind,*
Tiada bersaudara	*without relatives,*
Tiada beribu, tanpa berbapa	*without mother, without father.*
Semalam-malam, ku rasa sama	*Every night, I feel the same.*
Segala-gala, gelap gulita.	*Everything is in darkness.*

Q: You talked about your mother. What about your father?

Like many of those in his generation, my father gambled and womanised. During the Korean War, he became wealthy. All his working life, he worked as a storekeeper at the Hooglandt rubber godown at 12 Kim Seng Road. Originally Dutch, it was bought over by the Swiss trading company, Diethelm. The godown was down the road from Jiak Kim  Street, where the nightclub, Zouk, was located until a few years ago.

As a storekeeper, there were many opportunities on the side. At his peak, my father owned four or five bungalows at Braddell Heights. In secondary school and pre-university, I sometimes helped him deliver goods during school holidays. He owned two rickety lorries, and I would direct the lorry crew to pick up large boxes containing cartons of Kotex sanitary towels from the Kimberly-Clark factories at Tanglin Halt and deliver them to shops in various parts of town. There was no Google Maps then and I sometimes got lost. I remember my father being quite upset with me once for not delivering boxes on time.

There was a coolie gang at the Hooglandt godown. They were mostly Teochew, controlled by a head called the ka-pa-la, from the Malay word *kepala,* or leader. They must have found me curious. One of them had a son who later became a senior officer in the Economic Development Board (EDB).

The coolies knew I was good at my studies and were kind to me. I spoke to them in my limited Teochew and became fond of them. I think they were of me too. Years later, one of them helped to serve *satay beehoon* at the Lagoon Hawker Centre when it opened. We were happy to recall the godown days. My father also had an assistant storekeeper who was a PAP grassroots leader, which enhanced his stature. He was also a good source of information and gossip.

My father's godown abutted the Singapore River, where coolies would load and unload rubber bales, carrying these on their backs as they walked along narrow planks to lighters (*tongkang*). They worked hard and had strong team spirit. Next door was a rice godown, where sacks of rice were pulled up using handheld hooks. Everyone knew that the rice coolies often poked more holes in the gunny sacks than necessary, so that more rice grains would fall out and be swept up by destitute old ladies.

The lighters could only sail at certain times of the day to get to the ships anchored at sea. If the tide was too low, there was not enough water; if the tide was too high, they could not clear the bridges. It was important to know the day in the lunar calendar as this determined the time of high tide. In Teochew, the rhyme we used to remember this was: 初三流，十八水. This means the tide is highest on the third and eighteenth day of the lunar month. On both these days, the tide is at its highest roughly at noontime and midnight. For the other days, we interpolated accordingly.

The watchman, Ram Shakal, a kindly Indian from Uttar Pradesh, lived with his family at the back of the godown. It looked more like a

Old Singapore River full of tongkangs
Courtesy of ABN AMRO Collection, FY000620.

Back of my father's godown before it was demolished

Preserved godowns nearby which housed Zouk for many years

dark cave to me. I never went inside. On Chinese New Year, he would visit us with his family. Many years later, a young lieutenant greeted me with a smart salute at the Ministry of Defence (MINDEF). He said he was Ram Shakal's son, a Sandhurst graduate. I later learned from Nominated Member of Parliament (NMP) Shriniwas Rai that Ram was a Brahmin who had left India for some unhappy reason. I then realised why he and his young sons kept a short twirl of long hair at the back of their heads.

There was also a Malay woman who sold Malay rice to workers on a side road. The food was delicious. A piece of mutton was 30 cents, an egg 10 cents. The rice was bathed in light curry gravy, the original *nasi mandi*. On one Hari Raya, she invited my mother to her little zinc-roofed house across a stream. I tagged along as a kid. I remember the house being tiny but spotless. Malays are house-proud.

The outhouse for the godown was built in the river. It was best to do one's business at high tide when the water was high. At low tide, it was uncomfortable and not dissimilar to the scene in the movie *Slumdog Millionaire*. One had to walk on a plank to get to the outhouse. My father lost his balance once and fell into the river at low tide!

As a gambler, my father took positions in rubber futures. He was both a punter and runner, and also sometimes a bookie, in horse racing. On weekends, our house at East Coast Terrace was carefully locked in case of police raids. Additional telephone lines would then be laid. He also played Russian poker and dominoes.

To earn extra income, my mum occasionally let the house out as a gambling den for dominoes. As kids, we partook in the wonderful suppers provided. The casino itself was in a smoke-filled room which I peeked into occasionally. On the table were wads of cash in large denominations. I still keep two high wooden stools from that gambling den as a memento.

When my father lost his wealth to gambling, my mother struggled to keep the family together. She often had to pawn her jewelry. Father's gambling and womanising caused her great stress. He had a bad temper and was hard on my older siblings, though by the time I grew up, he had mellowed. He was also proud of my academic achievements and attended all my school prize-giving days with my mother. I don't remember my father ever raising his voice at me.

My father went on a holiday to the United States (US) in the 1950s and was dazzled by how advanced the country was. His ambition was for his children to emigrate to America. One of my brothers studied in the US after his 'O' levels and became an American citizen. Others followed, although my sixth brother decided not to accept a green card after getting it approved. Migrating was never a consideration for me as I was a scholarship holder and bonded to the government. My parents were green card holders themselves and spent about three months in San Francisco, where we have relatives from branches on both sides of the family, every year. My mother went along but she never enjoyed America. In their winter years, both my parents had a change of heart. My mother, in particular, regretted that so many of her children ended up emigrating there.

My father witnessed the transformation of Singapore under Lee Kuan Yew's leadership. Our family's old house was at 298 River Valley Road, where I lived the first three years of my life. Lee Kuan Yew lived nearby at Oxley Road. He was already a well-known political leader. My father bumped into him occasionally. In 1957, we moved into a large bungalow at East Coast Terrace.

Although our family appeared wealthy, my parents were financially strapped for many years. In the 1970s, I looked after my father's finances when he was in America. Bank interest rates reached 20% before Paul Volcker, the then-Chair of the Federal Reserve, clamped down on inflation. It was scary watching how my father's bank debts soared during that period.

As children, our sympathies were with our mother. We did not think father treated her well, but mother would never allow us to criticise him. Her unhappiness with him was between them as husband and wife, she said. We had to respect him as a father. It was classic Confucianism

Opening of the kindergarten in Xianxi built by my father in my mother's memory

which would not find currency today. After my father retired from his work and stopped gambling, he treated mother better.

I remember my mother's last days at National University Hospital (NUH) when she was dying of cancer. My father was never more affectionate towards her. After she passed away, he visited her grave frequently. Burial is kinder on the living. I told my wife that I would like to be buried when I die.

On a visit to the kindergarten with my four children in the 1990s

My father decided to spend some money to build a kindergarten in my mother's memory in Xianxi. My cousin's husband helped him to secure governmental approval and oversaw the construction. When it finally opened, I accompanied my father for the opening ceremony. I gave a speech in Teochew which I first practised with Dr Ker Sin Tze. Many local officials were in attendance.

Since then, the kindergarten has outperformed our expectations. At one point, enrollment was falling and it seemed as if the kindergarten had no future. However, in recent years, its performance turned around and it is now considered a tier-one kindergarten in Guangdong province. During my last visit there at the end of 2019, my wife and I visited every class. The kids were bright-eyed, energetic and intelligent. Their lively faces cheered us greatly.

A cross my parents had to bear was my eldest brother's schizophrenia. Joseph Yeo Han Pio was 17 years my senior, born in 1937. The symptoms surfaced when he was in secondary school in SJI. My parents thought that it was bad behaviour and sent him to school in England. He was later diagnosed with schizophrenia and sent to a mental institution in the village of Shenley. I never knew him as a normal person. All I knew before primary school was that I had a brother in England who was not well.

In 1961, when I was in Primary One, my mother left us to go to

Delighted to see the kindergarten full of bright-eyed children at the end of 2019

緣起

I took this picture of my mother's bio in the kindergarten

London on her own. There, she made
daily visits to my brother in Shenley for
six months while staying in London with
her god-sister, Auntie Rose, whose
husband ran a boarding house. Somehow
she managed to make the daily journey to
Shenley on her own. She always referred
to that journey as her 苦路 (*ku lu*), her *Via
Dolorosa*. My father joined her in the last
month of her trip and brought her and my
eldest brother on a pilgrimage to Lourdes
in France and Fatima in Portugal in hope of a cure.

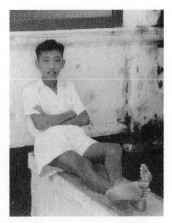

My eldest brother, Joseph

My brother's return to Singapore at age 24 disrupted our family life.
He was a difficult young man and was occasionally violent. We were
terrified of him. From time to time, he had to be sent to Woodbridge
Hospital. One one or two occasions, my father had to call the police and
Joseph was administered electronic shock treatment which left him dazed
for a few days. He did not like the medicine he was prescribed and often
pretended to take them. My father's sister who lived with us and helped
raise me, my third auntie Polly (三姑), nagged him occasionally and
was even beaten up once. As a young boy, I sometimes wished that the
authorities would just lock my eldest brother up in the asylum.

I grew up with this great stress in the family. When Joseph was in
Woodbridge Hospital, I sometimes accompanied my mother to bring
him food. The old Woodbridge
Hospital was set in spacious grounds;
the wards were arranged like
herringbones, and the sheltered
corridors were interconnected. I did
not look forward to the visits. I did
not understand then how my mother
felt. As he grew older, my brother
mellowed, and we no longer feared

*Celebrating Auntie Polly's birthday.
She helped to raise me.*

Family members with IMH doctors and nurses who cared for Joseph over long years

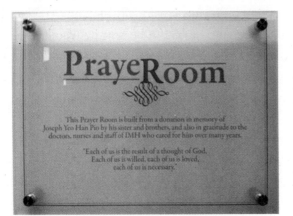

IMH prayer room

*Consecration of
Prayer Room*

but pitied him. My parents' neighbours at Palm Beach Garden were understanding and helpful.

For a time, I was ashamed of my brother's condition. I never denied it if someone asked, but it was not something I wanted to talk about if I could help it. My parents felt a great sense of responsibility towards him. They agreed in their will that whoever died first would transfer the entire estate to the other and use it to care for Joseph. After both of them passed away, the entire estate was willed to him. It was only after he had passed on that the remaining estate was distributed to the surviving siblings. My fourth brother and his wife then cared for him till he died.

When he died in 2008, I wrestled with the meaning of his life. My brother's condition caused my parents much pain, especially my mother. As a Member of Parliament, I was keenly aware that many families bore similar crosses. By that time, I was happy to tell those who sought my help about my brother's own situation. For his obituary, I found consolation in the words of Pope Benedict XVI: "Each of us is the result of a thought of God. Each of us is willed. Each of us is loved. Each of us is necessary." When the estate was distributed, my siblings and I decided to pool some of the money to remember Joseph by dedicating a room in the Institute of Mental Health (IMH) to him.

My only sister, Nellie Yeo, died in 2021 from a sudden heart attack. She had graduated as a staff nurse from Singapore General Hospital (SGH), batch 55. She later went to England to do her midwifery training, cycling to deliver babies in the countryside. My fourth brother later sponsored her to work in California.

Nellie was kind-hearted, frugal and a shrewd investor. She never married, lived alone and had few friends in San Francisco. Because of work-related disabilities, she retired early. She had bad knees and was on painkillers all the time. All of us surviving brothers are undeserved beneficiaries of her estate.

Like with my eldest brother, I often wonder about the meaning of her life. We flew her urn back to Singapore and interred it in the Holy

My only sister, Nellie   *Nellie as a young nurse at SGH*

Family Church columbarium together with those of our eldest and third brothers. Our second brother had died during the Second World War without a proper burial.

When my youngest son was diagnosed with leukaemia in 1997, our plans for the family came to a screeching halt. For many years, we had to fight for his life. Suffering is part of the human condition. However unpleasant my family's experiences, many families endure much worse. Philosophically, I am inclined to the view that it is suffering, *pathos*, which forges the identity of individuals and of groups.

Q: Did your personal identity conflict with your political identity?

I hope not. It is better to be yourself and be true to your own values. With social media, those who fake their public persona get discovered quickly.

In my application to join the PAP, I stated that my values were Chinese and Christian. Being Chinese means having values related to Confucianism and Taoism. In Confucianism, civilisation is impossible without human effort. This means education, human relationships and discipline. Human beings have to be organised, for which an operating system — culture — is needed.

As a philosophical Taoist, I see history as cyclical. There are cycles within cycles. Those which are beyond our control, we must abide by. Those which are within our control, we should work with. Without understanding of 道 (*tao*), 'the way', there can be no achievement of 德 (*de*), or virtue. These philosophical musings are deep in Chinese culture. I am not saying anything new here.

I am also a Christian. In Taoism and Buddhism, love means attachment, which leads to suffering. In the world of Confucius, love is calibrated according to the degree of one's relationship with a person. Christianity teaches that we should love others as much as we love ourselves, even our enemies. Confucius taught that we should not do to others what we don't want them to do to us. Christianity takes this a step further, insisting we have to love others as we love ourselves, which is of course very difficult. While I do not consider myself a fervent Catholic, I am happy to be identified as one.

Before I became Health Minister, Lee Kuan Yew called me on the telephone. He was worried about my Catholicism interfering with my responsibilities. He asked me about the government's plan to introduce legislation on the Advance Medical Directive (AMD), under which individuals could state in advance that they do not wish extraordinary life-sustaining treatment to be performed even when terminally ill and unconscious. I replied that I had no problems with the legislation. I

With Lee Kuan Yew around 1990

added that I would not do anything that I was not prepared to defend in church. He then asked me about my views on the current abortion regulations. I replied that it was settled policy. I don't think he was happy with my answers.

In 1996, someone complained to Lee Kuan Yew that I had been unduly influenced to favour one hospital over another. He called Dr Kwa Soon Bee, Permanent Secretary and concurrent Director of Medical Services, to his office and questioned him about me.

With Dr Kwa Soon Bee at the Jurong Bird Park. He was Permanent Secretary and Director of Medical Services when I was Health Minister.

Dr Kwa was much my senior and the younger brother of Mrs Lee. He played a major role in the development of Singapore's healthcare institutions. I knew of him when I was in secondary school through one of my brothers, who was a doctor. Later, in the Singapore Armed Forces, I got to know him in his role as the head of the Army Medical Corps. He was most proper in his dealings with me. On my first overseas trip as a young health minister, he saw me off at the airport in the VIP lounge. I was bewildered. Why was this senior official sending me off? I told him it was unnecessary but he insisted that it was the right thing to do.

In his conversation with Dr Kwa, Lee Kuan Yew said he had two concerns about me: that I was a Teochew and a Catholic. Although he was asked not to tell me, Dr Kwa reported the conversation to me in tears. I was profoundly troubled. Lee Kuan Yew's concerns related to my deep identity. There were many Teochews and a few Catholics in the Cabinet at the time, but perhaps they did not identify with either as strongly as I did. When my mother passed away, Lee Kuan Yew wrote me a condolence message saying that he knew how much my mother meant to me. I was touched by this.

Q: Why is identity important?

Identity centres our entire being. A person's identity is multi-faceted and often subconscious. We are not defined by the present but by our collective past. We are products of cultural, historical and familial influences flowing down generations. They make up the countless lines of code in our operating system when we become adults. Without this software, we are no better than apes.

In the old Yeo house, there is a signboard with the characters 光前裕后 (*guang qian yu hou*), which roughly means that by honouring our ancestors, we bless our descendants. Recently, on the BBC, I heard a story of how an indigenous Canadian found new purpose in life when he learned of his ancestors' achievements. If we attempt to change people's identities by force and rob them of their past, it will destabilise their sense of self and demoralise their spirit. Instead of changing them, we will break them.

Four characters at the Yeo ancestral house in Wenli Village reminding us that by honouring ancestors, we bless our descendants.

I witnessed this with horror on a trip to Australia. For a period after leaving politics in 2011, I was an informal advisor to the then-Western Australian Prime Minister Colin Barnett. As part of my familiarisation with the economy of the state, I was brought on a study visit to a huge iron mine in Pilbara operated by Rio Tinto. In the late afternoon, I saw a group of Aborigines coming together on open ground. My host told me that they were gathering to drink, and would drink until they were all drunk. This happened daily.

Australia once had a policy of forced assimilation, whereby Aboriginal children were taken from their parents and educated in special schools in the hope that they could be pole-vaulted into the 20th century. It was a disaster. Cut off from their roots, they had nothing to stand on. This was the tragedy of the 'stolen generation'. We are only slowly understanding how remarkably the Australasian aborigines adapted to an extreme environment over thousands of years.

In a recent sermon given by Archbishop William Goh during online Sunday Mass, he said that if we do not know our own identity, we cannot respect the identities of others. If we are insecure about our own identity, we become uncomfortable with the strength of another person's identity. I have a great curiosity about people's identities. I don't know why. Maybe it is inborn. I have said publicly that if my children do not feel Chinese, I would have failed as a father. My children have all been baptised as Catholics and identify as such. Whether they practise their faith is, however, their own decision to make.

CHAPTER 3

❖

Big Singapore

George Yeo discusses the importance of seeing Singapore's diversity as integral. It requires Singaporeans to have big hearts and minds so that we accept those who are different from us as also being a part of us. We are one, not despite, but because of our differences. In this chapter and the next, he sets Singapore's diversity within a global context.

Q: Is it really possible to separate one's political identity from one's cultural identity?

While it is always difficult, we must strive to do so. Just bearing in mind this separation is helpful even when we can't fully achieve it in practice. It does not mean that one should be placed higher than the other. It depends. We should never lightly ask a person to choose between his nationality and his race or religion.

As a Member of Parliament (MP), I handed out citizenship certificates to new citizens every three months. They hail from different parts of the world. My speeches invariably revolved around the theme of inclusiveness. We are happy that they have chosen to become part of the Singaporean family, but want them to continue cherishing their links to their ancestral lands. However, as new Singaporeans, we also require them to open their minds and hearts to others who are different from them. Being Singaporean means being bigger than what they were before in China, India or Indonesia.

We often talk about enlarging common space in Singapore. This, however, suggests a zero-sum game, implying that common space can only be enlarged when individual spaces are restricted. Such a framing is negative. Singaporeans should not have to suppress their cultural and religious identities in order to become Singaporean. Being Singaporean should enlarge a person, not diminish him. Common space is small when our hearts and minds are small. It is large when our hearts and minds are big. But, of course, we need boundaries on bad behaviour.

Q: How important is the use of multiple languages?

In 2018, the Asian Civilisations Museum (ACM) curated an exhibition of the 9th century Belitung shipwreck. The acquisition of the wreck began when I was Minister for Trade and Industry. We succeeded in negotiating the price down because there was no competing bid at that time. The money came from the Singapore Tourism Board reserve fund and the Khoo Foundation. It was a 9th century Tang wreck, probably the most important from the Tang Dynasty in the world today, containing some 65,000 pieces of pottery from different kilns in China intended for the Middle East. Many pieces have Arabic characters. A small gold and silver collection was in the Islamic style. There are a few, very precious precursor blue-and-white plates with a date palm motif.

Fortunately for us, the Chinese did not have much interest in this collection at that time. Were we trying to acquire it today, we would have no chance of getting it because Chinese museums would pay much more for it. I was interviewed by Chinese TV in Hong Kong about the acquisition some years after I left office. They were wistful. When President Xi Jinping opened the summit for the Belt and Road Initiative, he mentioned the Belitung wreck at the beginning of his speech.

I was invited to visit the exhibition at ACM, but was dismayed to find that there were no Chinese explanatory texts accompanying the exhibits. Everything was in English. I asked the curator why this was so. He told me that if they were to have explanations in Chinese, they would have to have them in Malay and Tamil too. He said, however, that there were Chinese brochures at the counter. Examining them, I realised they were only broad summaries of little value to the serious visitor.

First exposure of a few pieces from the Tang Treasures in 2005

THE TANG SHIPWRECK

Art and exchange in the 9th century

Exhibition of the Tang Shipwreck in ACM in 2020

This rigid conceptualisation of fairness harms Singapore. Visitors most interested in the Belitung wreck are likely to be Chinese and would appreciate having explanations in Chinese. Many pieces are not available to them in China or elsewhere. If we had an exhibition of Chola bronzes, it would be important to have Tamil explanations but not Chinese. It would be good if an exhibition of Korans included Arabic explanations. Diversity in Singapore should not be rigid or legalistic.

It is of course inconvenient to use multiple languages. Administrators don't like it, but it is not good for Singapore to avoid this. In the seven years I served on various committees in the Vatican, it was standard practice for translations to be provided. The Catholic Church would not be Catholic if it were monolingual. It is universal only because it speaks multiple languages. There was one exception when the chairman of a special task force, a senior gentleman from England, suggested that only English be used for convenience. Everyone was too polite to disagree. The result was that those not fluent in English did not participate fully, and the recommendations of the task force could not be well implemented because practical problems were not freely surfaced.

During election time in Singapore, candidates speak in different languages and dialects to communicate with residents and connect with them not just intellectually, but also emotionally. During Covid-19, when effective communication is a matter of life and death, all languages and dialects have to be used. Among those from older generations, there is significant alienation because of the predominant use of English today. Many from the pioneer generation feel alienated in their own country.

I saw this in my own mother. Having worked in government for most of my working life, I understand the problems of using multiple languages. We need a practical approach. The objective is effective communication directed at both the mind and the heart. There will always be Singaporeans who complain of unfairness. Their complaints should be carefully considered and adjustments made if necessary. We will never stop debating culture, language and religion in Singapore because diversity is in our core. Singapore will not be Singapore if these issues cease to bother us. If this happens, we will not be a Big Singapore but a small Singapore.

Among Singaporeans, it is essential that some of us master Chinese, Bahasa and other languages. It is right that English is our common language and the principal language of administration. We should not, however, become principally monolingual in English. As a population, we will never be able to master English like the British, Americans or Australians.

Singaporeans are embarrassed when Westerners praise our command of English, thinking that it is our second language, when it is in fact, for many of us, our first.

However, when we travel to China, Indonesia or Malaysia, our command of Chinese or Bahasa is often inadequate. Within our own delegations, we find it increasingly difficult to find or include those who know those languages well. Loss of language facility is also accompanied by reduced understanding of culture, history and politics. I was delighted when my calligraphy teacher, Tan Siah Kwee, was able to explain every word on my parents' Chaozhou marriage certificate to me. If we cease to have Singaporeans like him, we will be a poorer place.

Projecting 10–20 years ahead or more, Singapore will be much better placed to ride the growth of Asia by being a linguistic and cultural hub. The use of multiple languages enables Singapore to access different countries economically, culturally and politically. Singapore thrives by being a centre of arbitrage. The most difficult arbitrage involves culture. Language is key to this.

Q: Can diversity be enforced? When does it become dysfunctional?

Kuo Pao Kun's first English play, *The Coffin is Too Big For The Hole*, satirises the pursuit of standardisation in the name of efficiency. In the play, when the titular coffin was too big for a standard-sized hole, the bureaucratic solution was to cut the coffin down to size. Pao Kun's cry was for greater diversity in Singapore.

Kuo Pao Kun inspired many people, not only artists, including Sim Wong Hoo who wrote a book about him after he died in 2002

He was a profound man who had great influence on a generation of artists. He appreciated my support of the Substation arts facility. When he died, the founder of Creative Technology, Sim Wong Hoo, wrote a book to remember him. Wong Hoo attributed part of his success to Pao Kun. As a young man, while taking music lessons at Practice Theatre, he was inspired by Pao Kun. I came to know Wong Hoo because of a donation he made to Practice Theatre which is now headed by Pao Kun's daughter, Jian Hong.

Pao Kun's daughter Jian Hong and Practice Theatre at Waterloo Street today

There are limits, of course. Unconstrained diversity leads to disunity. We need laws to mark out limits or else extremists will have a free hand to polarise society. Social media has weakened hierarchies everywhere, leading to social and political fragmentation in many countries. If society has no common values, diversity will break it up. If there is no unifying core, force will be needed to ensure unity — but enforced unity is a false unity that cannot endure.

Singapore has laws and regulations to encourage mixing in our neighbourhoods, schools, military units, hawker centres and other common spaces. But they only take us so far. If we are like oil and water to each other, stirring the mixture only makes the blobs smaller temporarily. We will never melt into one solution. In a crisis, we will not gel.

Unity begins with respect for the other. Respect springs from interest and knowledge. As the Chinese like to say, I have you in my heart and you have me in yours. This applies as much to groups as it does to individuals.

As Foreign Minister, I was keen to build Singapore's friendships with other small countries. In the United Nations (UN), most countries are small. The solidarity of small countries is an important aspect of our foreign policy. I disliked how Singapore was described as punching above her weight, as if we have become too big for our boots. Such boasts do not endear us to other small countries. The higher we climb, the more we have to turn back and help others move up the ladder.

I enjoyed visiting other small countries. Visiting big countries, I was sometimes made to feel like a supplicant. After one World Economic Forum in Davos, I visited Liechtenstein, a tiny nation of 38,000 people sandwiched between Austria and Switzerland. There is a joke that if you take a nap in the car, you might miss the country completely. My host, Foreign Minister Aurelia Frick, could hardly believe her ears when I said I was going to spend a night there. I was intrigued by her beautiful little country and wanted to get a sense of it. We became good friends. Long after I left government, she would still ask after me. Till today, the wallpaper on my iPad is a picture of Liechtenstein.

Aurelia shared Liechtenstein's policy on immigration with me. Despite its tiny population, Liechtenstein is careful in whom it takes in as new citizens. Citizenship is conditional on the acceptance of the individual by the local community. Only a few dozen residence permits are given every year. All new migrants must learn German. Most importantly, local Liechtensteinians must feel that you can be one of them.

I have been floating a similar proposal to former colleagues in the Singapore government. Before approving new citizenships, why not run candidates past a jury of ordinary Singaporeans? Let them be interviewed first. We can tell the jury that they should not blackball too many candidates, maybe, let us say, 2 out of 10. They should be provided with the applicant's background and allowed to ask whatever questions they wish.

Let us say a wealthy businessman from China wants to become a citizen. Our jury can ask him about his knowledge of Malays and Indians in Singapore. Does he know what halal means? When an Indian walks in, they can ask him how he would relate to local Indians, many of whom might have descended from castes lower than his. Of course, words are just words. What have they actually done to benefit ordinary Singaporeans?

Such a process would alter the psychology of new citizenships. Word would get around with lightning speed among applicants that they have not only to impress the Economic Development Board (EDB) and Ministry of Manpower (MOM), but also ordinary Singaporeans. Ordinary Singaporeans will feel that they have a say in who can become fellow Singaporeans. Like anxious parents wanting their children to get into good schools, prospective citizenship applicants will build up a track record of local involvement. I would suggest a further step: that the status of new citizens be provisional for, say, five years.

In 2010, a year before the civil war in Syria (which was fuelled and fanned by outside forces), I made an official visit to Syria as the guest of Foreign Minister Walid Muallem. The Grand Mufti of Syria, Sheikh Ahmad Bareddin Al Hassoun, whom I had met in Singapore, invited me to visit him in Aleppo. His son, also a man of the cloth, received my wife and me at the city gate of Aleppo. The Grand Mufti hosted us with utmost courtesy for lunch at his house, to which he invited other religious leaders. As it was Friday, he invited me to join him at his mosque and to address the congregation through an interpreter. In the afternoon, he picked us up at our hotel and brought us to the Catholic Armenian Cathedral, where a special mass for women was held. I was invited to speak. When he spoke, I could see that the Catholic congregation was full of admiration and affection for him.

Invited to Friday prayers by Chief Mufti of Syria in 2010

Visit to Aleppo Armenian Catholic Church with Chief Mufti

Lunch at Chief Mufti's house with Armenian Catholic Bishop

Sheikh Ahmad's sermons were always suffused with compassion and love. "There was a father with five sons — one a Buddhist, another a Christian, the third a Muslim, the fourth a Jew and the fifth a Hindu. Who does he love the most? Surely the son who loved his brothers."

If we love only those whose beliefs are the same as ours, that is a conditional love, not a true love. Love is loving a person for what he is, not for what we want him to be. Since we are all unique individuals, diversity is natural. Acknowledging a common Creator Father means acknowledging that we are all brothers and sisters.

Cardinal Jan Schotte was a Synod Secretary to Pope John Paul II. My wife and I were introduced to him by Father Frank DePoorter from the Congregation of the Immaculate Heart of Mary (CICM) Mission in Singapore. He was visiting Australia and stopped over in Singapore on the way back to Rome, giving us an opportunity to have him over for dinner.

Cardinal Schotte once drafted a speech for the Holy Father which included the line "Despite our differences, we are one." The Pope said, no, crossed out the word 'despite', and replaced it with the word 'because'. That story was imprinted on my mind. A unity that is not based on diversity is a brittle one. Unity begins with respect for the individual as a unique creation.

Q: Countries have managed diversity in different ways. Is there a best way to embrace diversity?

I often use the human colonisation of space as a thought experiment. Imagine a time in the future when Earth decides to colonise Mars as a multinational project. How will the human colony on Mars be governed? Perhaps the colonisation of the Americas by the European powers in earlier centuries might give us some insights. Will the colony on Mars be organised like the United States (US), the European Union (EU) or Singapore? While it cannot be organised like China or India, many in the colony will be Chinese and Indians. There is already a

After the Berlin Wall was returned to its American owner, we brought back the original artists of Kings of Freedom, Niklas Bo Beckert and Dennis Kaun, to do a new painting with the words from Pope John Paul II.

quiet race between the US and China to send men to Mars. Such a future may not be that far away.

What makes us human is the human brain. The human brain is the most complex assembly of atoms in the known universe. What distinguishes us from chimpanzees, with whom we share about 98.5% of our genome is our ability to collectively organise and reorganise. The collective brain of human beings — past and present — has the potential to understand everything, or so we want to think. The more we are able to network past and present brains, the more amazing the collective brain becomes. Each human brain is like a computer. The operating system which connects human brains is culture and civilisation. Apple has iOS, Google has AndroidOS and Huawei has HarmonyOS. Our destiny in the stars is only limited by our ability or willingness to work together. What will the human operating system be like on Mars? For sure, like the Starship Enterprise in *Star Trek*, it will have to accommodate considerable human diversity.

The use of multiple languages expresses respect for diversity. The Malays have a common saying, *bahasa jiwa bangsa*, which means that language is the soul of a race or nation. For the EU, diversity is the starting point. At every meeting, political leaders put headphones on in order to understand one another. Former European Commission President José Manuel Barroso once highlighted that translation is at the core of Europe. That indeed was my experience in the Vatican.

It is, however, unclear whether the EU will endure for centuries. The Europeans are a collection of tribal peoples, each fiercely proud of its history, language and culture. In a multipolar world, Europe's complex governance is both a strength and a weakness. European nations remain unwilling to cede defence and foreign policy fully to the EU.

Singapore has to find our own way to manage diversity. We can't be like Europe because we are price-takers in the world and have to react quickly and decisively to threats and opportunities. We can't be like China, which is remarkably homogeneous for such a vast country. The challenge is always one of balance, which is not autonomously determined. Singapore's balance has to be found in relation to the region and world in which we make a living and protect ourselves. It has to be a dynamic balance.

It is not enough to tolerate diversity. Tolerating diversity carries the connotation that we have to suppress our natural emotions in order to be civil. Sooner or later, we will run out of patience and blow up. There has to be respect for the other and an appreciation of their strength and goodness. Singapore is only as big as we are able to cultivate such an attitude within ourselves. Cultural education must be an integral part of being or becoming Singaporean.

I must first know who I am and be comfortable with my own identity. Only then am I able to appreciate others who are different from me. Curiosity begets curiosity. When we deny a person's identity, they become uptight and angry. When we acknowledge it, they become relaxed and even able to joke about it. The old Malaya was a little like that before race became politicised. The Malaysian cartoonist Lat manages to poke fun at racial differences without causing offence because underlying all his depictions is an affection for all races.

Debate about Singapore's diversity will never cease. It can be healthy. Leadership is always vital. Extremists should never be allowed to hijack the common agenda, though I accept that defining extremism might itself be contentious. At an abstract level, defining extremism leads to endless argument. The test is the person's attitude in ordinary life. Does he cherish other Singaporeans? If we walk past our neighbours every day without showing interest in their customs and culture, we are not one community. We are only co-existing. Chinese New Year should always be a happy event for all races. If nothing else, we will all be happy when our neighbours' children line up to receive ang pows. In the same way, Hari Raya should be a day of celebration for all Singaporeans. New citizens have to be inducted into such a wonderful way of life. If they are not prepared to, it is better that they do not become citizens.

My old Baha'i friend, Jamshed Fozdar, and his wife, Parvati, have been lobbying for Nowruz, the Spring New Year celebrated by many

Celebrating Nowruz in Azerbaijan

A popular Nowruz game is to see who can use an egg to break his opponent's egg

people from the Balkans to Central Asia and Afghanistan and which falls on or around 21 March, to be made a national holiday in Singapore. I did encourage Nowruz to be celebrated in Singapore, but replied to him that until many Singaporeans celebrate the festival, it would be hard to justify making it a national holiday.

Left: Birthplace of Zoroasterianism near Baku. On the mountainsides are flames fuelled by natural gas that never burn out. I was in Baku with Philip Yeo for the groundbreaking of Keppel's shipyard.

Centre & bottom: For the first time, Nowruz was 'officially' recognised in Singapore in 2010 when President Nathan attended the celebration dinner organised by Parsi Zoroastrian Association of Singapore.

Photo credit: Ministry of Communications and Information Collection, courtesy of National Archives of Singapore.

Q: What are some of the practical issues you encountered, especially when you were a Minister?

Let me give a few examples.

As Minister for Information and the Arts, I inherited the Speak Mandarin Campaign. In Chinese, its tagline was "用华语表心意", but in English, it was rendered as "If you're a Chinese, make a statement — in Mandarin". The English slogan caused considerable offence among non-Mandarin speakers because of its double meaning. We changed the slogan to "讲华语·受益多" the following year. The English version was "Speak Mandarin. It helps." That was palatable to everyone. A little sensitivity in thought, word and deed makes all the difference.

We used to have Christian broadcasts on Sundays. It was a practice inherited from colonial times. Non-Christian groups felt that this was unfair. For a long time, we had Muslim programmes on the Malay station but that was uncontroversial. Lee Kuan Yew struck a bargain with Muslim leaders early on that in return for mosques not making public calls to prayer on loudspeakers, Malay radio would broadcast the *adhan* instead. A Muslim intellectual argued that since many Singaporeans were switching to English, English radio should also carry Muslim broadcasts. He was not persuaded when I countered that Muslims already had their fair share of airtime on Malay radio. Not long afterwards, Buddhist groups made similar requests.

This issue was a hot potato. The more the subject was discussed, the more dissatisfied various groups became. I did not raise the matter with Cabinet because a decision taken there would give me no room for manoeuvre. I decided to move gingerly towards a more even outcome. We cut down Christian broadcasts on Sunday and introduced some on Buddhism, especially at festivals like Vesak. On Malay radio, apart from the *adhan*, we reduced broadcasts that were religious in nature. Tamil radio was not controversial even though many Tamil songs had references to Hindu gods. On Guru Nanak Day, we had a programme on Sikhism. I kept religious leaders informed of the direction we were moving in. If the issue blew up, I was prepared for a full debate in Parliament. All this was done over a number of months, slice by slice. No group got everything it wanted, but everyone had something. It was rough justice which was good enough for religious leaders and made possible only because of a tradition of compromise in Singapore.

On some issues, we had to act decisively. For example, we banned *The Satanic Verses* by Salman Rushdie without a second thought. In the case of Paul Schraeder's *The Last Temptation of Christ*, however, we did nothing. On such issues, Christians and Buddhists did not react the same way as Muslims. We were not wedded to abstract equality. The considerations were completely practical.

One day, I received a request from MUIS, the Islamic Religious Council of Singapore, to ban publications by the Ahmadiyya, a movement that some consider heretical. Ahmadiyya followers are persecuted in some countries but they are free to practise their religion in Singapore. I remember authorising a reply to MUIS stating that the Ministry was not in a position to judge which sects were heretical.

Such tensions will never go away in a diverse society. We will always have debates on subjects like Special Assistance Program (SAP) schools, madrasahs, tudungs, turbans and the Administration of Muslim Law Act (AMLA). If we want to quarrel, there are many reasons to do so. Better to give and take. Crucial is trust that the government is not partial and tries to be fair even if decisions taken are not all to our liking.

Laws can mark out the perimeters of debate, but for society to be harmonious, there has to be mutual respect. In Singapore, we are incredibly blessed to have the Inter-Religious Organisation (IRO), a social organisation representing 10 religions. They are a treasure to Singaporean society. I will never forget the day I officiated at the inclusion of the 10th religion — Jainism — for which I wore Gujarati clothing, including long pointy shoes which curved upwards. Not being used to wearing Gujarati pants, I kept pulling them up, fearing that they were not properly fastened at the waist. My wife told me afterwards that she wondered what I was doing.

After my defeat in the 2011 General Election, there was a macabre series of suicides in Bedok Reservoir over a number of months. A sudden gloom fell over the entire area. As I was still an adviser to grassroots organisations, I got the IRO to come down and say prayers. It gave comfort to local residents. There was one more incident after that before the suicides stopped.

Celebrating inclusion of Jainism into the IRO. First time I wore Gujarati clothes and shoes.

IRO praying at Bedok Reservoir after spate of suicides following the 2011 General Elections

CHAPTER 4

❖

Reflecting the World's Diversity

Q: Diversity is a challenge everywhere. Is there something that Singapore can show the world?

We should never presume to do so. Singapore is a little experiment which others would naturally want to study for its successes and failures. We will never be able to declare complete success. We should also not stop learning from others. With modern transportation, the world has become much smaller. With the Internet, we are connected all the time. There has never been greater movement of people on this planet than in this current period. Thus, all societies have become more diverse, faster than their cultures are able to evolve in response. Singapore is by no means alone in having to grapple with such challenges.

Across the world, many experiments are running concurrently. The national motto of the United States (US) is *E Pluribus Unum* (from many, one). The ideal is the US as one great melting pot. The huddled masses who arrive are progressively absorbed. They learn English. They revere the Constitution. They sing the Star-Spangled Banner and wave the flag. It worked for European immigrants who had common roots in Greece, Rome and Judeo-Christianity. African Americans are still not fully enfranchised despite the Civil War and the civil rights movement. New migrants from Latin America and Asia cling tenaciously to their old cultures. The American cauldron continues to bubble, sometimes threatening to boil over. By the middle of this century, whites will be in the minority.

Historically, the US has been able to re-invent itself again and again. The American experiment is of interest to the entire world. It began as a new creation of Europe. Whether it will be a new creation for the world, no one can be sure. European immigrants who came to America in serried waves took time to fit in. It was only after the First World War that a common white American identity emerged.

During the Second World War, Japanese Americans were interned for fear of them becoming a fifth column. To earn the trust of white Americans, over 12,000 second-generation Japanese Americans volunteered to fight under the 442nd Regiment, which became the most decorated unit in US military history. American Senator Daniel Inouye of Hawaii lost his right arm fighting the Germans in Italy. Japanese Americans were, however, only trusted with combat missions in Europe, not in Asia. The trauma of their experience after Pearl Harbour hastened their assimilation into American society.

It is harder for minority races which are not European to melt into the American pot. The Hispanic community has become so large that their complete assimilation may not be possible. In many districts, political candidates speak Spanish to reach out to them.

Chinese Americans are at a crossroads. As US–China relations become more fraught, many in that community are distrusted. Unlike Japanese Americans, they are unlikely to give up their ancestral ties so readily. China plays up the difficulties faced by the Chinese community in the US. It is good for China if talented Chinese turn their backs on the US and return to China. It is also natural for China to make use of Chinese networks in the US to gather information and recruit agents of influence. In recent years, US security agencies have become obsessed with the challenges posed by China. Negative sentiments against the Chinese among ordinary Americans rub off on other Asian Americans like Koreans, Vietnamese and Southeast Asians. Chinese American leaders find themselves between a rock and a hard place. Athletes like Gu Ailing, who won two gold medals in the 2022 Beijing Winter Olympics, are caught in opposing loyalties.

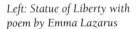

"Give me your tired, your poor, your huddled masses yearning to breathe free. The wretched refuse of your teeming shore. Send these, the homeless, tempest-tost to me, I lift my lamp beside the golden door!"

Left: Statue of Liberty with poem by Emma Lazarus

Bottom: President Trump's wall on the Mexican border

Unlike Chinese Americans, Indian Americans are less conflicted. There is no distrust of Indians as the US government sees India as an ally against China, even though India will always have its own agenda. Muslim Americans are still small in numbers. Should their proportion in the general population increase like in Europe, ethnic relations in the US will become more complicated especially given longstanding US support of Israel.

The US is now caught between the high ideals expressed in the poem of Emma Lazarus inscribed beneath the Statue of Liberty, "The New Colossus", and fears that the country may be inundated by non-white immigration — between the lines *"Give me your tired, your poor, your huddled masses yearning to breathe free, the wretched refuse of your teeming shore. Send these, the homeless, tempest-tossed to me, I lift my lamp beside the golden door!"* and President Trump's wall.

In France, the growing Muslim population is shaking the foundations of society. French Muslims are over-represented in the national soccer team but under-represented in the cultural and political establishments. Islamic values do not align well with the national ideals of an "indivisible, secular, democratic, and social Republic", as stated in the Constitution of 1958. While nude sunbathing is commonplace, burqinis are disallowed by law, a matter still being litigated. More seriously, the large number of unemployed and underemployed Muslim youth in major cities is not only destabilising, but a potential recruitment ground for extremists.

Policing beaches in France

The EU is founded on diversity but held together by common European values. Although much of Europe is stridently secular today, many European values have Christian origins. It is unlikely that Turkey, with its large Muslim population, will ever be admitted, although neither side will openly say this. The growing Muslim population in Europe is a challenge to the idea of European solidarity. Migration from the Middle East and Africa is creating a backlash in a number of European member states.

Europe, however, is a union more in name than in fact. It is more a confederation than a federation like the US. European states are still not prepared to cede the most critical powers to Brussels. As American power in the world recedes — as the world becomes multipolar — this may change. Some Europeans want to establish a separate European army, without which there cannot be a common European foreign policy. This is not likely to happen soon, for it would conflict with the Transatlantic Alliance, which has its strongest expression in the North Atlantic Treaty Organization (NATO). Conflict with Russia over Ukraine has united Europe as never before in a long while. Its internal divisions are however, never far beneath the surface.

India's diversity is similar to that of Europe. It inherited a centralised system of administration from the British Raj. For four decades after independence, the Congress Party took an inclusive approach, which kept ethnic, language, caste and religious conflicts within bounds. Since then, India has seen a a strong Hindutva reaction led by the Bharatiya Janata Party (BJP) and the Rashtriya Swayamsevak Sangh (RSS).

The demolition of the Babri Mosque in Ayodhya in December 1992 began a new phase in Indian politics. The Hindutva mission to right 'historical wrongs' creates insecurity among Muslims and Christians. The leadership of the Army and Administrative Service is also being affected. Power has been progressively devolving to the states because of economic forces and electoral politics.

Historically, the Indian sub-continent has always been diverse. While it has never been fully united, even under the Mauryas, it is also not

Babri Mosque in the 19ᵗʰ century, before its demolition in December 1992

prone to revolution. India in some ways is more like a civilisation than a nation.

Indonesia is arguably as diverse as India, but it has a strong core in Java, which accounts for more than half its population. Despite this, its national language is not Javanese but Bahasa. On 28 October 1928, in a house owned by an Chinese Indonesian, the second Indonesian youth congress pledged that Indonesia would be one country, one nation and one language (*satu tanah air, satu bangsa, satu bahasa*). Similarly, although Muslims make up 80% of the population, the proclaimed national philosophy is not Islam but Pancasila. In the Indonesian Army, Christian officers are disproportionately represented. The Sanskrit motto *bhinneka tunggal ika* means 'unity in diversity'. Indonesia would not be a single nation if its majority population were not Javanese. Without Javanese wisdom, not only would there not be one Indonesia, but the Association of Southeast Asian Nations (ASEAN) as we know it would probably not have come about.

However, there is a 'Chinese problem' in Indonesia, as there is in all of Southeast Asia. Though a small minority, ethnic Chinese in Southeast Asia play a disproportionate role in the economy and are over-represented among the wealthy. The Thai King Rama VI called them the "Jews of

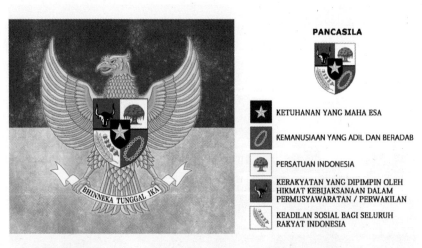

Pancasila:

Ketuhanan yang Maha Esa (Belief in the Almighty God)

Kemanusiaan yang adil dan beradab (Just and civilised humanity)

Persatuan Indonesia (The unity of Indonesia)

Kerakyatan yang dipimpin oleh hikmat kebijaksanaan dalam permusyawaratan/perwakilan (Democracy guided by the inner wisdom in the unanimity arising out of deliberations among representatives)

Keadilan sosial bagi seluruh rakyat Indonesia (Social justice for all of the people of Indonesia)

The pledge [edit]

In Indonesian, with the original spelling, the pledge reads:[5]

Pertama
Kami poetra dan poetri Indonesia, mengakoe bertoempah darah jang satoe, tanah air Indonesia.
Kedoea
Kami poetra dan poetri Indonesia, mengakoe berbangsa jang satoe, bangsa Indonesia.
Ketiga
Kami poetra dan poetri Indonesia, mendjoendjoeng bahasa persatoean, bahasa Indonesia.

In Indonesian with current spelling:

Pertama
Kami putra dan putri Indonesia, mengaku bertumpah darah yang satu, tanah air Indonesia.
Kedua
Kami putra dan putri Indonesia, mengaku berbangsa yang satu, bangsa Indonesia.
Ketiga
Kami putra dan putri Indonesia, menjunjung bahasa persatuan, bahasa Indonesia.

In English:

Firstly
We the sons and daughters of Indonesia, acknowledge one motherland, Indonesia.
Secondly
We the sons and daughters of Indonesia, acknowledge to be of one nation, the nation of Indonesia.
Thirdly
We the sons and daughters of Indonesia, uphold the language of unity, Indonesian.

Pancasila and Sumpah Pemuda

the East". From time to time, they are discriminated against, sometimes actively through national policy, sometimes more subtly. Like the Jews in Europe, their sense of insecurity made them stronger. With China in the ascendant, they are playing a more prominent role in the regional economy. ASEAN is already China's top trading partner, overtaking Europe and the US.

China's population is unusually homogeneous, being made up of over 90% Han Chinese. This is by design, not accident. Its system of governance has evolved over thousands of years. It relies on a political culture which is sometimes described as Confucianism. The nation is conceived as a big family, with Chinese learning how to behave as family members from a young age.

China has always been largely self-sufficient. Today's dual circulation economy is not new. With its large population, China has always depended more on internal circulation than the world outside. It protects itself by building walls — not just physical, but cultural and economic ones. With Covid-19, it has built the greatest wall of all — the great biological wall of China.

The current Western fear that an ascendant China will become imperialistic shows an inability or unwillingness to understand China in the context of its long history. Minorities in China do not pose a threat to the Han people. When they do, they are suppressed. When they are peaceful, they receive better treatment than ordinary Han people. China's political system is not exportable. It is built on a political culture that is quintessentially Chinese. Unlike US exceptionalism, China's civilisation has no missionary instinct.

In the case of Xinjiang, China left Muslim minorities to their own devices for too long. The Chinese government restored Uighur names. Road signs were in Chinese and Uighur scripts. Uighurs were allowed more children than Han families. The education system did not require their young to learn Chinese. The Chinese government took too long to realise that Salafi thinking was seeping into the Muslim population and changing it. It was only when Islamic terrorism went from bad to worse, causing local Han Chinese to arm themselves and fight back, that the central government acted decisively.

No doubt, the re-education camps are not Sunday schools, but to describe them as concentration camps and the measures taken by Beijing as genocidal is tendentious. The fact of the matter is that Xinjiang is once again peaceful, and its local tourism is booming. Outsiders may be tempted to teach China how to manage Islamic extremism, but they should remember that no country has found an easy solution. Muslim countries understand this and are slow to criticise China. We are still finding our own way in Singapore and are certainly not in a position to judge others. Better we learn from the experiences of others — both their successes and failures.

Q: What should we do to manage diversity in Singapore?

Be it living with fellow Singaporeans or interacting with foreign friends, we should always try to put ourselves in the shoes of others. It is not easy to empathise, but we should always try. When we do, they feel they are in us, and we are then in them too. The intensity varies with the relationship. The closer the relationship, the greater the need for empathy. I like the Taoist Yin-Yang symbol. In the black, there is a spot of white. In the white, there is a spot of black. In this way, opposites find their unity.

Singapore should be like a crystal with many facets reflecting the diversity of the world. That is when it sparkles. When we seek homogeneity, when we turn inwards, we stop shining and become a dull stone.

For example, when the Japanese visit Singapore, they feel partially at home here. There are Japanese restaurants, supermarkets, schools and clinics. They can gather with fellow Japanese on the golf course or mix with non-Japanese in a bar. Singapore has a special place in the minds and hearts of Australians because of the Second World War. Near where I live, the old Changi Prison wall is well preserved. Every year, Australians remember their forebears who suffered and died in that prison. Australian heritage is all over Singapore, as is the heritage of other peoples. Australians are welcome in Singapore as old friends.

Just about everyone in the world can find themselves reflected in Singapore, even small European communities like the Nordics and the Swiss. Singapore has profound links to all of Asia and the West. Singapore is also the most ASEANised country in ASEAN. The other nine countries have substantial communities living in Singapore, contributing not only to our economy but also to the arts. Naturally, our blood is also mixed as a result.

In his classic 1992 text, *Tribes*, Joel Kotkin explained the importance of cities being home to members of trading communities like the Chinese, Jews, Parsees, Sindhis, Armenians and Lebanese. Members of such tribes operate in multiple domains. They maintain international networks which are powered by information. They know where to buy cheaper and where to sell dearer. Their internal network of trust reduces the cost of capital. Singapore was one city so identified by Kotkin.

As a city-state, we enjoy a special advantage: we have control over our borders. That which is healthful should be able to come and go freely. That which is harmful should be kept out. Singapore is a bubble with a sophisticated semi-permeable membrane. Creating and maintaining this semi-permeability requires much investment in immigration and quarantine control. It requires good intelligence. Within the bubble, we try to create salubrious conditions for economic and cultural activities. This includes good infrastructure, laws which enforce contracts and protect property rights, a sense of safety and a wholesome environment. We also need cultural amenities which nourish the spirit. Cities which are part of larger countries are less able to provide equivalent conditions because urban and rural interests are not always aligned.

The heart of Singapore's economy is arbitrage. The most important arbitrage is not in trade or finance, but culture. Arbitrage in commodity and financial markets can be reduced to algorithms. Cultural nuances are hard to codify. Dealing with Japanese trading houses is different from dealing with Southeast Asian ethnic Chinese businessmen. Commu-

Changi Prison where many Australian prisoners suffered and died during the Second World War

Prime Minister Kevin Rudd visiting Changi Chapel

nicating with Australians is different from communicating with Javanese. In many Asian cultures, there are a hundred different ways to say 'no' without actually saying 'no'. Without cultural sensitivity, nuances are missed and mistakes are easily made. In Singapore, we have a multichannel capability. We switch channels all the time depending on whom we deal with.

We develop this sensitivity not through formal study but by growing up in Singapore. From a young age, we learn what the taboos are. For example, every native Singaporean knows that Muslims do not eat pork and shy away from dogs. When we invite Muslim friends for a meal, we have to be sensitive. Some have stricter requirements, whereas for others, so long as the food does not contain pork or lard, it is okay. A few might even appreciate a glass of wine. All in all, it is better to find out in advance. If necessary, we can order in food which is halal-certified.

More Singaporeans have become vegetarian or vegan. I don't mind eating vegetarian occasionally, but I would resent having to do so every time I am with a vegetarian guest. There was a time when Muslim and non-Muslim Members of Parliament (MPs) sat at separate tables in the Singapore Parliament because of dietary requirements. When Lee Kuan Yew saw it happening, he was alarmed. We then switched to buffet dining. MPs would collect their food from separate buffet tables, which could be halal, non-halal or vegetarian, and then sit together at mixed tables.

What seems obvious to us in Singapore may not be at all in other countries. When Mohammad Maidin joined the Young People's Action Party (PAP) delegation on its visit to China, I promised him that we would arrange halal food for Muslims in the delegation. At one of our first meals, a steamed fish arrived beautifully garnished. My eyes popped out when I saw thin slices of ham slotted into the side of the fish. Maidin was just as quick to notice. We looked at each other. He was gracious and signalled that it was not a problem. For the rest of the trip, he stuck to the readily available vegetarian food. I felt very bad for his inconvenience. I learned that in China, if one wants to be sure that food is halal, it is best to go to a 清真 (halal) restaurant.

Singapore has many interesting small communities like the Jews, Parsees, Bohras, Sikhs, Arabs, Malayalees and Baha'is. Not only are they all internationally connected, they enrich our society and strengthen our global network. After I lost my seat in the 2011 General Election, both the Jewish and Parsee communities hosted me for dinner. For the Jewish community, it was partly to thank me for helping them with the establishment of a Jewish School which teaches Hebrew. Recently, the Deputy Australian High Commissioner told me that her child was studying there, which gladdened my heart. The Parsee community knew that I had always admired their high-mindedness. These small communities add colour to our lives in Singapore. The Baha'is had previously requested my help about the persecution of their members in Iran. On one visit to Israel, I asked to visit their Headquarters in Haifa and met a number of Singapore volunteers there.

Q: Can we ever be too sensitive? What is an ideal Singapore to you?

Yes, of course. This is my gripe with the 'woke' culture which is creeping into our own society. If we are overly sensitive to slights, even when they are not intended, we will gradually start to fray. Too much political correctness is suffocating. We become hypocrites. At an abstract level, it is often difficult to reach agreement. In practice, however, mutual respect can dissolve most difficulties.

The problem arises when one side insists on his rights while refusing to see the same problem from the other person's point of view. Everything then becomes a power struggle. For example, many Singaporeans take their dogs out and sometimes groom them on void deck or park benches. Seeing this, Muslims avoid using them. If the authorities put up notices saying that benches cannot be used for such a purpose, non-Muslims will be unhappy. Debating issues like this will only get everyone hot under the collar. A little thoughtfulness, like cleaning up after we use a public bench or table, goes a long way

What is ideal? We should be more rooted in ASEAN, and I personally

Jewish Welfare Board hosting me after the 2011 General Election

Visit to the Waterloo Street Synagogue

Singapore's vibrant Malayalee community

Habib Hassan of Ba'alwi Mosque hosting a Hari Raya reception

Meeting young Bohras

Arabs, mostly Hadramis, in Southeast Asia

Parsee community hosting me to dinner after the
2011 General Election

Meeting members of the Sikh community

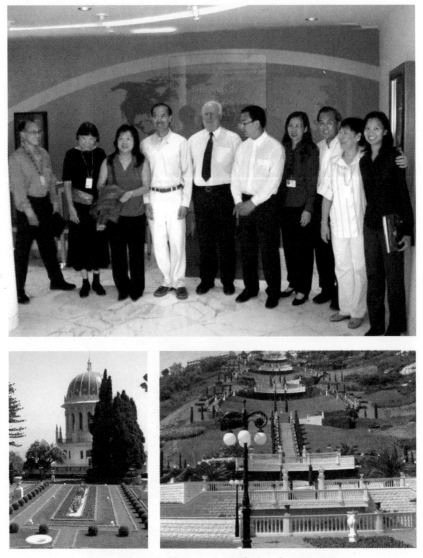

Visit to Baha'i World Centre in Haifa, Israel in June 2003

like the Swiss spirit. Switzerland should be an inspiration to us. Many of us are vaguely familiar with the story of William Tell and the formation of the Helvetic Confederation over 700 years ago. The Swiss are made up of four different communities — German, French, Italian and Romansh (a tiny community) — gathered in different cantons. Over the centuries, they were determined to stick together and not be dragged into larger conflicts around them in Europe, including religious wars between Catholics and Protestants.

They take their security most seriously. As the Head of Air Plans, I once visited the Pilatus Aircraft factory in Zurich to look at a turboprop trainer replacement for the Republic of Singapore Air Force (RSAF). Before the chief executive officer (CEO) began his briefing, I told him I regretted not having asked for a briefing from the Swiss Air Force. It was too late now. He said he was a Colonel in the Swiss Air Force and proceeded to give me a briefing not on Pilatus, but the Swiss Air Force. I was hugely impressed and thought that he could not have done better marketing for his company.

Like us, the Swiss recognise four official languages. Like us, each of their cantons is distinct but connected to a wider world. There is a palpable camaraderie that all Swiss share. The Swiss have an emergency fund which distressed citizens abroad can make use of to return home. Everywhere they go, they bless their host community and do a disproportionate amount of philanthropic work. The Red Cross is a Swiss creation. The World Economic Forum is a Swiss Foundation. I had a Swiss classmate in Harvard Business School who graduated with me in 1985. He told me he was going back to the Swiss Army for four months, or one trimester, so that he could become a Captain. (Their year is divided into three trimesters of 17 weeks each, and those who qualify for promotion must first put in an extra trimester to earn it.)

Singapore must re-root itself more strongly in the region. Our sudden independence stripped us of our traditional hinterland. We had to leapfrog the region and plug directly into the developed world. Investments from MNCs enabled us to grow rapidly for over 30 years

Switzerland in Singapore — St Gallen Symposium

Swiss granite sculpture at Botanic Garden to mark the 700th year of the Helvetic Confederation in 1991

The Swiss Club in Singapore

and streak ahead of other countries in the region. In the process, we lost our sense of the region, especially Malaysia and Indonesia.

Other countries in ASEAN sometimes feel that we look down on them. I received this feedback most strongly after I left government. There is some truth in it. With the geopolitical shifts around us, we need ASEAN more than ever. By ourselves, bad relations between the US and China can put us in a tight spot. Other countries in ASEAN fear a similar situation. By banding together, we create a collective buffer. Faced with pressure from one side or the other, we can seek refuge in a common ASEAN position.

For ASEAN to be robust, its integration must be both top-down and ground-up. All of us in ASEAN should steadily develop a stronger sense of ASEAN citizenship. Singapore students should spend more time visiting other ASEAN countries, learning more about their people and making friends. Singapore should strive to be a capital city for all of ASEAN. A Singapore at ease with the diversity of ASEAN will find itself at ease with the diversity of the world. Our schools should teach ASEAN history, geography and cultures more — much more than they currently do.

My colleague and old friend, Zainul Abidin Rasheed, once remarked to me that every race in Singapore feels itself to be in the minority. Chinese Singaporeans are acutely aware that the Chinese in Southeast Asia are a minority race who are bullied from time to time. Zainul's insight is worthy of reflection. This sense of everyone being part of a minority community is good for Singapore. It is also good that no religion in Singapore is in the majority. We thus have no choice but to live with one another. We have to be sensitive to one another as fellow Singaporeans and we must teach our children to be the same. New citizens have to understand this imperative and do their part.

Singapore's political culture is much influenced by Chinese Confucianism, as Chinese Communism is today. In Chinese political tradition, ministers have to serve everyone. Whatever their individual origin and affiliation, once in office, they have to take a higher view and treat everyone equally. It was for this reason that Han Yu (韩愈), the

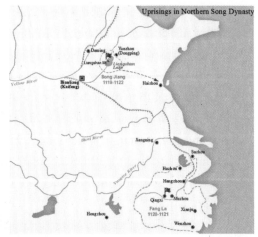

Song Jiang, leader of the 108 heroes   Outlaws of the Liangshan marsh

Wu Song beats the tiger

patron saint of Teochews, memorialised the Chinese emperor against being too caught up in worshipping one of Buddha's bones. This is the same ideal which the PAP, and now other political parties as well, subscribe to. No one can easily win a seat in Parliament by appealing only to sub-groups. For this reason, we should never adopt a system of proportional proportion which encourages candidates to focus narrowly on particular communities or causes. The group representation constituency (GRC) system has done us more good than harm.

Most of all, we need to have a big heart and a big mind. In the Ming romance, *The Water Margin* (水浒传), a band of rebels led by a historical figure, Song Jiang, sought refuge in a mountain called Mount Liang (梁山). At that time, the leader of Mount Liang was small-minded. He told Song Jiang that the mountain was too small and tried to wave Song Jiang's little group on. In response, Song Jiang decided to take over the mountain himself. Under his leadership, there were never enough heroes on the mountain. Much of the story was about how he persuaded many like Wu Song to join him. The 108 Outlaws of the Marsh, a truly diverse bunch, have since captured popular imagination in China. Singapore is of comparable size and should do likewise.

❖

The Eurasian Prawn Paste

> *Despite being tiny, the Eurasian community has a special place in Singapore society. It is the magic sauce that puts zing in our multi-ethnic salad.*

Q: Why is the Eurasian community so important to you?

Scanning through the summary of the 2020 census, I was disappointed that the Eurasian community was subsumed under 'Others'. I can understand statisticians doing this because Eurasians make up less than 1% of Singapore's population. But, it is wrong.

For many years after independence, many of our national symbols showed four components. The one I like most was of four arms locked together, representing the four races, which appeared on postage stamps and our old $10 currency note. Over time, we became sloppy and resorted to using CMIO for Chinese, Malay, Indian and Others. The sub-text is that numbers matter and the Eurasians count for little. The official identification of four races, like the recognition of our four official languages, should be a cardinal principle, the way it is for the Swiss.

Happily, in recent National Day Parades, we no longer leave out the Eurasian community. In Switzerland, the Romansh community also accounts for less than 1% of the Swiss population, but is always proudly listed as Switzerland's fourth community with links going back to Ancient Rome.

Four Interlocking Arms

Joseph 'Joe' Conceicao was a Member of Parliament and one of our ambassadors. He was a teacher at St Patrick's School before my time. In the last years of his life, J. Y. Pillay, the senior public servant, and I took him out for lunch regularly. Many years ago, Joe said publicly that it was better for Singapore Eurasians to melt into the major communities. It was a comment spoken out of despair as he felt that the Eurasian community was shrinking and demoralised.

Joe was a prolific writer. On one occasion, he asked me to run through a draft of his autobiography, which I did with relish. Joe was an exquisite writer with an impish sense of humour. His book, *Flavours of Change*, chronicled his life, including the period he spent as a young child misbehaving in the Bahau Eurasian camp in Johor during the Second World War. The only thing was that his autobiography was strangely written in the third person. I did not think it appropriate and told him so. He then re-wrote it in the first person.

Joe Conceicao

I found Joe insightful, unconventional and interesting. He peppered me with questions about world politics, which always fascinated him. We enjoyed our meals together. He told me that his Portuguese surname should properly be pronounced as "kon sang sung", which I knew, but we also knew better than to try changing the way it is commonly pronounced in Singapore, as "kon saeng seo". Gradually, as Eurasian identity went through a revivification, I was glad to see Joe delighting in his Eurasian-ness.

Among themselves, Portuguese Eurasians affectionately call each other *grago*, or, more accurately, *geragok*, which is the name of the tiny shrimps used for making the fermented shrimp sauce *chinchalok*. Many Portuguese Eurasians were shrimp fishermen in Malacca. Rex Shelley wrote a wonderful book about them called *The Shrimp People*. That said, *grago* can be derogatory and non-Eurasians should not use it on Portuguese Eurasians unless they know them well. It is not unlike the use of *gwailo*, meaning 'devil', in Hong Kong for white people. Cantonese people are wont to use it on all foreigners with equal opportunity, although many white people in Hong Kong don't mind the term and some even refer to themselves as such. With strangers, however, one should be careful about causing offense.

My family moved to Siglap when I was three years old. Like Joe, I grew up as a Katong boy. Till today, our family church is the Church of the Holy Family. My first four years in primary school were at St Patrick's. The Katong area always had a significant Eurasian community. The Fatima Block Rosary Movement, later called the Pilgrim Virgin Movement, was started there. Its founders were Cecil Klass (father of the radio DJ, John Klass) and Caetano Xavier Furtado (a botanist from Goa with an encyclopaedic mind). I don't know how my father became the treasurer of the movement. We lived in a big house and he was considered a man of means, so perhaps, they assumed he could be trusted with the money.

Every 13 January, the movement organised a party at our house to celebrate the first apparition of the Virgin Mary to three children in

Katong Block Rosary (latter Pilgrim Virgin Movement). My father is seated in the middle of the second row, next to Cecil Klass on his left, the leader of the movement. On his right is my Confirmation Godfather L. V. Stewart. I am kneeling in front on the left.

Annual 13 January celebration of the Katong Block Rosary Movement. Cheering with Framroz soft drinks.

Family picture before the altar. With Father Amiotte.

My father leading the rosary prayers

Fátima, Portugal in 1917. The Eurasian owner of the soft drinks company, Framroz, provided the drinks. Satay was freshly roasted and in plentiful supply. In time, my father got his sons to deputize for him at the monthly meetings. Eventually the job was passed to me as the youngest in the family. When I had my Confirmation in Primary Six, Lionel V Stewart, a Eurasian member of the movement, became my sponsor. I still keep the crucifix he gave me in my study.

On the 13th of every month, there is a Fatima procession at St Joseph's Church in Victoria Street. The procession stops at the grotto of the Virgin Mary in Fatima to recite a rosary decade and to sing some hymns. I accompanied my parents at these processions for many years. There are two St Joseph's churches in Singapore. This one was called the PM church because it belonged to the Portuguese Mission and answered to the Bishop of Macao, unlike the other churches in Singapore which came under the MEP (French Mission) and reported to the French Archbishop.

After the Portuguese revolution in 1974, Lisbon offered to return Macau to China immediately. Beijing, wanting to settle Hong Kong first, asked Lisbon to hold on for the time being (till 1999). Not long afterwards, St Joseph's Church (PM) was brought under the Singapore Archdiocese. I remember the last Portuguese priest, Father Bata, being appointed an Honorary Consul General for the Portuguese government. Today, the Church is under the care of Opus Dei, which has pledged to maintain its Eurasian character.

It must have been through a process of osmosis over many years that the imprint of the Eurasian community became a sub-conscious part of me. Many of the teachers and brothers were Eurasian. Thinking back, it is remarkable that the majority of my school principals were Eurasian — John Snodgrass, Brigadier Campbell (Singapore's first Brigadier), Harry Sociago, Brother Justinian and TO Aeria (the vice-principal of St Joseph's Institution).

Q: How did you come to represent the Eurasian community in Cabinet?

Boris Theseira from the Ministry of Defence's Security and Intelligence Division (SID) became a close friend when I was in the Singapore Armed Forces (SAF). At the time, then-Deputy Prime Minister (DPM) and Defence Minister Goh Chok Tong had asked me repeatedly to enter politics. I repeatedly declined because I was too young and needed to establish myself independently first. Meanwhile, Boris merrily told his Indonesian friends, General Benny Murdani and General Try Sutrisno, that I was going into politics and would become a minister, and they should therefore cultivate me.

In early 1988, Boris arranged for me to visit Indonesia as the Director of Joint Operations and Planning. I don't know what Boris told them, but the Indonesian military high command accorded me special hospitality. The first time I played golf (disastrously) was at the Halim golf course outside Jakarta. I also had my first taste of *mee bakso* (肉胖面) during that Indonesian army golf tournament.

Well, I was finally persuaded to stand for election a few months later. Boris turned out to be right, which only improved his standing in the eyes of the Indonesians.

General Murdani, a Dutch Catholic Eurasian whom everyone affectionately called Pak Benny, became like an uncle to me. I called on him when he was clearing out his office in the Defense Ministry after falling out with President Suharto. He gave me a Seiko watch with his name and four stars engraved on it and a box of orange golf balls (also with four stars), both of which I still treasure in his memory. He was a good commander. I saw him off at Paya Lebar Air Base once. He took care to shake hands with everyone sending him off, including low-ranking administrative staff. In his distinguished military career, he must have made three or four operational parachute jumps.

He told me how East Timor was being mishandled. Being Catholic himself, Pak Benny was acutely aware of local sensitivities. For 400

My wife, Jennifer, looking at Boris Theseira playing the piano up in the highlands of Tanah Toraja in Sulawesi

Group picture in Rantepao, Sulawesi

General Benny Murdani's golf balls   *General Benny Murdani's watch*

years, East Timor was under Portuguese rule. During his time, he made sure that Catholic priests sent to East Timor were fellow Melanesians who came from Flores. After he left service, Catholic priests from Java were despatched instead. They did not relate to the local population as

First and second editions of the Kristang dictionary

well. Eventually, under President Habibie, Indonesia had to disgorge East Timor.

Culture is often deeply rooted. In 2004, two Eurasian women, Valerie Scully and Catherine Zuzarte, published a dictionary of Kristang, the Portuguese dialect spoken by the Portuguese Eurasian community. It was a labour of love. Kristang was seen as a dying language, and they wanted to record as many words as possible before the language disappeared forever. They spent many months interviewing older Eurasians who still knew the language.

When they invited me to pen a foreword, my first thought was: why were they doing this? The more I reflected on their effort, the more my admiration for them grew. Although the Eurasian community was small, they showed an indestructible spirit. In the end, I wrote in my foreword:

> *"Kristang is a dead or dying language, so why bother? Culture is a strange thing. It has a tenacious life force that often defies understanding. We may think that the tree has died and all we have left is a piece of deadwood; then, one day, after a little rain, green shoots suddenly sprout from it."*

Indeed, they have. The Eurasian Association (EA) is currently conducting Kristang classes, and a second edition of the Kristang Dictionary was published in 2017, for which I wrote an additional foreword.

In the age of globalisation, we are rediscovering our links to many parts of the world. The Kristang dictionary became a diplomatic asset when I was Foreign Minister. I happily presented it to visitors from Lusophone countries, especially Portugal, Brazil and East Timor. When the Portuguese Foreign Minister, Luis Amado, was in Singapore with his Prime Minister (PM), José Sócrates, I passed him two copies, one for him and the other for his PM. His PM was transfixed by the many words he could recognise and talked about the dictionary when he called on our PM. PM Lee Hsien Loong was surprised to hear about it too. To my discredit, I had not informed him about the dictionary, thinking it was too small a matter.

When Celso Amorim, the Brazilian Minister for External Affairs and Trade, received a copy from me, he was bowled over. Many phrases in Kristang were archaic but completely comprehensible. He started speaking to me in Portuguese thinking that I knew Kristang. I beat a hasty retreat and confessed my complete ignorance. At every subsequent meeting, Celso would somehow come back to the dictionary. In diplomacy, culture goes straight to the heart.

When I was in the Republic of Singapore Air Force, I got to know Lieutenant Colonel Tim De Souza, a graduate of SAF Training Institute's (SAFTI) first batch and one of Singapore's first fighter pilots. He was from SJI and a classmate of two of my brothers. He was passionate about reviving the the Eurasian Association. I remember having many conversations with him about it. Tim appreciated my enthusiasm. He found me a strong supporter even though there was nothing I could do to help him at that time. As fate would have it, after leaving the SAF to join politics, I took charge of the then-newly-created Ministry of Information and the Arts (MITA) and became responsible for heritage work.

We had a programme to help every ethnic group build its own cultural centre. For the Malay community, it was at Kampong Glam, and for the Chinese community, at the old Nanyang University Administrative Block. The Indians would later have one at Farrer Park. For the Eurasians, MITA found two old bungalows at Mountbatten Road

*Brian Davenport who took over from Tim de Souza as the
Eurasian Association President*

*After losing the 2011 General Election, I stepped down as minister
and could no longer represent the Eurasian community in Cabinet.
This was after the EA appreciation dinner for me.*

Appointment of President S. R. Nathan and myself as Patrons of the EA

Eurasian Community House

Eurasian food

Sugee cake

as a temporary facility until we had the land and the money to build the Eurasian House at Ceylon Road, across from where President Nathan had lived.

It was around that time that Tim asked me to represent the Eurasian community in the Cabinet. After E. W. Barker, one of Singapore's founding fathers, stepped down in 1988 (which was when I entered politics), there were concerns that the Eurasians would be slowly forgotten: out of sight, out of mind. Tim told me that Mr Barker supported his proposal. Mr Barker had met me at a few social events, and must have quietly observed and thought me not unsuitable. I took up the role with great pride. It was a rare honour, one that I will always cherish. After I left government, the EA made me its patron. When new trustees were appointed recently, I was invited to be the witness.

I supported naming the centre 'Eurasian House'. First, the name recognises the smallness of the community. Smallness is an advantage. The EA is able to track every Eurasian family that needs help. As a self-help group, the EA has succeeded beyond expectations.

Second, the name 'Eurasian House' also connotes openness. Being a good host is an important part of Eurasian culture. Of all the four heritage centres, Eurasian House has the most intimate and welcoming feel to it. On the top floor, there is a gallery of Eurasian history and heritage, including the story of Eurasian men and women who contributed much to Singapore's development in different fields. On the ground floor, there is a restaurant, Quentin's, which serves good Eurasian food, including dishes like devil's curry, prawn bostador, feng and, of course, sugee cake.

Q: What were your impressions of E. W. Barker?

He had no airs about him at all. It was a privilege for me to know and earn the respect of a man who played a major role in creating an independent Singapore. Beneath the bonhomie was a man of serious purpose. When he passed away in April 2001, I was asked by his family to deliver a eulogy, which ended with these words:

> *"We are still too young as a nation to have our founding myths well etched in stone. One day we will, and Eddie Barker's contribution to the creation of modern Singapore will find its proper place. He drafted an independent and multiracial Singapore Constitution in August 1965, an act that cannot be repeated. It was fitting that it was not a Chinese or a Malay or an Indian who crafted the words, but a member of our smallest community, the Eurasians."*

E. W. Barker. On the left is Eurasian Association President Tim de Souza.

Adhering to his wishes, the funeral was made a joyous event to celebrate all life, not just his. There was music and happy recollections which did not seem out of place at all.

Q: What do the Eurasians represent here in Singapore?

It is necessary to revisit history. During the colonial era, the Eurasians enjoyed a position of privilege which they lost after independence. This is best illustrated by the two sports clubs flanking the Padang. On one side is the Singapore Cricket Club, which was exclusive to whites. On the other is the Singapore Recreation Club, which was for Eurasians.

Decolonisation created mixed feelings among the Eurasians, a community created by western intrusion into the region. Many wanted the British out, but independence also meant that their higher status among British subjects would be lost. Not surprisingly, a certain gloom descended on the community when the People's Action Party took power. In the 1960s and 1970s, a significant number of them emigrated, principally to Australia.

It was only in the 1980s that the tide turned. A new spirit emerged, which led to Joe Conceicao's change of heart. The EA provided needed leadership. Its magazine was aptly called *The New Eurasian*. Despite efforts to broaden the definition of Eurasians to include those with maternal European ancestry, those with paternal Asian ancestries tend to be re-absorbed into these ancestral Asian communities.

Eurasians are still largely marked by their European names. A Eurasian friend remarked to me that younger Eurasians look more Chinese because of inter-marriage with Chinese women. Though many speak Mandarin, they are not considered Chinese because of their European name. In recent years, more Eurasians have been researching genealogy and finding the exercise to be educational, fascinating and spiritually important.

In more relaxed moments, I use the metaphor of rojak to describe Singapore. However much the ingredients are chopped up, they are still separate. Each has its own distinct flavor. What pulls everything together is the prawn paste. Without Eurasians, Singapore would become a harsher place. Jesus Christ said that we are judged by how we treat the least among us. Well, maybe not least but the littlest. By affirming Eurasians as a distinct fourth community, we affirm that all communities in Singapore are respected in their separate identities, whatever their size or contributions.

Eurasians make an outsized contribution to Singapore. When Joseph Schooling won Singapore's first Olympic gold medal, many Singaporeans thought that he was an imported talent, but he was not a new citizen. He was born and bred here. His father was Eurasian, and his mother is Chinese. As a schoolboy, he trained at Tanah Merah Country Club. His father, Colin, had told me that Joseph was swimming faster than the Olympic medallist Michael Phelps did at the same age, and that he would one day be a gift to Singapore. I gave a polite reply, but did not imagine that he would one day become world number one.

Colin had said that Joseph spent so much time in the water his legs were wobbly on land, for which a doctor prescribed tennis. The first

Screenshots of Joseph Schooling and his father that I posted on Facebook after he won the Olympic gold medal for Singapore

time I met him was after he played tennis at the club. The morning Joseph won the 100m butterfly event at the 2016 Rio Olympics, Singaporeans were delirious with joy. My wife and I jumped out of bed to sing *Majulah Singapura*.

Like Barker, Joseph belongs to Singapore's tiniest community. Barker drafted Singapore's constitution, which established our beginning as an independent nation. Joseph brought us to Olympian heights in sports. Reports of Joseph's gold medal in China and other countries provided background into Singapore's Eurasian community, which many were not aware of before. As a result, the world came to understand Singapore better.

Eurasian identity in Singapore is dynamic. The children of European fathers and Singaporean mothers do not automatically identify as Eurasian. On a visit to Istanbul with Lee Kuan Yew around 1990, I had tea with a group of Singaporean women who married Caucasian men. They made a request that their children be granted the same right to citizenship as the children of Singaporean men. When I mentioned this to Lee Kuan Yew, he agreed that we should change our law to effect this. We also facilitated the use of double-barrel surnames in birth registrations.

In a sense, we are competing to win the hearts and minds of children of mixed marriages. Those who grow up in Singapore will develop affection for Singapore and eventually identify themselves as Eurasian. The vitality of Singapore's Eurasian community is a measure of our success as Big Singapore.

❖

Passages to India

George Yeo talks about some of the visits he made to India over the years and his impressions of this great land, including a short section on Sri Lanka. There is an important community of Jaffna Tamils in Singapore, who are generally considered part of Singapore's Indian community.

Q: Tell us about your early visits to India.

I made my first visit to India in 1986 to attend the wedding of a Harvard classmate in Madurai. When my wife and I landed in Chennai, there was a long queue to clear immigration and customs. There were many Indians standing in line, hand-carrying large bags and parcels. Tariffs in India were high and returning Indians took advantage of this by bringing in whatever they could without paying duty. The officers took their work seriously, checking every entry in the forms. Curiously, the one processing us used green ink. It was my first brush with Indian bureaucracy.

We spent two days in Chennai visiting tourist sites. The one I remember best is St Thomas Cathedral Basilica. Thomas was the apostle who doubted Jesus' resurrection. He said that he would only believe it when he was able to put his fingers into Jesus' wounds. When he finally did so, he exclaimed, "My Lord and my God." Thomas went on to preach the gospel in India. He landed on the Malabar coast, where there was a Jewish community from biblical times. He crossed southern India to the Coromandel coast and was eventually martyred outside Chennai. When St Francis Xavier was in Chennai, he prayed over the tomb of Thomas in the Cathedral.

St Thomas Cathedral in Chennai

As a result, Thomas is beloved in Kerala. Many Malayalees are named Thomas, either as first name or as family name. An example is Tommy Thomas, the recently retired Attorney General of Malaysia.

While in Chennai, we made a day trip to Mahabalipuram, an ancient Pallava temple town by the sea. It was a pleasant outing. The site was interesting and the sea air wafting in from the Bay of Bengal provided welcome relief from the bustle of Chennai.

In 2019, Prime Minister (PM) Narendra Modi invited President Xi Jinping for a retreat in Mahabalipuram. It was the first time most Chinese had heard of the place. The purpose of the trip was to recall early contact between India and China. One of the temples has walls adorned with the figures of thousands of gods and human beings, one of which is clearly Chinese. He is believed to be Faxian, the Buddhist monk who visited India and Sri Lanka in the 5th century. Mahabalipuram is also the birthplace of Bodhidharma or Damo (达摩) who brought Chan (禅) or Zen Buddhism to China and *gongfu* to Shaolin. I congratulated then-External Affairs Minister Jaishankar on an exquisite choice of location. He is a Tamil and must have originated the idea.

No ethnic group celebrates weddings the way Indians do. The wedding in Madurai was the first of five weddings I attended in India. It was South Indian Christian. The rituals were similar to those of the Catholic Church. Rock sugar was part of the offerings and coconuts were smashed to release bad luck.

While we were there, my host arranged for us to visit Sri Meenakshi Temple, which is huge. Meenakshi is an avatar of Parvati, the wife of the god Shiva. Tamil Nadu is famous for its great temple towns. The *gopurams* (entrance towers) and tanks in these temples dwarf those we find in Hindu temples in Singapore and Malaysia.

Tamil culture has a long history. Some historians believe that Tamil civilisation was pre-Vedic and descended from the Indus Valley civilisation. Recent excavations outside Madurai, which date back centuries before Christ, support such a point of view. Regardless, the Tamils were one of the earliest human groups to become literate. They

Xi Jinping and Narendra Modi meeting in Mahabalipuram in December 2019

Wedding of Raj Chellaraj and Ponni in Madurai. I am in the background of both pictures, fascinated by the proceedings.

Sri Meenakshi Temple gopuram in Madurai

are an ancient people and attempts to put them down in Sri Lanka only engendered a ferocious resistance.

After Madurai, we took an Ambassador taxi to Kerala. The Ambassador was a sturdily Indian-built car with firm coconut coir upholstery. Spare parts for the car were available in every town. We made an invigorating short stop at Kanyakumari at the southernmost point of India, where the waters of the Bay of Bengal, the Indian Ocean and the Arabian Gulf meet. From there we were driven to our hotel at Kovalam Beach, a short distance from Trivandrum, the capital of Kerala. I had a number of Malayalee friends and had long wanted to visit their ancestral land. From my Cambridge days, I knew that Kerala often voted in the Communist Party.

Most of the guests in our first-class beachside hotel were Russians on the rupee account. During the Cold War, India kept close links with Russia, which supplied much of its advanced weaponry. Under a bilateral agreement, India was allowed to pay in rupees, which Russia used to purchase Indian goods and services. A bellhop at the hotel complained to me that the Russians were lousy tippers. South of Kovalam Beach was a strange beachside colony with nude and skimpily-clad white men and women.

The landscape in Kerala, with its beaches, backwaters, coconut trees and foothills reminded me of Malaya. The Malayalees are a talented race. They are Hindus, Muslims and Christians. They generally do well in Singapore and Malaysia. Many of the Indians working in the Gulf are from Kerala, and remittances from Malayalees working overseas are an important part of the Kerala economy. Without them, the Gulf Cooperation Council (GCC) economies would be seriously impaired. The government of Kerala alternates between the Communist Party and Congress. Their population has one of the highest education levels in India.

In 1988, I made my second visit to India as Director of Joint Operations and Planning in the SAF. My destination was the Indian National Defence Academy at Khadakwasla in Maharashtra. At that time, I was responsible for the construction of our new tri-service officer training school. The new SAFTI was a major project of long term importance, as we were not going to build a second one. We thus had to conceptualise it carefully and wanted to learn from the experiences of other military forces. Liu Thai Ker was our architectural adviser. We visited and studied many military academies like Duntroon, Sandhurst, West Point, Annapolis and Colorado Springs. However, these were all single-service schools, while ours would be tri-service. As the Indian Military Academy was tri-service, we took a special interest in it.

Coincidentally, the Superintendent at the time, a Lieutenant-General, had previously served as India's Defence Attache to Singapore. He gave us a warm welcome. During lunch at the huge cadet mess hall, he invited me to address the cadets, who hailed from all over the sub-continent.

Aerial view and cadet mess of India's National Defence Academy at Khadakwasla

Some were tall and fair, others lanky and dark, yet others squat and yellow. A few looked Chinese to me. It was a mini-United Nations.

All of them went through a common core curriculum. The Indian Army is a veritable institution, a pillar of stability for a vast sub-continent. General elections in India are conducted in phases according to geography. Their integrity is ensured by the Indian Army, which is re-deployed with the movement of polling booths and counting centres.

We were shown various facilities. In the laboratory classrooms, I was surprised to see the same test tubes, pipettes, burettes, calorimeters and Bunsen burners I had used in school. During the days of the Raj, Singapore was an extension of British India, and the legacy of British India in Singapore is profound. When I was an officer cadet, during a lecture on military law, the lecturer told us that in the event of a lacuna in the Singapore Armed Forces Act, the thin document which established the SAF, we were to refer to the Indian Army Manual (a big fat red book). The standards used by the central supply office in India also became our standards. Over time, the SAF became less British (Indian) and more American. I remember when we changed from the British salute to the American salute.

Much of what we started with in Singapore came through India, including the pomp and ceremony of our military parades, although we thankfully never had a horse-riding tradition. Every officer of the Indian Armed Forces must learn to ride a horse. We were told that if an officer cannot command a horse, he cannot command men. At Khadakwasla, there were over 3,000 rides (horses). Indian Administrative Officers have to learn riding too for the same reason.

India and Singapore were once part of a common larger system. Our old schools, hospitals, military and police messes, government buildings and law courts in Singapore were mostly scaled-down versions of similar facilities still found all over India. If India was the jewel in the crown of the British Empire, Singapore was only a little gem on its side.

The English language connects us to both the United Kingdom and the United States (US). Singapore moved quickly after independence to become more American. India, being a large country, still maintains many traditions from the days of the Raj. However, among the top academics, business leaders and professionals, there is a strong reorientation towards the US. A significant proportion of India's smartest graduates go there for further studies and work. Many do well, some extremely. They also bring along their passion for cricket.

Q: Why did you attend so many weddings in India?

I attended only five, but they were all memorable. Indian weddings are elaborate affairs. They are an important reason for the resilience of Indian society. Till today, educated Indians accept matchmaking. Marriage is not just a union of individuals, it is also a union of families. As such, both sides conduct their due diligence. The elaborate rituals also express the seriousness of the undertaking, which is never to be entered into lightly.

In so-called modern societies, much is made of individual choice and romance. The failure rate of such couplings does not inspire confidence in the criteria used. India has one of the lowest divorce rates in the world.

Captain Satish Sharma was a dear friend whom I visited almost every time I was in Delhi. He told me he was the best friend of Rajiv Gandhi, the former PM. Both were happy-go-lucky Air India pilots before Rajiv's brother, Sanjay Gandhi, was killed in an air crash. At various times, Satish was a Member of Parliament for the two Gandhi family seats of Amethi and Raebareli. He told me that he was only holding those seats in trust for the family. At his son's wedding, which was a relatively smallish affair, the entire Gandhi clan turned up, as did Manmohan Singh and others.

It rained unexpectedly at the wedding. As the shelters provided were only for shade and were not waterproof, I was invited to retreat into the house, which was reserved for a privileged few. It gave me an opportunity to observe important members of the Gandhi family and the Congress Party at close range and to speak to some of them. Being from Singapore was a plus.

In June 2011, my wife and I made a quick trip to Bengaluru to attend the wedding of the son of an old friend, Narayana Murthy. In keeping with his down-to-earth style, the wedding was a simple affair by Indian standards. I remember being preoccupied at the time with the call to enter the Presidential race in Singapore.

The fourth wedding was in Jodhpur, for the marriage of N. K. Singh's

Wedding in Delhi in December 2008

Captain Satish Sharma and Sterre, parents of the groom

Greeting the father of the groom, Narayana Murthy, founder of Infosy. Wedding in Bengaluru in June 2011.

Vegetarian lunch

My wife and I with the bride and groom

With the father of the groom, N. K. Singh

Wedding cocktail in Jodhpur in May 2014

With Montek Singh Ahluwalia

Pandit Jasraj whose singing was spellbinding

Fairyland wedding in Jodhpur

son. N. K. was a distinguished Indian Administrative Service officer from Bihar who entered politics, joined the Bharatiya Janata Party and became a Member of the Rajya Sabha (the Upper House of the Indian Parliament). I got to know him well when we were working on the revival of Nalanda University. He is a Rajput. As his wife's brother was the Maharaja of Jodhpur, the wedding was held in the palace, which was decked out like a fairyland. The bride was from another Maharaja family. That evening, all the Maharajas of Rajasthan turned up with their retinues.

It was a glittering affair, the most splendid wedding I have ever attended. It included a spellbinding hour-long performance by a great Indian singer, Pandit Jasraj. Somehow the desert air in Rajasthan enables musical notes to travel farther.

While attending a Nalanda board meeting in Delhi, I took the opportunity to attend the wedding of Finance Minister Arun Jaitley's daughter. I had known Arun as Trade Minister and kept in touch with him when he was in the Opposition. It was an honour for me to be invited to one of the wedding receptions. That wedding felt like a political event, not unlike Chinese New Year parties at the Istana. A river of guests streamed in and out. They congratulated the couple, had their meals and left. Politics is the same everywhere.

Q: You enjoyed India?

India is a huge canvas. It is the great land, the *Maha Bharat*. I don't enjoy India the way I do Bali or Switzerland. In fact, oftentimes on arrival, the abject poverty, messiness and pollution hit me like a blast of hot air. After a day or two, however, India gets inside me and I enjoy it for what it is. My wife likes India too and is always happy to accompany me whenever she can. My daughter learned Indian dance in school and spent much time working there as a fund manager. All my three sons have been to India too for different reasons.

I made many visits to India, officially as minister, and after leaving government, as a business executive. In the next two chapters, I will

Wedding of Finance Minister Arun Jaitley's daughter in Delhi in December 2015

talk about the main ones in the context of Singapore's relations with India and my involvement in the Nalanda project. For now, let me recount a few trips I made off the beaten track in the Indian sub-continent.

Amritsar

The British called the Sikhs a martial race. I knew a few Sikh officers in the SAF. Colonel Gurcharan Singh, from SAFTI's first batch of graduates, was my Commandant when I was a student in Singapore Command and Staff College. As Lat always portrayed in his cartoons, Sikhs are part of our local landscape. On one of my trips to Delhi, I made a side trip to Amritsar and flew back to Singapore directly from there with Singapore Airlines.

Jallianwala Bagh, the site of the Amritsar Massacre, was a stark reminder that the British Empire everywhere was ultimately maintained by violence. Less than 30km away is the border with Pakistan, and Lahore is only 50km away.

In 1992, PM Nawaz Sharif, who was keen for Lee Kuan Yew's advice, invited him to visit Pakistan. Lee Kuan Yew and I were hosted by him and his Finance Minister, Sartaj Aziz, for the horse and cattle show in Lahore. I remember him tuning his radio to an Indian station to hear then-Indian Finance Minister Manmohan Singh giving his budget speech.

The people of the Punjab were cruelly divided by the Partition of India in 1947, causing the death of hundreds of thousands and the displacement of millions. At the Wagah border, the daily enactment of mock confrontation between Indian and Pakistani border guards satirizes a senseless conflict which has gone on for decades with no end in sight. No matter how far they are from the Indian sub-continent — whether in the US, Europe, Hong Kong or Singapore — Indians, Pakistanis, Bangladeshis and Sri Lankans know they are culturally one people.

At the Golden Temple, our guide, Kuldip Singh, had me wrap a cloth

Golden Temple in Amritsar in January 2007

around my head and wash my feet before I could enter barefoot. As it was a January evening, I kept to the jute carpet to avoid the cold marble. Pointing to a side gate on the left, Kuldip explained that it was from there that the army tanks rolled down to the edge of the lake. Their turrets then turned towards the temple where the militant leader, Jarnail Singh Bhindranwale was holed up and fired their main guns. This was Operation Blue Star.

I looked at Kuldip and asked, "Are you still angry?" He replied, "No. God has punished all of them," by which he meant Bhindranwale, Longowal and Indira Gandhi. (I had also been to the site in Delhi where Indira Gandhi was gunned down by Sikh guards.)

Recalling the entire tragic history, I was pensive and decided to visit the temple a second time the following morning to see it in full daylight. Kuldip was surprised and happy to see me again. "You're back!" he exclaimed. He brought me to see the dining hall, where free food was provided 24/7. I remember the piece of *prashad* given to me as I was leaving the temple to be particularly delicious. Kuldip then went to a shop and bought me a steel bangle which I still keep.

Calling on Madhya Pradesh Chief Minister Shivraj Singh Chauhan in April 2008

Great Stupa in Sanchi, April 2008

Like the Jaffna Tamils, Singaporean Sikhs were deeply affected by the conflict in India. Following an incident there, one of our respected High Court judges, Justice Choor Singh, who had then just retired, wrote me an angry letter protesting against the actions of the Indian government and asking for a response from our government. It showed the depth of his emotion. I wrote him a polite reply. Separating our political identity from our cultural identity is never easy.

Bhopal

In 2008, I visited Bhopal and called on the Chief Minister of Madhya Pradesh to explore opportunities for Singapore. It was an opportunity for me to visit Sanchi, an important Buddhist site. Its Great Stupa was built by the Mauryan Emperor, Ashoka. Surrounding the stupa are four ornamental gates called *toranas*, which reminded me of *torii* gates at Shinto shrines. The site and its many monuments were well maintained by the Archaeological Survey of India. I encountered a tour group from Taiwan who spoke Hokkien, but there were far fewer tourists than I expected. With better amenities and promotion, Buddhist tourism in India could be many times bigger.

We passed by the old Union Carbide site. In 1984, a gas leak at their factory in Bhopal killed thousands of people. My guide told me that chemicals were still being stored there. Even after 24 years, litigation was still ongoing. Doing business in India, one has to be aware of its legal system. The wheels of justice turn slowly.

Jamshedpur

In 2007, at the invitation of one of Ratan Tata's senior executives, I made a side trip from Kolkata to Jamshedpur, which is now in the new state of Jharkhand. It is ranked as one of the cleanest cities in India.

I had learned about Jamshedpur in geography class in secondary school and the name stuck in my mind. It was established as a steel

Jamshedpur in January 2007

town by Jamsetji Tata, the founder of the Tata Group, over a hundred years ago. Tata was a great entrepreneur who believed that India could develop its own indigenous capability in manufacturing at a time when the Raj was at its height. Tata was incredibly far-sighted, introducing polices which Indians today associate more closely with Singapore. When the town was being designed, he said, "Be sure to lay wide streets planted with shady trees, every other of a quick-growing variety. Be sure that there is plenty of space for lawns and gardens; reserve large areas for football, hockey and parks; earmark areas for Hindu temples, Muslim mosques, and Christian churches." Tata also introduced a system of social security for employees, and water could be drunk from the tap in the city.

The Tatas are Parsees, a remarkable tribe. When Muslim rulers in Persia persecuted the Zoroastrians, they fled to India. Some of them sought a new home in Gujarat. They pleaded with the local raja to take them in. The raja pushed a full cup of milk to them, hinting that he could not accommodate them. In response, the Parsee leader scooped up a fistful of sugar and slowly sprinkled it into the milk. As the sugar dissolved, not a drop of milk overflowed. Indeed, wherever the Parsees settle, they sweeten the society into which they become a part.

I have often wondered why other cities in India are not more like Jamshedpur. Maybe it is simply a matter of time. In the early 1990s, Hong Kong businessmen looked down on their fellow Cantonese in Guangdong. I used to hear it being said that they could not make white handbags in the Pearl River Delta because the workers there did not have clean hands. No one talks about Chinese workers in this way any more.

Thanjavur

On my way to see P. Chidambaram, the former Finance Minister of India, in his hometown of Chettinad in May 2010, my wife and I spent a day at Thanjavur to visit the old Saraswathi Mahal Library and the

Top: Received by police quarter guard in Thanjavur in May 2010

Left: Chola Brihadeswara Temple in Thanjavur

famous Chola Brihadeshwara Temple. It was hot, very hot, and dusty. After an hour at the library, we proceeded to the temple. My wife was exhausted and decided to rest in the car. Ambassador Gopinath Pillai quickly said that he would accompany my wife. I think he, too, was tired out.

I like having Gopi as a travel companion. He is knowledgeable and practical. The temple was built a thousand years ago by the great Chola King Raja Raja. It was he who, in one monsoon period, launched a fleet which crossed the Bay of Bengal and destroyed Srivijaya. Historians now believe that one reason the war was fought was for control of the lucrative trade of the Southern Song. Raja Raja Chola's ships entered the Sunda Strait and, with the winds blowing in his favour, sailed up the Strait of Malacca, destroying Srivijayan settlements one at a time. They could not be reinforced from upwind. His victory is recorded in bas-relief on the side of the temple which I wanted to see.

A year after the trip, I was defeated in the 2011 General Election. Someone wrote in Tamil Murasu that I had committed a grievous taboo when I entered the temple in Thanjavur by the main gate. No one had told me this at the time.

Chettinad

It was extraordinarily kind of Chidambaram to invite my wife and me to visit Chettinad for three days. He had invited me a few times before, but I was always too busy. In 2009, in front of my wife, he said that if I was too busy, my wife could visit Chettinad by herself and he would host her without me. It was a rebuke by one of India's most famous litigation lawyers. I hastened to make arrangements to visit Chettinad the following year.

Chidambaram was born there. At that time, he was India's Minister of Home Affairs, but he still found time to be with us despite his heavy responsibilities.

Chettinad is the home of the Natukottai Chettiars. They are patrons of many Hindu temples in Tamil Nadu and Southeast Asia, including Singapore. In Chettinad, Chettiar families have big, deep houses, many built from money made in British Burma. They conduct business at the front of the house, while the living quarters are at the back. In between are vaults secured by enormous locks, which are used to store precious possessions.

Chidambaram brought us to his local Congress Party branch, a village cooperative where housewives came together to make brass souvenirs, and a Rishi Valley school where more advanced students helped to pull along less advanced students, thus creating a different spirit in the classroom. On the last day, we drove to Madurai, where my wife and I visited the Sri Meenakshi Temple a second time.

Before we left for the airport, Chidambaram bought my wife a bunch of beautiful bangles. As scarves were given to us everywhere we went, I ended up bringing home a whole suitcase of them. We had so many that I could have opened a shop after that. Eventually, the scarves were sent to the Hougang Community Club for distribution to the local Indian community. Some were of high quality.

Chidambaram knew that I had an affection for India and once joked at a social gathering that I had been Indian in my previous life. It was a high compliment. He got his son, Karti, to receive us in Chennai and accompany us to Chettinad, where he would meet us directly.

That evening in Chennai, a group of Chettiar businessmen hosted us for dinner. One of them asked for my help. There is a Hindu temple in Ho Chi Minh City which was established by the Chettiars and named after a celibate avatar of Lord Murugan, Thendayuthapani. I was told that this particular avatar was chosen for many temples in Southeast Asia to remind Chettiar men to stay faithful to their wives while overseas. In 1975, when South Vietnam fell to the North, the temple trustees were told to remove jewels which adorned the deities because the new government did not want to be responsible for safeguarding them. As India had high import duties, the jewels were brought to Singapore and kept in a Chettiar temple here. I was asked if I could help arrange for

At one of the Chettiar mansions in Chettinad

Brought by Minister Chidambaram to visit a business run by housewives making brass objects

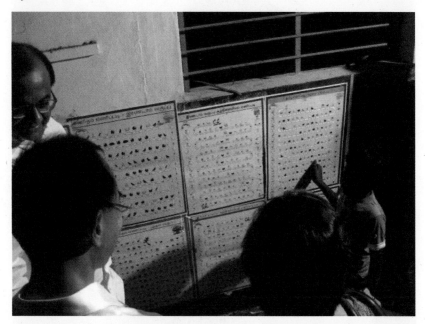

Minister Chidambaram introducing me to a school using the Rishi Valley method of teaching

Visiting Sri Meenakshi Temple with Minister Chidambaram

the jewels to be returned to the temple in Ho Chi Minh City, which had continued to function without priests all this while.

I discussed their request with K. Shanmugam, who is Chettiar. He was not aware of the Vietnamese jewels and was happy to do some research. Later, on a visit to Vietnam, he visited the temple. We agreed that the less valuable jewels could go back first, but only when conditions were ripe. When I met the Vietnamese Foreign Minister some weeks later, I raised the matter with him. He was not familiar with the subject and was probably wondering how I got involved, but he did promise to follow up. I left office a year later and never found out what happened afterwards.

Chettinad is in the district of Karaikudi. Many of the chefs cooking banana leaf curry in Singapore comes from there. Spicy Chettinad chicken is world famous. Chettinad is also known for its vegetarian cuisine.

Jaffna

In Singapore, Jaffna Tamils are overrepresented in the legal and medical professions. All four of my children were delivered by Jaffna doctors — the first and fourth by Prof S. S. Ratnam, the second and fourth by his nephew Dr Anandakumar. My relatives in China were surprised to hear this. Birthing is a sensitive matter for older Chinese people, and even more so for the Japanese. Japanese mothers in Singapore used to go back to Japan to give birth until we allowed Japanese doctors to practise in Singapore, though they could only see Japanese patients. Happily, in Singapore, most Singaporeans choose doctors and lawyers not on the basis of race but of competence.

The long war in Jaffna was heartbreaking for Jaffna Tamils overseas, including those living in Singapore. My old tutor in Christ's College Cambridge, Dr Vis Navaratnam, is a Jaffna Tamil and a contemporary of Prof S. S. Ratnam from Colombo University. At dinner hosted by the Master of the College in my honour in late March 2009, Dr Navratnam's

Old picture of Chettiar Temple in Saigon

Viewing the temple jewellery safely kept at the Holy Tree Sri Balasubramaniam Temple with President S. R. Nathan, Minister K. Shanmugam and Ambassador Gopinath Pillai

wife pulled me aside and pleaded for help from the Singapore government. It was the final days of the war. Fighters and supporters of the Tamil Tigers were being surrounded and killed in Mullaitivu. Many were innocent civilians. Could Singapore not do something? My old tutor did not say anything, but I knew from his expression that he felt the same way. Less than two months later, the 25-year civil war ended.

Not long afterwards, I received a delegation from Sri Lanka and recalled my meeting with Dr Navaratnam and his wife in Cambridge to them. Sri Lanka's then Foreign Minister, Rohitha Bogollagama, was reassuring and promised to get in touch with Dr Navaratnam. After so many years of bitter conflict, reconciliation would take time.

In late 2009, a few months after the war ended in May, I made an official visit to Colombo as Foreign Minister and visited Jaffna while I was there. I felt I had to make the effort on behalf of Singapore's Jaffna Tamil community. I asked Tharman Shanmugaratnam and leaders of our local Jaffna Tamil community for ideas on how Singapore could support rehabilitation. He suggested that we help rebuild the Jaffna Public Library. The famous library, with its large collection of books, had been burned down by a Singhalese mob in 1981 and was only partially restored by the Colombo government many years later.

We first flew to Mannar to observe mines being cleared with the help of dogs. My host was a young Major General. He told me how the fighting spirit of the Sri Lankan Army was transformed when Gotabaya Rajapaksa took over as Defence Minister. The Tigers were a formidable opponent and used electronic chips to make smart mines. Chinese weapons made a decisive difference. Mannar was being restored as the rice basket of Sri Lanka. Tamil engineers, who could do nothing for years because of the war, briefed me on their plans to repair the irrigation system, which consisted of a system of connected tanks (square ponds).

By chance, we arrived in Jaffna on Deepavali. When we entered the Jaffna Library, facing the main entrance was a copy of the Thirukural, an ancient Tamil book on ethics and morality. As we lit the oil lamp at noon, a nearby temple bell sounded. Everyone thought it an auspicious sign.

Observing mine clearance in Mannar in October 2009

First visit to Jaffna Library in October 2009

Breaking a coconut outside Nallur Kandasamy Temple in Jaffna

At the Nallur Kandaswamy Temple, I was invited to break a coconut. Unlike the well-shaved Singaporean coconuts that are easy to smash, the one given to me still had some husk on it. Someone whispered that I had to aim it at a metal spike protruding from the ground. If the coconut didn't break, it would be considered bad luck. I was greatly stressed by this and gave it all I got. Someone managed to capture a photograph of the exact moment and recorded the relief on my face.

I noticed all the Hindu temples had fresh coats of paint. A semblance of normalcy had returned. However, my Jaffna Tamil friends told me that the wounds were still raw. There were many grievances, not least concerning rights to old properties.

Later in the afternoon, I was brought on a visit to a camp for internally displaced persons (IDPs). It housed over 10,000 people. I was in a battered, bulletproof limousine with Minister Douglas Devananda. In front and behind us were army trucks with soldiers holding assault rifles at the ready. All that security was not for me, but for my host. Nonetheless, I did not feel safe at all. When we entered the IDP camp, he was greeted by the wails of women crying to be reunited with their families.

Douglas left the Tamil Tigers some years earlier and went over to the government side. They tried to assassinate him over 10 times. Despite sustaining many wounds, he miraculously survived. He told me that he looked much older than his age.

The Singaporean Jaffna community raised money to turn a part of the Jaffna Library into a children's library and donated many books. It was right to prioritise education. By the time the children's library was ready to be opened, I had left government. With the support of our Jaffna Tamil community, the Ministry of Foreign Affairs invited me to do the honours. I agreed enthusiastically.

When Sri Lanka became independent in 1948, it was significantly ahead of Singapore on all social and economic indicators. Difficult medical cases in Singapore were referred to doctors in Colombo. A fateful decision was taken to adopt Sinhala as the sole official language. As one Sri Lankan minister lamented to me, that began the great unraveling.

Visit to an IDP camp in October 2009

Second visit to Jaffna Library in July 2011 for the opening of the children's section

One language meant two nations. For there to be one nation, two languages had to be recognised. Under stress of war and terrorism, the Sinhalese community was also fractured. It took decades for that lesson to be learned.

In 2012, as part of the Kerry Group, I attended the ground breaking ceremony of two Shangri-La hotels in Colombo and Hambantota. Defence Minister Gotabaya Rajapaksa, who was also responsible for Colombo, was determined to jump start the economy and gave Shangri-La the land by the sea which the Defence Ministry was vacating. On a subsequent visit, I was invited by President Mahinda Rajapaksa for breakfast. Before seeing me off, he showed me his personal shrine room. Amidst Buddha statues were Hindu deities. I read he made speeches in Tamil. Unfortunately, Sri Lanka continues to be afflicted by political instability. Covid-19 and the Ukraine war have added to the country's economic woes. The new Prime Minister is Ranil Wickremesinghe. I have met him a number of times when he was in office and in opposition, in Sri Lanka and in Singapore. Sri Lanka does not lack men of ability. It will however take time for the wounds of the past to heal.

Groundbreaking ceremony of Shangri-La Hotel in Colombo in 2012

✢

CHAPTER 7

India and Singapore

George Yeo talks about the evolution of Singapore's relationship with India and India's place in the world.

Q: Why was your visit to India in 1993 so important to bilateral relations?

India was entering a new phase of reform and opening up. In 1991, Rajiv Gandhi was assassinated in Tamil Nadu. The outpouring of grief returned the Congress Party to power. Indian finances, however, were in dire straits. Under Prime Minister (PM) Narasimha Rao, the country changed course.

In late 1991, Finance Minister Manmohan Singh and Commerce Minister P. Chidambaram visited Singapore to talk about India's new direction. I was then a Second Minister in the Ministry of Foreign Affairs. I was surprised one day to read a request from the Indian government asking us to run courses for their joint secretaries. For Mother India to make such a request of little Singapore was significant. Interestingly, China made a similar request in 1979.

My visit to India in January 1993 was against that backdrop of change. I led a large delegation (by Singapore standards), including members from the private sector. From the government, we had Lim Boon Heng, K. Shanmugam, Dr Michael Lim, Kishore Mahbubani (then Deputy Secretary at the Ministry of Foreign Affairs (MFA)), Professor Tommy Koh and others. From the private sector, I remember Ameer Jumabhoy, Murli Chanrai and Ashok Melwani.

Left to right: Manmohan Singh, Narasimha Rao and Sonia Gandhi.
Facing grave financial difficulties, India under PM Narasimha Rao embarked on a new path of reform and opening up in 1992. He was supported by Sonia Gandhi, wife of Rajiv Gandhi who had been assassinated earlier in Tamil Nadu. The two ministers driving change were Finance Minister Manmohan Singh and Commerce Minister P. Chidambaram.

With P. Chidambaram in his office at North Block

I attended the World Economic Forum (WEF) first and flew directly to Delhi from Zurich. Before I left Singapore, Murli Deora, the head of the Congress Party in Mumbai, met me at MFA. He arranged for me to meet members of the Confederation of Indian Industry (CII) at Davos, where I first met P. Chidambaram.

On our first day in Delhi, we called on PM Rao at his residence. Comfortable chairs were arrayed on a lush green lawn for the meeting. It was a pleasantly cool winter morning, and we lined up to shake hands with PM Rao. When he came to Kishore, PM Rao did not extend his hand and went on to greet the next person. He thought that Kishore was a member of his staff. I have never stopped ribbing Kishore about this diplomatic snub since. It was clear from our meeting with PM Rao that he wanted Singapore to be part of India's new journey.

Later in the evening, Salman Khurshid, Minister of State for External Affairs and one of India's most senior Muslim ministers, hosted us to a grand dinner at Hyderabad House. He was charming and gracious. Hyderabad House was the residence for the last Nizam, the former rulers of Hyderabad from the 18th to the 20th centuries. Designed by Edwin Luytens, it was taken over by the Indian Government in 1947. The princely state of Hyderabad had been unwisely reluctant to be fully integrated into India and was annexed in 1948.

After Delhi, we made the usual side trip to Agra and Jaipur. Although the distance was not long, the condition of the roads made for an exhausting journey. Our tiredness evaporated when we arrived at the Taj Mahal, which was as beautiful as we expected. Although the Taj Mahal was normally closed to visitors at night, through an Indian friend, Tommy Koh was able to wrangle a night visit for us. His reputation as a diplomat is not for nothing. Ameer was out somewhere when our delegation left in the evening. When he heard from the hotel staff that we were visiting the Taj, he quickly hailed a taxi to join us. Under a full moon, marble walls glittered as water in the pools shimmered.

From Agra, we travelled by road to Jaipur. The Maharaja — who was nicknamed Bubbles and later became India's ambassador to

Jama Mosque in Delhi

At the Taj Mahal in Agra

Buland Darwaza, gate built by Akbar at Fatehpur Sikri

Fatehpur Sikri built by Akbar

Delegation picture, probably in Jaipur

Chennakeshava Temple at Somanathapura near Mysore

Brunei — was Ameer's polo buddy. We were grandly received in his palace. We then flew to Mumbai, where we were hosted by Murli Deora.

Before delivering my speech to the Mumbai business community, Murli, who sat on my left, nudged me to say that the Mayor, who was sitting on my right, was "one of them". "We made a deal *with* them," he whispered. It took me a few seconds to realise what he meant: Murli was a *baniya* from the Marwari community, who are disproportionately represented in big business. During the Raj, the Marwaris dominated the economy of Kolkata.

India's caste system is hard for foreigners to understand, but caste consciousness is an inseparable part of India and woven into its politics. Few marriages take place without caste being a consideration. Murli's son, Milind, belongs to a younger generation of Congress leaders. Murli was pleased when I told him that he was increasingly being referred to as Milind's father instead of Milind as Murli's son.

My speech cited a long piece written by Larry Summers in *The Economist* on the rise of China. To Professor Summers' credit, he saw China's upward trajectory early on. I thought China should be an inspiration to India now that it was adopting a similar policy of reform and opening up. I was wrong. The audience's response was polite but not enthusiastic. Indians do not like being compared to China.

That evening, Adi and Jamshyd Godrej hosted us to dinner on the roof of the Godrej House. They are Parsees. The streets were unusually quiet that night. Mumbai had a curfew in the late evening because of rioting which followed the dismantling of the Babri Mosque in Ayodhya by Hindu extremists the previous December. In Mumbai, it was clear to us that the captains of Indian industry were gearing themselves up for a different future. As in Delhi, there was much warmth shown towards Singapore.

Our next stop was Bengaluru, where the burgeoning information technology (IT) industry was attracting global interest. It was explained to me that the emergence of Bengaluru's status as a new tech hub had two main reasons. First, Bengaluru was a thousand metres above sea level and enjoyed cooler weather. Second, it had an initial boost from the Indian Institute of Science (IISc), which was established in 1909 with the active support of Jamsetji Tata. I saw in the visitor's book that Lee Kuan Yew had visited it some years earlier. A staff member told me that following India's defeat in the 1962 Sino-Indian War, the government was determined to build up its military technology and chose a location far from the China border, with the IISc as nucleus. The history of high tech in Bengaluru was thus similar to Silicon Valley, which also began with military research.

The policy secretary for IT flew down from Delhi to brief us. He was obviously competent and most persuasive. A new spirit was evident. Not long afterwards, Philip Yeo worked with Ratan Tata to build the International Tech Park, which opened in 1996 and has since expanded a number of times. Its main partners are the Tatas and Singapore's Ascendas. Singapore's links with Bengaluru have become broad and deep.

From Bengaluru, we made a side trip to Mysore. Along the way, we visited Srirangapatna, which was the capital under Hyder Ali and Tipu Sultan. We made a short stop at an important Vishnu temple where the Brahmins were Tamil. We also visited the Mysore Palace, which was beautifully lit up with electricity supplied from a nearby dam. We were accompanied by a bright-eyed District Collector (a junior Admin Officer).

The son of the last Maharaja of Mysore hosted us for tea. He was unshaven and did not look the part, despite the glare of his ancestors whose portraits hung around us. At St Philomena's Cathedral, the Bishop himself gave us a briefing. I remember Shanmugam being impressed by him.

Our final stop was Chennai where we called on Chief Minister J. Jayalalitha. Security was tight after Rajiv Gandhi's assassination by the Tamil Tigers. We were escorted into what looked like a small fortress with Black Cats guarding every corner and parapet. When I remarked that the Chief Minister looked comely, someone whispered that she was wearing a Kevlar jacket beneath her outer clothes. I wasn't sure if he was joking. The Chief Minister proposed a Madras–Singapore corridor, an idea which had been floated before. We visited a large piece of land which was earmarked for it. Though prone to flooding, its level could

Calling on Maharaja Srikantadatta Wodeyar of Mysore

be raised. While that project never came to fruition, Singapore's links to Tamil Nadu have remained strong. For many years, the leadership of Tamil Nadu alternated between J. Jayalalitha of the AIA-DMK Party and Dr M. Karunanidhi of the DMK Party. I had the honour of hosting Karunanidhi during his official visit to Singapore in 1999. He was a master of the Tamil language and delivered a lecture on it at Singapore's Indoor Stadium. I remember being told afterwards that the Chief Minister was somewhat disappointed that only six thousand people attended. In Chennai, there would have been tens of thousands, but, for Singapore, that attendance was not small at all and should have been considered a sell-out.

At the suggestion of K. Kesavapany, then our ambassador to the United Nations (UN) and World Trade Organization (WTO) in Geneva, who had been with me in Davos, we visited Kanchipuram to the north, near the border with Karnataka. It was the seat of the Pallavas, just as Madurai was the seat of the Pandyas and Thanjavur the seat of the Cholas. Pany said that I should meet the 'living god' of the *mutt* (*monastery*) in Kanchipuram.

We were greeted by a police quarter guard on arrival. The guard commander was a female police officer. She saluted me smartly, gave her name, and added that she had been centrally recruited. Central recruitment meant rigorous selections and difficult exams for applicants. The process applied as much to Indian Police as it did to the Admin Service and the Armed Forces. We were also accompanied by the Kanchipuram District Collector, who was as enthused about the new policies as the one who looked after us in Mysore.

The *mutt* was a humble complex, without marble flooring or a chandelier. In India, there are four *mutts* headed by four shankaracharyas. In the *mutt* at Kanchipuram, in addition to the shankaracharya, the head of the monastery, there was a 'deputy' and a 'trainee'. The 'trainee' was a young priest who greeted us politely. The 'deputy' was seated and about to greet his *darshan*. He greeted and gave each of us a small bag of rock sugar. When a member of our delegation extended his left hand to

With Ameer Jumabhoy, who taught me much about India

Meeting Salman Khurshid again after many years in 2012. He was my host on my first official visit to India in January 1993.

Head of the Mumbai Congress Party Murli Deora and I at an investor's meet in January 2011. He saw me in Singapore at the end of 1992 and arranged my meeting with CII leaders in Davos in January 1993. Murli and I became close friends. I got to know his son Milind and told the father one day that he was increasingly referred to as Milind's father.

The Mutt at Kanchipuram

Calling on Chief Minister of Tamil Nadu J. Jayalalitha

Hosting Chief Minister Karunanidhi to lunch at Oberoi Imperial Hotel in 1999

At Sriperumbudur where Rajiv Gandhi was killed

At Indira Gandhi's residence in Delhi where she was gunned down by Sikh guards

receive it, he asked for his right hand instead, firmly saying 'Asian custom'. When it came to my turn, he proclaimed "Chini Hindi bhai bhai" meaning that Chinese and Indians are brothers. It was interesting that he saw me as Chinese.

We then went down a flight of steps to meet the *shankaracharya*, who was bed-ridden. We stood at the door while an acolyte whispered our names in his ear, one by one. Even though the bed was some distance away, his piercing eyes looked at each of us individually, like laser beams. Some years later, to my dismay, I read that the 'deputy' and 'trainee' were embroiled in scandals. *Shankaracharyas* are deeply respected figures in South India.

On the way back to Chennai, we made a brief stop at the site where Rajiv Gandhi was killed by a woman suicide bomber at Sriperumbudur. He had just unveiled a statue of his mother, Indira Gandhi, across the field. In 1987, Rajiv made a fateful decision to intervene against the Tamil Tigers in Jaffna for which they plotted revenge. Chidambaram normally translated for Rajiv Gandhi whenever he visited Tamil Nadu. On that fateful day, he had been called off to do something and therefore lived.

My 1993 trip to India was part of a new chapter in Singapore's relationship with India. Our common past was drawing us together again.

Q: What followed this historic visit?

Kishore prepared a report of our visit for Cabinet. It gave an optimistic assessment of India. Joe Pillay told him that it was unwise of him to write such a positive report about India. Indeed, Lee Kuan Yew was unconvinced. He spoke about the dead hand of Indian bureaucracy and doubted that India could be changed so easily. As he had long experience of India, I took his reaction to heart and checked myself. From time to time, Lee Kuan Yew sent me articles he had read which were critical of India, but his mind was not closed to new information. Every time I returned from India, he quizzed me on my impressions.

When the signs were clearer that India was indeed set on a new course, and after our joint project led by Philip Yeo and Ratan Tata in Bangalore took off, Lee Kuan Yew became less negative. At one Cabinet meeting, he said that we should be prepared for changes in government, which happened regularly in India.

In 2009, Sunanda Datta-Ray conducted four interview sessions with Lee Kuan Yew. and wrote a book entitled *Looking East to Look West: Lee Kuan Yew's Mission India*. The book talked about Lee Kuan Yew's long interest in India and his effort to get India more engaged with East and Southeast Asia.

True enough, the Chief Minister of Karnataka, Veerappa Moily, whom we met in Bengaluru, lost his position when the Janata Dal party won. Deve Gowda became the new CM. He later became Prime Minister but for less than a year. Gowda was as interested in Singapore as his predecessor. When PM Goh Chok Tong attended a conference in Kolkata, Gowda flew there to show his commitment to Singapore. He assured PM Goh that he would be even more supportive than Moily, which was true.

PM Goh was favorably disposed towards India. The Indians were glad that he was less sceptical than Lee Kuan Yew and cultivated good ties with him. As PM and Senior Minister, Goh was close to all three Indian PMs who followed Rao — Atal Bihari Vajpayee, Manmohan Singh and Narendra Modi. They related well to PM Goh's frank and disarming ways.

PM Goh also saw India as strategically important for Singapore. He said that he was keen to fan an Indian fever among Singaporean businessmen and described India as Singapore's other wing to China. Tarun Das, CII's Director General for many years, was indefatigable in promoting closer ties.

Q: Tell us about CECA, the India–Singapore Comprehensive Economic Cooperation Agreement.

When I was Minister for Trade and Industry, Singapore's approach to international trade and investment followed two tracks. The first was the multilateral system with the WTO at its core. However, we knew that it was not easy to make progress multilaterally as this required consensus in an increasingly fractious world. As such, we also pushed along a second track of securing bilateral and regional trade agreements with as many countries and regions as possible.

Building up stronger economic and political links to India was an obvious objective. India will soon become the most populous country in the world. It is only a matter of a few decades before India becomes the world's second or third largest economy. India's long-term importance to Singapore is a no-brainer.

But dealing with India is never easy. Unlike China, which has a centralised system, India is more complicated. It is not homogeneous. Although more power is devolving to the states, the central government can often block what states want to do. India's litigiousness is well known. The wheels of justice in India turn slowly. It is hard to do business in India without detailed knowledge of local conditions. Having a local partner helps, but the choice of partner then becomes critical. The widespread use of English can be deceptive. The fact is, India has its own nature.

In preparation for a visit by PM Vajpayee in 2002, PM Goh asked me whether he should try to launch free trade negotiations with India. I consulted my colleagues in the Ministry. Their reactions ranged from scepticism to cynicism. When I reported this to PM Goh, he smiled and nodded. I did not expect him to convey my negative comments to PM Vajpayee.

It turned out PM Vajpayee himself was keen to have a trade deal too. Accompanying him was Arun Shourie, the Minister for Dis-investment. He asked to have a separate breakfast meeting with me. I thought it was best for me to be completely frank. We did not think Indian officials were really interested. It would be a waste of time. Arun listened carefully and assured me that he would take up our concerns with his PM. As it turned out, the Indian side was, or became, serious.

Negotiations were launched soon after. On the Singapore side, I normally left it to my permanent secretary, Heng Swee Keat, to propose a chief negotiator. I was surprised when Swee Keat volunteered himself. I did not think he knew much about India and suggested that he bone up quickly. I remember even recommending a couple of books for him to read, including a new book by John Garver on India–China relations called *Protracted Contest*. Swee Keat absorbed knowledge like a sponge and was more than up to the task.

Negotiations were tough but made steady progress. I remembered Lee Kuan Yew's advice to prepare for a change of government and took care to brief Sonia Gandhi and Manmohan Singh in Delhi. They assured me that Congress supported CECA negotiations. In the end, the negotiations were concluded with a Congress government.

I had gone over to the Foreign Ministry by then, with Lim Hng Kiang as my successor as Minister for Trade and Industry, but joined the delegation which went to Delhi for the signing ceremony in 2005. PM Lee Hsien Loong and PM Manmohan Singh signed the agreement, for which the stack of documents must have been a metre high.

After the signing, we shook hands in turn. When I shook PM Singh's hand, he said in his soft voice, "We would not have been able to do this without you." I was touched, but I did not expect that CECA would one day become a controversial agreement in Singapore. It is said that success has many fathers but failure is an orphan. I am happy to claim some responsibility for CECA, despite the current adverse reaction.

CECA was India's first comprehensive bilateral free trade agreement in the world. Our objective beyond the bilateral agreement was to support a larger agreement between Indian and all of the Association of Southeast Asian Nations (ASEAN), which was achieved in 2009. India's initial Look East policy was later strengthened to an Act East policy under PM Narendra Modi, who made a special effort to attend Lee Kuan Yew's funeral in 2015 to show respect and friendship. Our relations with India are now multi-faceted, including cooperation over defence matters. A strong, friendly India is a force for stability in our region and an essential part of ASEAN's strategic architecture.

Q: Why is there such an adverse reaction to CECA in Singapore now?

When my team lost in the 2011 General Election (GE), immigration from China was a big issue. We had let in too many too quickly to feed our economic growth, which incurred a strong domestic reaction. I sensed widespread anger while campaigning and told PM Lee about it. I was surprised he subsequently made an apology to Singaporeans.

In the 2020 GE, immigration from India became a big issue, especially among those in the professional, managerial, executive and technical (PMET) sector. But CECA never provided an open door. I was glad that Minister Ong Ye Kung, who was the Director of Trade when I was Minister for Trade and Industry, confirmed this to be the case in Parliament in 2021.

In my view, there are two separate issues we should be mindful of. First, we should control the quantity and quality of the people we admit, whether as citizens, permanent residents or Employment Pass holders. We should monitor whether they are helping to create jobs for Singaporeans or taking jobs away from them.

Second, there must be a clear expectation of good behaviour on the part of foreigners. Many are prepared to help Singaporeans with money or time. This should be facilitated in an organised way. We want to treat guests well, but we have every right to turf them out if they misbehave. As for the approval of citizenship, the applicant should first show that he would make a good Singaporean. In an earlier chapter, I proposed that a jury of common Singaporeans could make the assessment. Like the example I gave of the Parsees, immigrants should sweeten Singaporean society, not sour it.

I was once told that Singapore had the most Indian Institutes of Technology (IIT) and Institutes of Marketing and Management (IMM) graduates of any city outside India. India's IITs and IMMs produce some of the smartest scientists, technologists, engineers and computer scientists in the world. An increasing number of United States (US) multinational corporations (MNCs) are headed by Indians, including

Greeting PM Manmohan Singh

With Ratan Tata who started the International Tech Park in Bengaluru with Philip Yeo

PM Goh Chok Tong with PM Vajpayee in Singapore on 8 April 2002. PM Goh was keen to start an Indian fever in Singapore and pushed for the launch of CECA with PM Vajpayee.

Tarun Das who contributed greatly to Singapore–India relations

Arun Shourie presenting me his book Does He Know A Mother's Heart?, *which I will refer to in* Musings Series Three

PM Modi signing a condolence book in Delhi before flying to Singapore for the state funeral of Lee Kuan Yew

Amartya Sen and Sugata Bose when I gave a lecture in Harvard comparing India and China in March 2012

the current and previous Dean of my old business school in Harvard. By contrast, Chinese are increasingly distrusted in the US.

We have to manage this international Indian network in Singapore consciously and carefully. It is a powerful one which we should not just leave to market forces. Managed well, that network adds considerably to our influence in the world.

Q: How do you see relations between India and China?

In 2012, I spent a week in Harvard as an Ezra Vogel Fellow, during which I gave a speech comparing China and India. Ezra Vogel himself, Amartya Sen and Sugata Bose were in the audience.

China is like a giant redwood. It grows several feet every year and looks magnificent from a distance. It will stop growing one day, but everyone will continue to reference it. One day in the distant future, the tree will fall, and the entire forest will hear its collapse. A large area of forest will also be affected.

India, by contrast, is like a giant bush. It is everywhere and hard to make sense of. Some parts will flourish while others will languish. Even if a section is burned by fire or blighted by disease, the rest of the bush will continue growing. It never dies; it just goes on. Yet, the biomass of the tree and the biomass of the bush are comparable.

Unlike Chinese history, which has clear cycles, India's history is more like Europe's. Historians and political scientists argue about whether there was one India before the Raj. There is, however, no disagreement that the entire Indian sub-continent constitutes one connected civilisation whatever the changing political configuration, and despite divisions of race, religion, language and caste. Chidambaram once told me that stories of Shiva differ all over India but do not contradict one another. So far as the gods are concerned, there has only ever been one India.

There is no aspect of the human condition that has not been explored or philosophised over in India. I don't think India can ever have a

Left: Xi Jinping showing Narendra Modi the Big Goose Temple in Xi'an in 2015

Bottom: Li Keqiang and Narendra Modi at the Temple of Heaven witnessing simultaneous display of yoga and taiji

revolution or the sort of upheaval that we see in China from time to time. India is never as good as it looks; it is also never as bad as it sometimes appears. Dealing with India, one needs to move to its rhythm.

The civilisations of East and South Asia are separated by high mountains, wide deserts and Southeast Asia. In the long history of India and China, there has been no major war between them. The border war in 1962 which lasted a few weeks left a scar in India, but has been long forgotten in China. Although recent border skirmishes have reopened old wounds, good sense and diplomacy should be able to heal these. There is no deep historical antipathy between the two countries. Each respects the other as an ancient people.

PM Modi and President Xi Jinping made great efforts to build up their relationship. Modi invited Xi to his hometown in Ahmedabad and made reference to a Gujarati monk, Dharmagupta, who brought Buddhism to Sui China. Xi reciprocated by hosting Modi at his hometown in Xi'an and accompanied him on a tour of the Big Goose Pagoda, which was the monastery Xuanzang returned to after spending many years in India. When Modi arrived in Beijing, Premier Li Keqiang hosted him at an event at the Temple of Heaven, where a simultaneous display of yoga and *taiji* was presented. Modi's hosting of Xi in Mahabalipuram was in the same vein. Historically, India's great contribution to China was Buddhism, which transformed the texture of Chinese civilisation.

The main issue between them is the delineation of their common border. In the east, India recognises the McMahon Line, which was agreed between the Raj and the local Tibetan authority at a time when London recognised Qing suzerainty over Tibet. China claims most of Arunachal Pradesh as part of southern Tibet. To the west, there was never any agreement between the Raj and China. India claims Aksai Chin, while the conflict between India and Pakistan over Jammu and Kashmir adds to the complexity. Both Mao Zedong and Deng Xiaoping offered a simple swap of the two, Aksai Chin for Arunachal Pradesh, but India was unwilling.

By the time India came around in the 1990s, China had hardened its position, especially over Tawang in Arunachal Pradesh. The sixth Dalai Lama was born in Tawang. China suspects that India and the US want the next Dalai Lama to be reincarnated there in order to torment China for one more lifetime. Delhi's facilitation of the 14th Dalai Lama's visit to Tawang in 2018 added to Chinese suspicion.

It will take time and much goodwill before the 3,500km-long border between India and China is delineated. It went from being a central issue in their bilateral agenda to being only one of many items, until the recent interruption.

Border conflicts between the old Soviet Union and China were much more tense in the past. In 2008, Sergey Lavrov and Yang Jiechi signed the Sino-Russian Border Line Agreement covering a stretch of 3,600km. There is no more border conflict between the two countries now. President Kassym-Jomart Tokaev of Kazakhstan was once a Soviet diplomat involved in border negotiations with China. When he was Foreign Minister of Kazakhstan, I asked him who conceded more in the agreement. He said that maybe it was Russia, but just by a little. Once bilateral relations are cordial, border negotiations become much easier. So it will be too, between India and China.

The only land border China has not yet delineated is that with India and Bhutan. The border with Myanmar was delineated in 1960, largely along the McMahon Line. India's incredibly complex border with Bangladesh was finally delineated in 2015.

In recent years, the US has been trying to enlist India's support in its protracted struggle with China. India's participation in the Quadrilateral Security Dialogue, together with Australia, Japan and the US, sent an anti-China signal, but it will never allow itself to be made use of by others. It supported China's BRICS initiative, along with Brazil, Russia and South Africa, and joined the Shanghai Cooperation Organisation. India also maintains a strategic military relationship with Russia. It has taken delivery of Russia's S-400 air defence system despite US objections, and has dared the US to sanction it.

Welcoming Minister and Mrs Arjun Singh to the National Museum in 1994

Our first major exhibition on India in 1994

The Buddha relic which was the centrepiece of the exhibition

I believe that the relationship between India and China will gradually improve, but there will be ups and downs in the short term. Despite Indian government sanctions against Chinese tech companies, bilateral trade between the two countries continues to grow. China was keen for India to join the Regional Comprehensive Economic Partnership and encouraged ASEAN negotiators to help facilitate India's participation. Unfortunately, domestic politics in India made it hard for India to agree to this. India is rightly afraid that its market will be swamped by cheap Chinese goods.

Q: What about India and ASEAN?

Southeast Asia's relationship with India goes back to the early mists of history. In the first millenium, Buddhist–Hindu influence permeated all parts of Southeast Asia. All 10 countries of ASEAN have India in them. The name 'Singapore' is of Sanskrit origin and needs no explanation in India. When Thai King Vajiralongkorn was formally installed in 2019, the ceremony was both Brahmanic and Buddhist. Many court rituals in Muslim Sultanates were originally Hindu. Variations of the *Ramayana* and *Mahabharata* continue to be enacted all over Southeast Asia.

As India looks and acts East, India's relationship with ASEAN will naturally grow. ASEAN naturally welcomes a growing Indian presence for geopolitical balance. Neither threatens the other. We have no sensitive boundary disputes, whether over land or at sea. But both sides need to deepen their knowledge of each other and work harder for closer cooperation in all fields — political, economic, technological, cultural and military.

Singapore has been at the forefront in promoting closer India–ASEAN relations. It is in our strategic interest. Our museums organise exhibitions on India regularly. In 1994, India's Human Resource Minister and I launched *Alamkara* at the Asian Civilisations Museum. It showcased 5,000 years of Indian art and history and attracted over 120,000 visitors. The curator of Delhi Museum personally carried a precious Buddha relic

Hosting lunch for Minister Kamal Nath (centre) at Changi Point when Ambassador S. Jaishankar (right) pointed out to me that Captain Mohan Singh had been imprisoned across the water at Pulau Ubin

which had never travelled out of India before.

In 2007, in support of the Nalanda University project, Singapore organised a special exhibition *On the Nalanda Trail*, also at the Asian Civilisations Museum, which leaders of the East Asia Summit meeting in Singapore visited. It told the story of the spread of Buddhism in Asia. Malaysia PM Abdullah Badawi was pleased when I showed him Sriijaya artifacts from his home state of Kedah. Indonesia President Susilo Bambang Yudhono was particularly interested in a 9th century copper plate recording the donation made by a Sailendra king to Nalanda Mahavihara.

Q: What role did Singapore play in the Indian National Army?

It is good to remember that Southeast Asia, and Singapore in particular, played a significant role in India's struggle for independence.

When the Japanese moved into Southeast Asia during the Second World War, they sponsored nationalist leaders like Aung San, Sukarno and Subhas Chandra Bose (Netaji). Indian prisoners of war from the

British Army were released and armed once they joined the Indian National Army (INA), which was first led by Captain Mohan Singh. The Japanese soon found him recalcitrant and switched their support to Bose.

When the former Indian Trade Minister Kamal Nath visited me in Singapore, I hosted him for lunch at Changi Point. Indian High Commissioner Jaishankar (now External Affairs Minister) pointed to Pulau Ubin across the water and said that Captain Mohan Singh had been imprisoned there. I immediately replied that I knew exactly where, and declared that the building was still there. I used to patronise a seafood restaurant on Pulau Ubin which had thick walls and barred windows. The restaurant owner told me that the building had been used as a government opium distribution centre after the Second World War. Bingo!

Since then, I have repeatedly reminded the National Heritage Board to preserve the building as a historical site. It should be properly restored with historical material on how the Japanese incarcerated Captain Singh in order to give Bose a free hand in reorganising the INA, though I know my Bengali friends won't be pleased to hear this.

Singapore was the headquarters of the INA. The Padang and Farrer Park became its parade grounds. Not long afterwards, the women's regiment was formed and was named after the Rani of Jhansi, the Indian Queen and leading figure of the 1857 Indian Rebellion. In Myanmar (then known as Burma), the INA fought alongside the Japanese Army.

President S. R. Nathan was an admirer of Bose. He recounted some of his war stories to me, including an occasion where he saw Subhas Chandra Bose, Aung San, Sukarno and Hideki Tojo arriving at the Istana Bukit Serene in Johor, one at a time. On another occasion, he was on the same ferry with Bose crossing the Muar River. A young Nathan saw the silhouette of his nationalist hero silhouetted against the evening sky.

Before the war ended in 1945, the INA built a memorial on the esplanade beside the Padang bearing the Urdu words *Ittefaq* (unity), *Itmad* (faith) and *Kurbani* (sacrifice). When the British returned in

PM Narendra Modi paying respect to Netaji and the INA at Esplanade Park

Left: Replica of the INA Memorial at the house of Netaji in Kolkata

Bottom right: At Netaji's house in Kolkata. Behind me is the car which enabled Netaji to escape the British who were about to arrest him.

September, they immediately demolished the memorial. In Delhi, the British started prosecuting members of the INA as traitors. Nehru defended them as patriots. Indeed, without the INA threatening armed insurrection, Britain might have delayed giving India its independence. Winston Churchill was certainly not in favour of it.

In the end, with the clock to midnight ticking fast, the British abandoned the trials. Bose was a controversial figure in India but with the efflux of time, he is increasingly recognised as a great Indian patriot. Certainly, Netaji Airport in Kolkata, West Bengal, is named after him.

President Nathan shared another snippet with me. In 1947, when Nehru visited Singapore, he asked for a bouquet of flowers. His staff thought that they were intended for Lady Edwina, Lord Louis Mountbatten's wife. It turned out that the flowers were for Nehru to honour INA fighters at the site where the memorial once stood.

I got to know Sugata, Netaji's nephew, well because of our common involvement in the Nalanda project. He showed me Netaji's old house which is now a museum to the INA. It has a replica of the INA Memorial which the British demolished. In 1995, I unveiled a plaque to mark the site of the INA memorial at the Esplanade Park. After seeing the replica in Kolkata, I had proposed to the Cabinet that we should erect a full-size replica on the exact site. Some ministers objected as the INA was associated with the Japanese Army, which did terrible things during their occupation of Singapore. I understood their discomfort and later suggested that a replica be placed instead at the Indian Heritage Centre.

At a dinner I once hosted for India Deputy PM Lal Krishna Advani beside the Singapore River, he expressed interest in seeing the INA Memorial site. I said that it was a short walk from where we were, but as it was late in the evening, we arranged for him to visit the following day. Some years later, PM Modi also paid his respects to Bose at the Esplanade Park memorial.

Singapore's role in India's independence parallels our role in China's 1911 Revolution. As we are proud to recall Singapore's support of Dr Sun Yat-sen, so we should be too of the role Subhas Chandra Bose played.

President S. R. Nathan launching Sugata Bose's book on his grand-uncle in May 2011

Sugata Bose's book His Majesty's Opponent, *May 2011*

With INA veterans in Singapore who attended the book launch

However, we must take care not to forget the cruelties which his Japanese sponsor inflicted on innocent Singaporeans. In July 2011, President S. R. Nathan launched Sugata Bose's book on his grand-uncle, titled *His Majesty's Opponent*, at the Singapore Recreation Club. It was attended by a few Singapore INA veterans.

CHAPTER 8

On The Nalanda Trail

*George Yeo recounts his involvement with the revival of what
was possibly the world's first university, Nalanda.*

Q: How did you come to be involved with this historic project?

The first major exhibition of Indian artefacts in Singapore was called
Alamkara in 1994. Many of the visitors who came did so to venerate a
small Buddha relic, which was being exhibited outside India for the first
time. Many of the hundreds of millions of Buddhists who live in East
and Southeast Asia would love to visit Buddhist sites in India. This
potential will only grow as incomes rise. What holds them back is the
lack of good facilities.

When Indian Deputy Prime Minister (DPM) Lal Krishna Advani
visited Singapore in 2003, I was the Minister-in-Attendance to him.
Knowing that he wished to promote Singaporean investment in India,
I suggested Buddhist tourism. Tourism is a good way to generate
economic activity in a country as its benefits are spread widely. It also
exposes local people to foreigners, increasing their knowledge of the
world and broadening their minds. India's many Buddhist sites would
benefit millions of people once religious tourism takes off. These places
are an enormous asset. Meanwhile, as a tourism hub, Singapore can play
a role in promoting Buddhist tourism in India.

DPM Advani listened intently and said that he would follow up. He
was not the Hindutva radical I initially thought him to be from the Babri

With DPM Advani who asked to visit the Indian National Army memorial at Esplanade Park. My Nalanda trail began with him.

Advani's book about his time in prison

Mosque incident. Some years later, he gave me a copy of his prison journals and was proud of the glowing speech he gave on Jinnah in 2005.

A few months later, he sent India's Tourism Minister Jagmohan Malhotra to Singapore. We had good discussions. In early 2004, he invited me to attend the dedication ceremony of Bodh Gaya's Mahabodhi Mahavihar as a UNESCO World Heritage Site. It was under a bodhi tree here that the Buddha is said to have attained enlightenment.

Jagmohan said that I could bring guests along. The Buddhist community in Singapore was enthusiastic and chartered a SilkAir aircraft to fly participants directly to Gaya Airport. My Buddhist friends told me that this special occasion brought Buddhist groups from different traditions in Singapore together. In addition to traditional Chinese Mahayana, there are other Mahayana groups affiliated to Taiwan, Korea, Japan and Vietnam. Our Theravada groups are connected to Sri Lanka, Thailand and Myanmar. In recent years, Tibetan Buddhism has also increased its presence. Our delegation was led by a number of monks.

When I mentioned our upcoming trip to the late President S. R. Nathan, he gave me a book by an Oxford University graduate, Sun Shuyun, to read, titled *Ten Thousand Miles Without A Cloud*. It is a delightful introduction to the history of Buddhism in India. I bought all the copies available in our local bookshops and passed them to members of the delegation for background reading.

Sun Shuyun was principally interested in the journey of the great Tang Dynasty monk, Xuanzang, to India in the 7th century. It was a difficult journey full of dangers, which inspired the Ming Dynasty novel *Journey to the West*. All Chinese children are familiar with the story of the Great Monk and his helpers: the legendary monkey god, Sun Wukong; the pig-man, Zhu Bajie; and the desert monk, Sha Wujing. However, Sun Shuyun lamented her own ignorance of the actual historical basis of

Sun Shuyun's Ten Thousand Miles Without A Cloud

Journey to the West and decided to delve into it and retrace Xuanzang's journey. The book is written at three levels — the Great Monk's journey, the Buddha's journey and her own. It was the first time I heard of Nalanda, the university which Xuanzang attended and in which he later became a great teacher. Nalanda buzzed in my mind after that.

I went to Delhi to join Jagmohan for the International Conclave on Buddhism and Spiritual Tourism first before flying with him to Bodh Gaya, where I joined the Singapore delegation. After the ceremony ended, I flew with Jagmohan for a short visit to Sarnath before returning to Delhi. The Singapore delegation went on from Bodh Gaya to visit Nalanda and Vulture's Peak before returning home. I regretted not being able to join them in Nalanda, not knowing that I would one day become very involved in its revival as a seat of learning.

In 2004, there was a change of government in India and the Congress Party came back to power. In Singapore, I hosted dinner for the new Vice Chairman of the Planning Commission, Montek Singh Ahluwalia. The Chairman was the Prime Minister himself. We talked about Nalanda and I suggested its modern-day revival as an international institution.

Mahabodhi Mahavihara at Bodh Gaya, the spot where Buddha achieved enlightenment beneath a Bodhi tree

At its peak, Nalanda had over 10,000 students from all over Asia. Buddhist communities in China, Japan, Korea and Southeast Asia were all connected to Nalanda or inspired by it, one way or another. If we could get the leaders of the East Asia Summit to give their collective blessing, the new Nalanda could become an icon for a new Asia.

I must have been quite passionate in my advocacy. Montek looked at me, paused and requested a short paper on what I had just said

Top & centre: Tourism Minister Jagmohan in Singapore, 2003

International Conclave on Buddhism in Delhi, 2004

to him. I hesitated momentarily before agreeing. Within a week, I emailed a proposal to him. In Delhi, it was called the "Singapore Proposal".

Some weeks later, I bumped into N. K. Singh at Delhi Airport. He had been Montek's predecessor in the Planning Commission and was now helping Chief Minister Nitish Kumar in Bihar, his home state. N. K. told me that Montek had told him about my proposal. He had separately been working with Nitish on reviving Nalanda as a state university. The draft state legislation had already been prepared and he would send me a copy for my comment. I replied after a few days. In the legislation was a provision to defer to the central government should there be a decision to elevate the revival of Nalanda to a national project.

Q: What was the role of the Mentor Group chaired by Amartya Sen?

Not long afterwards, in 2007, the Indian government formed a Nalanda Mentors Group to conceptualise the new university and invited me to be a member. Prime Minister (PM) Manmohan Singh appointed Amartya Sen as its chairman. In his 2021 memoir, *Home in the World*, Amartya wrote about his fascination with the history of Nalanda from an early age. While studying in Santiniketan, he and his friends organised frequent outings to the nearby Rajgir Hills.

It is one of the blessings of my life to have had the opportunity of working with Amartya on the Nalanda project. When my book, *Banyan, Bonsai and the Tao*, was published in 2013, Amartya contributed a foreword and specially flew to Singapore from Kolkata to be the guest of honour for the launch.

The other Indian members of the Mentors Group were N. K. Singh, the politician and former Indian Administrative Service officer; Lord Meghnad Desai, the British Labour politician and economist; Sugata Bose, a Harvard historian and grand-nephew of Subhas Chandra Bose; and Tansen Sen, a graduate of Peking University and an Asian history professor.

Except for me, the non-Indian members were accomplished scholars.

Ikuo Hirayama was a famous Japanese painter who survived the bombing of Hiroshima. He had been with other students when he saw a United States (US) B-29 bomber drop a parachute with something attached to the end. He rushed from the balcony back into his classroom to beckon others to come out and see the parachute. Because he did so, he lived. Those who stayed out to watch were incinerated by the atomic bomb detonating in the air. Hirayama went on to dedicate his life to promoting the cause of peace in the world. After he passed away in 2009, Susumu Nakanishi, a Japanese scholar, was his alternate and successor.

With us too was Prapod Assavavirulhakarn, a scholar of religious studies from Chulalongkorn University, and Wang Bangwei, a historian of Sino-Indian cultural relations from Peking University. Wang Gungwu was initially my alternate. As I was Foreign Minister at the time, I wasn't sure whether I would be able to attend all the meetings. Very quickly, Amartya and other members of the Mentor Group decided that Prof Wang should be a member in his own right.

As funding for the Nalanda project came through the External Affairs Ministry, the Ministry's Joint Secretary (East) joined the Group as an *ex officio* member. The Ministry also appointed a Joint Secretary (Nalanda) to help us.

Many members of the Mentor Group knew Sanskrit and/or Chinese. Amartya was once criticised for not being too 'westernised' and not 'Indian enough' by an Indian politician. He shut up when Amartya invited him for a debate in Sanskrit.

My role was principally political. I was conscious that I was participating in an individual capacity and not as a Singapore minister. Nevertheless, I had the backing of the Singapore government even after I left government in 2011. The Singaporean Buddhist community cheered me on and our High Commission in Delhi was always helpful. Although some senior officers of Singapore's Foreign Ministry did not believe the project would take off, they were not openly critical because I was their minister. One day, I asked my Senior Minister of State, the late Dr Balaji Sadasivan, a man I had great respect for and was very fond of, whether the project was worth the effort. He immediately replied, "Of course." That gave me heart.

The undergraduate education system in India has to accommodate the need for caste preferences. Quotas are therefore often the subject of political debate. From the outset, Nalanda was conceived as a post-graduate university as a matter of practicality. Putting emphasis on quality rather than quantity also gave the project a clearer focus. South Asian University, which was established by the South Asian Association for Regional Cooperation (SAARC), provided a useful precedent. For Nalanda, the support of the member countries of the East Asian Summit was essential for the establishment of Nalanda as an international university.

In November 2006, Singapore organised a Nalanda Buddhist Symposium as part of our preparatory work for the launch of the project. India President Abdul Kalam addressed us by video-conferencing. He was an early advocate of Nalanda's revival. After learning of my proposal to Montek, he asked to see me during his state visit to Singapore in March 2006. He was only interested in talking about Nalanda. When he returned to India, he addressed the joint session of the Bihar Legislature and strongly advocated for the revival of Nalanda.

Also joining the Symposium by video-conferencing was Prof Tan Chung from University of Chicago. Tan Chung was the son of Tan Yun-

Tan Chung's magnum opus

Shan, a Chinese scholar whom Rabindranath Tagore recruited in Singapore in 1927 to establish the Cheena Bhavana, or China House, in Tagore's Visva Bharati University in Santiniketan. Both Chiang Kai-shek and Zhou Enlai visited it. Tan Chung was one of the two authors of a fascinating volume called *India and China: Twenty Centuries of Civilizational Interaction and Vibrations*. Prof Wang Gungwu also spoke. I gave a speech on the Asian renaissance.

At Amartya Sen's home in Santiniketan

Nalanda Mentors Group with Bihar Chief Minister Nitish Kumar in Patna

Landing in Rajgir. Left to right: N. K. Singh, Montek Singh Ahluwalia and Chief Minister Nitish Kumar.

Calling on President Abdul Kalam in Singapore. The entire conversation was on Nalanda.

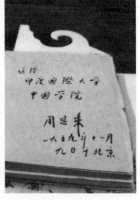

Cheena Bhavana in Santiniketan

Zhou Enlai's inscription

Nalanda Mentors Group inaugural meeting in Singapore

Bungalow owner, Wu Hsioh Kwang, on the right. Artist Tan Swie Hian standing. On the left is editor of Musings, *Woon Tai Ho.*

My wife with Amartya Sen. To his left is Minister of State Balaji Sadasivan, who encouraged me on the Nalanda project.

The inaugural meeting of the Mentors Group was held in Singapore in July 2007. On one evening, we had dinner at a bungalow owned by a Singaporean businessman, Wu Hsioh Kwang, which was solely used for paintings on Nalanda by a Singaporean artist, Tan Swie Hian.

Lee Kuan Yew read about the Mentors Group in the newspapers and called me in the evening to ask whether Amartya was still in town. If so, he would like to meet him. I replied that Amartya had already flown off, but would make sure to let him know the next time Amartya came to Singapore. I conveyed Lee Kuan Yew's request to Amartya. He was pleased to hear it as he had publicly criticised Lee Kuan Yew before. Lee Kuan Yew showed keen interest in the Nalanda project, remarking that it was a good thing. When I expressed the hope that it could build a bridge between India and China, he replied that that was expecting too much.

Q: An exhibition on Nalanda was held at Singapore's Asian Civilisations Museum in 2007/2008. What was the inspiration?

On the Nalanda Trail was organised by the Asian Civilisations Museum to coincide with the third East Asia Summit (EAS) held in Singapore in November 2007. We arranged for the leaders to visit the exhibition because their endorsement of the Nalanda project was an item on our agenda that year.

The exhibition was well put together by Gauri Parimoo Krishnan. Amartya liked the catalogue so much that he asked for 20 copies to be sent to him in Harvard. Objects from Srivijaya and other Buddhist kingdoms in Southeast Asia were displayed. There was a precious picture from the Kamakura period in Japan depicting the old Nalanda library towering into the clouds.

Before the leaders meeting, I lobbied EAS Foreign Ministers for their support. At that time, there were 16 countries in the EAS — the ASEAN-10, China, Japan, Korea, Australia, New Zealand and India. (The US and Russia joined later.) Except for Australia, New Zealand,

and the Philippines, the Nalanda project resonated naturally with countries which had a Buddhist heritage. Korean Foreign Minister Ban Ki-moon was particularly enthusiastic. I learned from him about the visit of a young Korean monk, Hyecho, from the kingdom of Silla to Nalanda in the 8th century. Hyecho studied Buddhism in Tang China from Indian monks who encouraged him to make the journey. A senior Indian monk in Chang'an, Vajrabodhi, described Hyecho as one of the six living persons who was well-trained in the five sections of the Buddhist canon.

Winning China's support was more complicated. When President Kalam spoke at the Nalanda Buddhism Symposium, he made an extended reference to the Buddhist heritage of Tawang. I had not heard of Tawang before and did some research. I learned that Tawang is in a part of Arunachal Pradesh claimed by China as part of south Tibet. It was the birthplace of the sixth Dalai Lama. I felt uneasy and mentioned to Amartya that it was important that the Nalanda project not be politicised. China's support was critical. Amartya thanked me for my advice.

Through Wang Bangwei, we tried to organise a Mentors Group meeting in China. Bangwei is a scholar without strong political connections. As there was no progress, I made a request through our embassy in China. On my subsequent visit to Beijing, in my call on State Councillor Dai Bingguo, I explained the background of the Nalanda project and expressed the hope that it would bring China and India closer together. He listened carefully and, after asking Vice Minister Hu Zhengyue for his views, declared that the Nalanda project was a good thing (好事). Our request to hold a Mentor Group meeting in China would be positively considered.

A few weeks later, Premier Wen Jiabao made an official visit to India. According to National Security Adviser Shivshankar Menon, who informed me immediately afterwards, right at the start of Wen Jiabao's meeting with Manmohan Singh, Wen said that China welcomed the Mentors Group meeting in China. In Delhi, Wen announced that China would make a US$1 million donation to the project. He found time to take an active part in a forum on Nalanda while he was there. Subsequently, the joint communique issued in December 2010 stated:

> *"Both sides agreed to work together on projects which strengthen bonds between the peoples of East Asia. In this context, China welcomed India's efforts to revive the Nalanda University. Both sides appreciated the work of the Nalanda Mentor Group and the progress made so far. India welcomed China's contribution of US$1 million for the Nalanda University."*

By the time we visited China, the University had been formally legislated into existence by the Indian Parliament and the Mentors Group had become its Governing Board.

We visited Xi'an first before adjourning to Peking University for our formal meeting. Xi'an was important because this was where Xuanzang, the monk, began and ended his journey. We spent a few hours at the Giant Wild Goose Pagoda where Xuanzang dedicated the rest of his life to translating sutras he brought back from India. Wang Gungwu was so inspired that he joined us in climbing many storeys up to the top of the historic pagoda.

At Peking University, Amartya gave a public lecture which was well-received. I saw a long line of male and female students lining up for his autograph after he spoke. We also called on China's Vice Foreign Minister Zhang Zhijun.

As a young monk in Chang'an (now Xi'an), Xuanzang felt that his knowledge of Buddhism was incomplete. He was particularly interested in the *yogacara* (yoga practice) taught by the great Nalanda monk Silabhadra, who appeared to him in a dream. Despite an order by Emperor Tang Taizong that no one was to leave China, Xuanzang slipped out and made the perilous journey to India. He went via the northern silk route between the Tianshan Range and the Taklamakan Desert, climbed snowy slopes into present-day Kyrgyzstan and rounded the

Pamirs into Afghanistan, where he saw the Buddha statues of Bamiyan. From there he entered India and finally arrived in Magadha (now Bihar).

In Nalanda, Xuanzang was welcomed by Silabhadra,who had anticipated his arrival in a dream. Nalanda taught many subjects, including theology, logic, grammar, mathematics, astronomy and medicine. It was probably the world's first university. It was established in the 5th century and lasted for 700 years before its destruction by Afghan invaders in the 12th century, not long after Oxford University was established (but before Cambridge).

In all, Xuanzang lived some 15 years in India and became a famous teacher in Nalanda. When he finally indicated that he planned to return to China, his colleagues asked why he wanted to return to such an uncivilised land. Xuanzang, who was a great debater, deftly replied that this was precisely why he had to return to China.

The return journey via the Southern Silk Route was easier but not without its dangers. In addition to sacred texts, Xuanzang brought back with him sacred objects. At Hetian, he requested permission to re-enter China. By that time, his reputation had spread in China. Tang Taizong, who was still the Emperor, despatched an imperial guard to escort Xuanzang back to Chang'an. He was welcomed by the Emperor himself and given resources to translate the sutras into Chinese.

The translation of the sutras from Sanskrit to Chinese was one of humankind's greatest intellectual efforts. It not only involved translating words, but phrases from one philosophical framework into another. As sutras are chanted, the translations also had to take into account vibrations in order to achieve equivalent meditative effects in Chinese.

Xuanzang declined the Emperor's invitation to be a high official in his court. However, in return for the resources given to him, he had to write a detailed account of his journey to India. His *Great Tang Records on the Western Regions* (大唐西域记) is one of the most important documents in world history. Spanning over 120,000 characters in 12 volumes, Xuanzang's history contains information on the geography, history, politics, economic life, religion and culture of different regions bordering China. It also described Nalanda in detail.

Xuanzang's account was written in a tradition first established by Sima Qian, who wrote the first of China's 24 dynastic histories, during the Western Han period. The histories contain a wealth of information. Names, places, dates, political events, wars, natural disasters, plagues and astronomical phenomena were generally recorded with a high degree of accuracy, though interpretations are naturally subjective and good and evil deeds often exaggerated. On the whole, however, China's historiography over the centuries is exceptional. Much of the history of South and Southeast Asia was recovered through Chinese records.

After Xuanzang, there was another great monk, Yijing, who spent many years in Nalanda. In AD 673, he travelled from Guangzhou to Srivijaya, where he learned Sanskrit. He then crossed the Bay of Bengal and spent many years in Nalanda before going back to Sumatra to translate the sutras and other Buddhist texts.

After two years, he ran out of paper. However, when he stepped aboard a ship to give instructions to the captain on what to buy for him in Guangzhou, the monsoon winds suddenly started to blow. The captain declared that he had to set sail immediately and brought Yijing along. When the monsoon changed direction, Yijing returned to Sumatra. In 695 AD, he completed his translation, sailed to Guangzhou and arrived in Luoyang, where Empress Wu Zetian welcomed him extravagantly.

His 25-year journey culminated in the translation of over 400 Buddhist texts into Chinese. Yijing wrote two important books, *A Record of Buddhist Practices Sent Home from the Southern Sea* (南海寄归内法传) and *The Great Tang Chronicle of Eminent Monks who Traveled to the West Seeking the Dharma* (大唐西域求法僧传). The former text detailed monastic practices in India and Southeast Asia and became an important reference text in Tang China monasteries. The latter book recorded the journeys of Tang monks who went to India in search of Buddhist knowledge. Both Wang Bangwei and Tansen Sen had deep knowledge of Yijing's exploits, which were almost as remarkable as Xuanzang's.

Yijing's writings reached Japan, Korea and Vietnam. In the Buddhist *vinayas*, there was no provision for eating with chopsticks. Yijing argued that since no chopsticks were used in India during the time of the Buddha, this lacuna should not be made an issue in China.

At the end of the 12th century, the Turko-Afghan invader Muhammad Khilji destroyed Nalanda and other great monasteries in Bihar (which derives its name from *vihara,* or an early type of Buddhist monastery), killing many monks. Buddhism had been on the wane in India for some time. The great library of Nalanda burned for weeks because of the many books it housed.

When the British were in India, no one knew what the ruins of Nalanda represented, unlike those at Bodh Gaya. One day, the famous British archaeologist, Alexander Cunningham, was given an English translation of what Xuanzang had written over a thousand years ago. To his astonishment, it read like a tour guide of India. Cunningham established the Archaeological Survey of India, which remains a key institution in India and is responsible for all the major archaelogical sites. Following the realisation that China had detailed records of centuries of Indian history, a relatively small group of soldiers, administra-tors and adventurers recovered the lost history of Buddhism in India with the help of Chinese records. Charles Allen wrote a gripping account of their endeavours in his book *The Buddha and the Sahibs*.

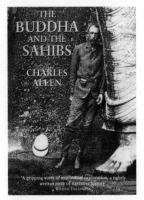

Charles Allen's The Buddha and the Sahibs *on India's recovery of its history from Chinese records*

Thus, in the 19th century, Nalanda was rediscovered in India. For East and Southeast Asians who grew up with the story of Xuanzang's quest for sutras in India, the rediscovery gave physical reality to what many had thought was legend. The Nalanda trail lead to Asia's recovery of a period of history when all parts of the continent were linked by a Buddhist web, which was religious, intellectual and philosophical. Without Buddhism, East and Southeast Asia would be a vast painting with one colour missing.

Q: But how do we connect the new to the old Nalanda? Is the new Nalanda secular or religious?

The revival of Nalanda was an idea whose time had come. Many people believed it should be done. Amartya Sen imagined it happening as a young man. Abdul Kalam pushed for it passionately. Nitish Kumar saw it as a mission. The Mentors Group therefore rode a wave of support not just in India, but across all of Asia. Even western scholars volunteered their services.

Although the inspiration for the new Nalanda was Buddhist, it was established as a secular institution. Making it a Buddhist institution would have immediately limited its compass. As Buddhist philosophy once united a wide region, the new Nalanda should also have a large conception of its mission. We live in an age where globalisation is sharpening conflicts both between and within countries. We share a planet which is threatened by man himself. Nalanda's mission should be to promote a philosophy of man living in harmony with his fellow man, of man living in harmony with nature and of man living as part of nature. The philosophy which suffuses Buddhism is of renewed relevance to the world today. In this way, the new Nalanda inherits the mantle of the old.

I became one of Nalanda's missionaries and took the opportunity to talk about it anywhere and everywhere. I knew some Ministry of Foreign Affairs officers were uncomfortable with this and I am sure some of my political colleagues also had reservations. But, on the whole, there was resonance. It became almost a romance.

In India, I did what little I could to lobby for Nalanda's cause. Arjun Singh was then the Human Resource Minister in India and responsible for education, including universities. He was a good friend from the Ministry of Information and the Arts days when we launched the Alamkara Exhibition together at the Asian Civilisations Museum. We kept in touch even when he left office. On his visit to Singapore in 2004, he brought his wife along. She was not completely ambulatory and did not usually travel. I did not want to tell him that my wife was in the US at the time, accompanying my youngest son for his bone marrow transplant at St. Jude Children's Research Hospital in Memphis. Had his wife known, she might not have come to Singapore, though I wanted her to. At the dinner I hosted for them, I asked my wife's sister to attend in her place.

On a cold winter day in Delhi, I called on Arjun and his wife. We sat before a brazier to keep warm. I gave a full background of the Nalanda project and asked for his support. He replied, "I have always supported Nalanda's revival and will not stand in the way."

Arjun was a man of few words. I thought 'not standing in the way' was a curmudgeonly expression and did not convey enthusiasm. It was only later that I realised the significance of his words. If the Human Resources Ministry objected to the formation of Nalanda University, the project would have stalled immediately before taking off. An unsupportive Human Resource Minister would have surfaced all manner of arguments against Nalanda. By not standing in the way, Arjun Singh enabled Nalanda University to be conceived in the womb of India's Ministry of External Affairs.

Remembering Lee Kuan Yew's wise words, I thought that I should also lobby the Opposition. When I spoke to Arun Shourie from the Bharatiya Janata Party about Nalanda, I realised that I was preaching to the converted. He had invited me to breakfast at his home. At the entrance, I was greeted by a collection of wheelchairs for his son, wife and mother, and many statues of the Buddha. Buddhism gave meaning to his suffering.

When the Nalanda University Bill was tabled in the Indian Parliament in August 2010, members from all parties in both the Lok Sabha and Rajya Sabha vied to show support with their eloquence, and in different languages. The bill was passed by a unanimous vote.

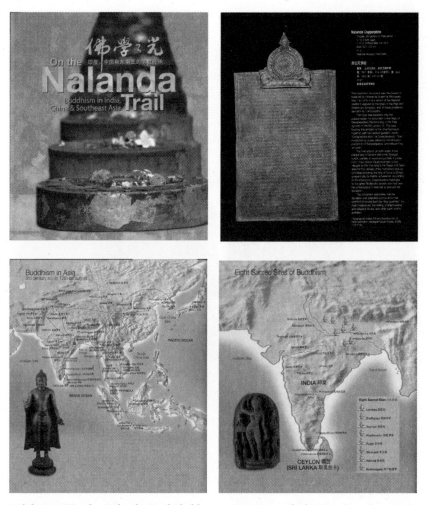

Exhibition "On the Nalanda Trail" held in conjunction with the East Asia Summit in Singapore in 2007. Top right shows the Nalanda Copperplate which recorded the monastery in Nalanda built by Sri Balaputradeva, a king from the Shailendra Dynasty of Srivijaya.

When Ban Ki-moon was Foreign Minister of Korea, he was a strong supporter of the Nalanda project and told me about the journey of Korean monk Hyecho to Nalanda in the 8th century.

Top and centre: Amartya Sen delivering a lecture at Peking University

Launching a book on India–China by Wang Bangwei and Tansen Sen at Peking University

Calling on Vice Minister of Foreign Affairs Zhang Zhijun in the China Foreign Ministry

Nalanda Governing Board visit to Xuanzang's Giant Wild Goose Pagoda in Xi'an

With Human Resource Minister Arjun Singh and his wife in Delhi. His support of Nalanda was critical.

Ruins of the old Nalanda

❖

CHAPTER 9

Revival of Nalanda after 800 Years

In this chapter, George Yeo describes the initial years of the university after it was established by an Act of the Indian Parliament in 2010. In 2012, Amartya Sen became the Founding Chancellor. Yeo took over the post as the second Chancellor in 2015 and the first Convocation was held in July 2016. In November of that year, Yeo resigned from his post.

Q: Tell us about the early beginnings of the new university.

Amartya Sen was appointed the Founding Chancellor of Nalanda in 2012. Members of the Mentors Group were appointed members of its first Governing Board, along with two state officials from the Bihar government. After its destruction 800 years ago and long forgotten, Nalanda was re-founded. It was a historic moment. In March 2012, Amartya Sen and I discussed the revival of the world's oldest university in Harvard.

The state of Bihar set aside a promising 400-acre site at Rajgir, a little over 10km from the ruins of the old Nalanda. Rajgir was the first capital of Magadha, the 'City of Kings' mentioned in the *Mahabharata*. This was land where the Buddha once traipsed. The site where King Bimbisara came down from his carriage to meet the Buddha is marked. The monastery built by him for the Buddha at Venuvana still stands.

The Buddha spent many months meditating and preaching at the nearby Rajgir Hills, at Gridhakuta. At Vulture Peak, he delivered perhaps the most important sutra in Mahayana Buddhism, the Lotus Sutra. The

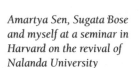

Amartya Sen, Sugata Bose and myself at a seminar in Harvard on the revival of Nalanda University

First Buddhist Council was held nearby in or around 483BC. Thus it is on sacred ground that the new Nalanda University, like the old, is sited.

Conditions in Rajgir for a new university were, however, difficult. For decades, Bihar was one of the most backward states in India. It was only after Nitish Kumar took over as Chief Minister in the year 2000 that the state began making steady progress. I have been up and down the country roads from Patna to Rajgir more than 10 times and saw the visible improvements for myself year by year. The fields looked lusher, the animals fatter and furrier, the sarees brighter and the village shops better stocked. Stretches of highways appeared bit by bit.

Gopa Sabharwal was the Founding Vice-Chancellor of the new Nalanda. She was a staff member of the Mentors Group, as Vice-Chancellor-designate, before the University was established. An able administrator, she had spirit and took many challenges in her stride. Nitish Kumar gave us a newly built conference complex in Rajgir to use as a temporary campus. The academic staff recruited had to put up with makeshift arrangements. Little by little, temporary accommodations for staff and students were found in Rajgir. However, health facilities were relatively backwards making it difficult for academic staff to bring their families along in the initial years.

The salary scale for Vice-Chancellor was deliberately set higher than for other public universities in India. This caused jealousy. Despite the Board's reluctance, Gopa insisted on drawing a salary lower than what she was entitled to. She did not want the issue of her salary to become a distraction from the work of the university.

After faculty were recruited through an international search for the first two departments and with their curriculums prepared, students were admitted. Naturally the university started out small, but it was a pregnant beginning. At all stages, Nitish Kumar did all he could to help the infant university take its first steps. At one meeting with him in Patna, I suggested that the Bihar state gift the university with additional land to be used as a long-term endowment. With economic development, and as Nalanda became more established, the land would grow in value

Nitish Kumar gave his full backing to Nalanda. Under his leadership, the economy of Bihar got steadily better.

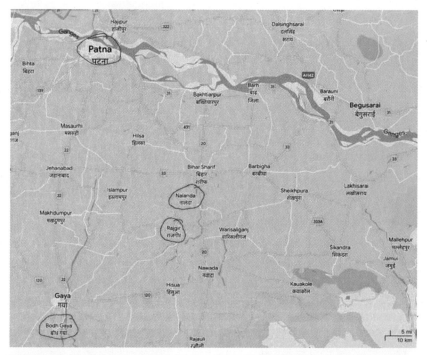

Map showing the relative positions of Patna, Rajgir, Nalanda and Bodh Gaya. Land where the Buddha traipsed.

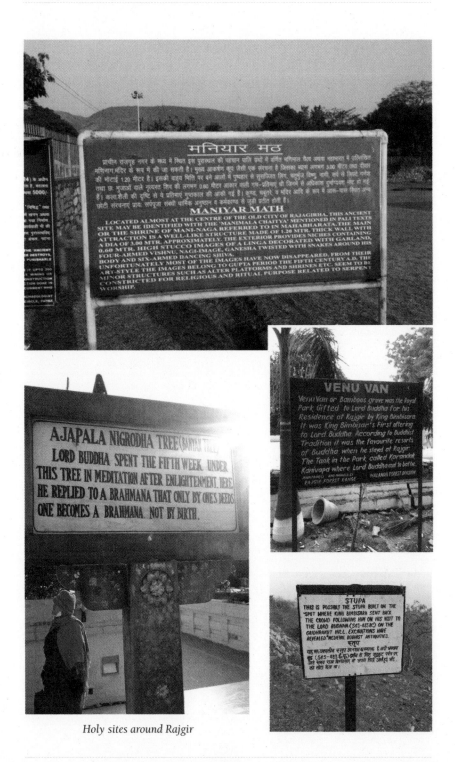

Holy sites around Rajgir

At Vulture Peak with Wang
Bangwei and Tansen Sen

Bihar countryside. Visible progress over the years.

and become an important revenue source for the university one day. The university should not rely only on government support in the long term. I cited other great universities as examples. The Chief Minister reacted positively and carved out an additional hundred acres for the university not long afterwards.

At one meeting, the Nalanda Governing Board decided to form an International Advisory Council. We wanted distinguished individuals to guide our work and help expand our international network. Amartya asked me to chair the Council. Our first member was Thai Princess Royal Maha Chakri Sirindhorn. I called on her in Bangkok to extend the Board's invitation. She knew Amartya and knew a lot about Nalanda. She accepted the appointment immediately, which was a great honour for Nalanda.

In July 2014, the Princess Royal visited Nalanda with a delegation, asking many questions. She also found time to visit a Thai monk in a little Thai temple nearby. Every member of the Thai delegation, down to drivers and porters, was invited to see the monk in her royal presence and to receive his blessing.

Our second member was Indonesian Presidential Adviser Pak Hassan Wirajuda. We were colleagues and became close friends when he was Indonesian Foreign Minister under Ibu Megawati and President Susilo Bambang Yudhoyono. He also visited Nalanda and was fascinated by the long contact between Nalanda and Buddhist kingdoms in Indonesia. He took particular interest in a copper plate which recorded the donation of a Srivijaya Shailendra King to Nalanda. There was also a famous Nalanda monk, Atisha, who spent many years studying under a Buddhist master in Sumatra, Dharmaraksita, before returning to India just before the Chola invasion. Some years later, Atisha went up to Tibet and transformed the practice of Buddhism there.

During my term as the Chancellor of Nalanda, I called on Dr Ban Ki-moon in New York, hoping that he would agree to chair the Advisory Council after his term as United Nations Secretary-General ended. He showed interest but the matter became moot after I resigned as Chancellor.

*Thai Princess Royal Maha Chakri Sirindhorn visiting Rajgir, Nalanda
and a Thai shrine in the vicinity*

Hosting my old friend and colleague, Indonesia Pak Hassan Wirajuda in Patna, Nalanda and Rajgir

Q: What happened as a result of the 2014 Indian general elections?

In the run-up to the 2014 general elections, the Bharatiya Janata Party (BJP) under Narendra Modi's leadership was the favourite to win. Modi was a controversial leader because of his Hindutva views and the belief by many that the state administration when he was Chief Minister was complicit in the 2002 Gujarat riots, which led to the death of hundreds of Muslims. He was even barred from entering the United States.

At the end of every Mentors Group and Governing Board meeting, Amartya would chair a media conference. He always had me beside him to answer questions on the involvement of the East Asia Summit (EAS). At the end of the Mentors Group meeting in January 2014, he did not ask me to join him. I wondered why but did not think much of it. I later learned that Amartya had criticised Modi's political views during the media conference. Amartya knew that Modi was likely to win, but strongly felt that he should speak out for what he believed to be right. I then understood why he did not want me at that media conference. He did not want me caught up in Indian politics.

At a Mentors Group meeting after the BJP took power and Modi became Prime Minister (PM), N. K. Singh, who is a BJP member, pulled me aside to say that it was unlikely that Amartya's three-year term as Chancellor would be renewed in 2015. I was troubled to hear this as Amartya's leadership was crucial. The new university was still finding its feet. Amartya himself was aware that senior members of the new government were against him.

Nalanda was founded as an autonomous university with an international remit. Its highest authority is the Visitor, who is the President of India. At that time, the position was held by Pranab Mukherjee, a much-respected political leader from Congress. It would be wrong to politicise the Chancellor's appointment. Furthermore, Amartya was greatly respected in India and had received the country's highest honour, the Bharat Ratna, in 1999 when a BJP-led government was in power. I never knew Amartya as a supporter of Congress or any political party. In fact, in private, he was often critical of Congress. In the ensuing months, however, the talk on the grapevine was that Amartya would not be re-appointed. Before his three-year term was up, Amartya indicated publicly that he did not wish to serve a second term as Chancellor.

A few weeks later, I received a phone call from N. K. Singh. He told me that PM Modi, External Affairs Minister Sushma Swaraj and the Visitor were in agreement that I should take over from Amartya as the second Chancellor. Would I consider it? If so, my candidacy would be put up to the Search Committee, which was unlikely to object.

Naturally, I felt honoured to be asked, but had grave reservations. Getting the new university up and running required much hands-on leadership, which Amartya provided. He spent months every year in India. I knew he was in constant touch with Gopa and would even personally call up Indian officials to clear roadblocks. I could never do what he did. Gopa, on her own, could only do so much.

N. K. assured me that it could work. The Ministry of External Affairs (MEA) would back me. Having a non-Indian Chancellor would send a positive signal to the EAS of the university's international character. As the Vice-Chancellor was Indian, it was a good combination.

I consulted Amartya. He was happy for me to take over leadership of the university from him, but worried that the government might interfere in its work. His concerns were not administrative; as funding for the university came from the Indian Parliament through the MEA, the university obviously had to abide by the government's rules and regulations. Rather, Amartya's concerns were political. He was worried that elements of the BJP would want to politicise university appointments, such as potentially wanting Gopa replaced. His advice was for me to get an undertaking from Minister Swaraj that the university would be allowed to run autonomously before accepting the appointment.

When I met Minister Sushma in Delhi, she assured me of the university's autonomy, adding that it was in that spirit that Amartya would be staying on the Governing Board as a member. It was either at that meeting or a later one that I reported the Governing Board's wish to renew Gopa's term as Vice-Chancellor. Minister Sushma showed no enthusiasm. In fact, she was critical of Gopa despite not being familiar with her work.

A few weeks later, the Foreign Secretary, S. Jaishankar, flew to see me in Hong Kong. Over dinner at my Mid Levels apartment, he expressed the hope that Minister Sushma's view of Gopa might become more favourable in the subsequent months before the matter of her renewal came up. I was surprised that Jaishankar had made this special effort to see me in Hong Kong, but took it positively. He also pointed to a provision in the university statutes that could be interpreted to set a term limit for the Vice-Chancellor, which I was not aware of before. We later found out that this provision had been inserted by the MEA without the Governing Board's approval, which was legally required.

I felt a growing tension between the Governing Board and MEA over Gopa's reappointment. Despite repeated affirmation of the Board's support for Gopa's extension, the MEA was opposed to it. Both sides sought legal opinions. The intensity of the dispute puzzled me initially as the Vice-Chancellor's appointment could not be all that important to the India government. I did not know then that there was a concerted move within the BJP government to change the leadership of India's educational and cultural establishments to reflect its Hindutva agenda of righting historical wrongs. Nalanda was a prize target. Nevertheless, Minister Sushma kindly agreed to launch my book in Delhi at Jawaharlal Nehru Bhawan, a facility which came under the charge of the MEA. When I invited P. Chidambaram to say a few words at the launch too, he asked me first to check with the MEA whether he would be welcome. I was startled by his response, not realising that politics in India was getting so badly polarised. In the end, I received the green light from the MEA, which must have been granted partly out of respect for me, and so Chidambaram was able to come as well.

In my short time as Chancellor, I had the pleasure of interacting

Minister of External Affairs Sushma Swaraj launching my book at the Jawaharlal Nehru Bhawan in Delhi

Vice-Chancellor Gopa Sabharwal and I addressing students of Nalanda University

with the first two batches of students of Nalanda University. Their vivaciousness inspired me and filled me with a sense of hope for the future.

*Students of
Nalanda University*

Students of Nalanda University

Students of Nalanda University

Q: Amidst all this tension, how did the First Convocation go?

Nalanda's first Convocation on 27 August 2016 went spectacularly well. Although the graduating class numbered only 13 students — five from the School of Historical Studies and eight from the School of Ecology and Environmental Studies — it was a grand affair. After its destruction 800 years ago, Nalanda was graduating students again!

As the Visitor and President of India, Pranab Mukherjee was the Chief Guest. Bihar's Governor Ram Nath Kovind and Chief Minister Nitish Kumar were also in attendance. The diplomatic corps was well represented, especially from EAS countries. Local Bihari cotton was used for the new academic robes.

President Mukherjee gave an inspiring speech. He said:

"Ancient Nalanda was known for the high level of debate and discussion it nurtured. It was not a mere geographical expression but it reflected an idea and a culture. Nalanda conveyed the message of friendship, cooperation, debate, discussion and argument. Discussion and debate are part of our ethos and life. They cannot be done away with. Universities and higher education institutions are the best forums for debate, discussion and free exchange of views. Though the main subjects of study were the Buddhist texts, importance was also given to critiques of Buddhism by various schools, study of Vedas and beyond. Nalanda was a melting pot of civilisations and modern India should remain the same. We should not close our windows and yet we should not be blown off by winds from outside. We should let the winds flow freely from all over the world and get enriched by them. We should embrace free discussion and debate leaving behind narrow mindsets and thoughts. Prof. Amartya Sen who is with us today has written about how our history and traditions have always celebrated the 'Argumentative Indian'. The lesson for modern Nalanda is

to ensure that this great tradition finds new life and vigour within its precincts. Universities must be the bastions of free speech and expression. It must be the arena where diverse and conflicting schools of thought contend. There should be no room for intolerance, prejudice and hatred within the spaces of this institution. Further, it must act as flag bearer for the coexistence of multiple views, thoughts and philosophies."

Amartya spoke too. My speech was largely to thank all those who laboured to make that happy day possible.

Historic first Convocation

Historic first Convocation

Q: And you resigned soon after that? What happened?

In November 2016, I was suddenly informed by the MEA that a new Governing Board had been appointed. Of the original members, only N. K. Singh was reappointed. Since my appointment as Chancellor was for a three-year term, I was to stay on as Chancellor, but my position was no longer tenable. I therefore tendered my resignation to the Visitor, President Pranab Mukherjee:

> "I have received your Order of 22 November 2016 creating with immediate effect a new Governing Board and your instruction of 23 November 2016 directing that the most senior Dean be appointed as interim Vice-Chancellor, thereby setting aside the old Governing Board's decision. As I was not consulted or even informed beforehand of this sudden change in the University's leadership, my position as Chancellor is no longer tenable. Accordingly, and with deep sadness, I tender my resignation to you."

With Rahul Gandhi. He wanted to speak to me after my resignation as Chancellor.

My resignation made headline news in India. Both Nitish Kumar and Rahul Gandhi wanted to speak to me on the phone. As I did not wish to be sucked into Indian politics, I made a Facebook post about the matter, which included a statement that I had released to the media:

> "The sudden dissolution of the old Nalanda Board is bound up with Indian domestic politics which I do not wish to be embroiled in. I am not an Indian citizen and prefer not to make further comments beyond what is contained in my statement of 25 November 2016 (see below). On the Nalanda project, I have worked closely with leaders of different political parties in India including the BJP and Congress.
>
> I remain completely committed to the original mission of Nalanda as supported by the leaders of the East Asian Summit in 2009 and as debated and unanimously agreed to by all political parties in India in both the Upper and Lower Houses when the Act was passed in 2010.
>
> Nalanda is an idea whose time has come. It is bigger than and will outlast anyone of us.

Statement by George Yeo, Chancellor of Nalanda University,
25 November 2016

> The Order which the Visitor approved on 21 November 2016 dissolving the Governing Board and creating a new one came as a complete surprise to me and to most members of the old Governing Board. I was neither involved in the preparation nor consulted beforehand.
>
> When I was appointed Chancellor in July 2015, I was told that a new Governing Board would be formed under an amended Act, core aspects of which the Ministry of External Affairs sought my views on. The amended Act

would have removed a major flaw in the current Act which in essence offers Governing Board seats to East Asian Summit countries making the highest financial contributions in the last three years. This provision, which was never recommended by the Nalanda Mentor Group, would not have been a good way to constitute the Governing Board and was the reason the Government of India requested the Nalanda Mentor Group to continue functioning as the Governing Board for a number of years until the Act could be amended. For reasons not entirely clear to me, the Government of India has decided to form the new Governing Board with immediate effect before the Act is amended. This is of course entirely the prerogative of the Government of India.

Pending the appointment of a new Vice-Chancellor, the incumbent Vice-Chancellor, Dr Gopa Sabharwal, whose extended term ended on 24 November, was to stay on as interim Vice-Chancellor until the new Vice-Chancellor is in place, to ensure that there is no hiatus in the leadership of the University. This is provided for in the University Statutes and fully supported by the old Governing Board. However, on 22 November, the Visitor overruled the Governing Board and directed that the senior-most Dean be appointed instead.

The circumstances under which the leadership change in Nalanda University has been suddenly and summarily effected is disturbing and possibly harmful to the University's development. It is puzzling why I, as Chancellor, was not even given notice of it. When I was invited to take over the responsibility from Amartya Sen last year, I was repeatedly assured that the University would have autonomy. This appears not to be the case now. Accordingly, and with deep sadness, I have submitted my letter of resignation as

Chancellor to the Visitor.

It has been an honour and a privilege for me to be associated with the revival of Nalanda over the last decade, to serve as a member of the Nalanda Mentors Group and the Governing Board under the leadership of Amartya Sen, and to be appointed its second Chancellor. Despite difficult circumstances, the University has made remarkable progress through the tireless effort of Dr Gopa Sabharwal and her colleagues.

The first Convocation in August this year presided over by the Visitor was a moment in history. Nalanda is an idea whose time has come and larger than anyone of us."

Q: What became of Singapore's involvement with the Nalanda project?

Nalanda Library

The Mentors Group decided very early on that we should try to source external financial support. This was important not so much because the Indian government could not afford to fund the university, but so that there would be international commitment to the university's success.

In my interactions with the Buddhist community in Singapore, I sensed a high level of interest in the project. Over lunch with Singapore Buddhist Lodge President Lee Bock Guan and Buddhist Federation Chairman Ven Kwang Sheng, I asked if there would be interest in funding the university library as part of Singapore's contribution to Nalanda's revival. The old Nalanda had a library with an incredible collection of books and its building was a landmark. With their agreement, I made an offer to the Governing Board that, working with the university's architect, the library would be designed and gifted by Singapore to the university, up to a limit of S$10 million. The Board happily agreed. If the cost went over the limit, the balance would come from the university's construction budget. I was proud that Singapore was able to put up its hand first.

Albert Hong was then the Chairman of RSP, the architecture firm, and agreed to do the project for us from the Singapore side. RSP had a successful practice in India and was familiar with the rules there. Liu Thai Ker was appointed as the architect for the library.

The details for the first phase of the project were formally approved by the Governing Board in January 2015. The library would be built on an island in a lake in the centre of the campus. A tripartite agreement between RSP, the university's architect, Vastu Shilpa, and Nalanda University was then signed in August 2015. With the help of Lee Bock

New Nalanda campus being built

Guan, Chua Thian Poh and others, we raised over S$4 million in cash and received commitments of a further S$2 million or thereabouts.

After I resigned, those commitments evaporated. When the new Governing Board took over, without informing me or the architectural team in Singapore, and in disregard of earlier Board approvals and the Tripartite Agreement, the library was completely redesigned. Over S$670,000 had already been incurred in design and consulting fees by then.

Although my involvement with Nalanda was not smooth, looking back, it made me many friends in India, Singapore and elsewhere. Singapore's ties to India are rooted in history and inseparable from our future. Our Buddhist links are bound to grow. There is, however, a rhythm to such matters which one cannot rush. On my part, I have learned to become more detached and philosophical.

Nalanda-Sriwijaya Centre at ISEAS

The Institute of Southeast Asian Studies (ISEAS), with the support of a donation from the Singapore Buddhist Lodge under Lee Bock Guan and the encouragement of President S. R. Nathan, Director K. Kesavapany (also a retired Ambassador) established the Nalanda-Sriwijaya Centre to complement the work we were doing in India. Not long after I resigned as Chancellor, ISEAS, by then under a new leadership, decided to shut the Centre down. My resignation probably inclined them to this.

Bodh Gaya

Another project I attempted without success was to secure a piece of land for the construction of a Singapore pilgrimage centre in Bodh Gaya. The Bihar Government, grateful for the role I played in Nalanda, was prepared to lease to the Buddhist community in Singapore a good piece of land in Bodh Gaya for the construction of a facility to service pilgrims from Singapore and Southeast Asia. Countries like Thailand and Japan already have such centres in Bodh Gaya. Religious pilgrimage to the

Mahabodhi Mahavihara grew rapidly after it became a UNESCO world heritage site. We are bound to see more Singaporeans going to the holy land of Buddhism. However, it was difficult to get a group together in Singapore to execute this project. Money was not the main issue. The concerns had more to do with a lack of familiarity with ground conditions in India and the fear of being cheated. No organisation was prepared to take the lead.

Sarnath's Chinese Temple

It was Tansen Sen who first told me that the Chinese Temple in Sarnath, an important Buddhist site near Varanasi in Uttar Pradesh, was built by a Singaporean.

The legend goes that when Buddha accepted a bowl of milk-rice pudding from Sujata, ending his six years of asceticism, his disciples were angry with him. When they saw him approaching them at the Deer Park in Sarnath, they conspired to ignore him. However, the Buddha, choosing the Middle Path, had achieved enlightenment after breaking his fast. When he came closer to them, his aura was so strong that his disciples completely forgot what they had planned to do and gathered around him. It was there, at Sarnath, that the Buddha delivered his first sutra, the Dharmachakra.

At the Dhamek Stupa in Sarnath marking the site where Buddha delivered his first sermon to his first five disciples

In the early 1930s, a Chinese Buddhist monk from Beijing, Ven Dao Jie (道阶), while on a pilgrimage to India, resolved to rebuild a dilapidated Chinese temple in Sarnath that had been established with the patronage of the Chinese Emperor in the 8th century during the Tang Dynasty. Unfortunately, he died before he could do it. A Singaporean businessman Lee Choon Seng (李俊承) decided to carry out the task, supported by Tan Yunshan (谭云山) and his disciple Ven De Yu (德玉), who came from Sichuan. Lee Choon Seng was the man who donated the land for the building of the Singapore Buddhist Lodge and was the first Chairman of the Singapore Buddhist Federation. He also founded the Poh Ern Shih Temple in Pasir Panjang.

He engaged an English engineer, A. H. King, to help in the restoration of the Sarnath temple. Construction was completed around 1939 and the result was the temple we see today in Sarnath, located next to the Deer Park. I got to know Lee Choon Seng's son, Boon Siong, who had emigrated to Canada. One day, with great excitement, he gave me a copy of the title deed to the Chinese Temple which he had found in an old family safe.

Tan Yunshan was very likely the man who got Rabindranath Tagore to write the following preface for the opening of the renovated temple:

> "The glorious history of the spiritual communication between China and India once raised its memorial on the sacred spot near Benares where Lord Buddha had proclaimed to his first five disciples his message of the emancipation of self in love. The architectural record of the two peoples' mingling of souls perished in course of time and its memory has lain obscure since then for series of obvious centuries. To-day when we feel deep in our heart the stir of a new awakening, let us rejoice in the fact that an attempt is being made to reconstruct the monastery in Sarnath originally established by the Chinese Emperor of Tang Dynasty 1300 years ago. Numerous are the monuments built to perpetuate the memory of injuries inflicted by one murdering race upon another, but let us, once for all, for the sake of humanity, restore one memorial of a generous past to remind us of an ancient meeting of countries in Asia for the exchange of

love, for the establishment of spiritual comradeship among nations separated by a vast distance in geography and race."

Tagore's words are precious today.

The Chinese Temple in Sarnath built by Lee Choon Seng

The Chinese Temple in Sarnath built by Lee Choon Seng

Q: What are your hopes for the future of Nalanda University?

I have two. Both are ideas which will take time to ripen.

I hope that a Bodhi tree descended from the original one at Bodh Gaya will be planted in Amartya's honour at Nalanda University. I was secretly working on this with Gopa. It could either be a sapling from the one at Anuradhapura, which was a sapling from the original tree brought to Sri Lanka by Ashoka's son, or the current one from Bodh Gaya, which was also a sapling taken from Anuradhapura after the original one died. I remember asking Vastu Shilpa's architect, Rajiv Kathpalia, to find a good location on campus for Amartya to plant the sapling.

Around 2014, while in Tianjin, I had a free morning and decided to visit the Dabei Buddhist Temple. To my delight, I discovered that it had a shrine housing a relic from Xuanzang. On arrival at the shrine, however, I was met by a signboard declaring that the relic — a piece of Xuanzang's cranial bone — had been taken out of the shrine in 1956 and presented by Premier Zhou Enlai to Indian Prime Minister Jawaharlal Nehru in Nalanda. I had not heard of this before and decided to look into it.

It turned out that the relic had been conveyed by the current Dalai Lama (who had not yet fled China) to Nehru at Nalanda in January 1957. It was intended for a Xuanzang memorial hall in Nalanda which China was to help build. The project was interrupted by the 1962 war and was only completed in 2006, when it opened to great fanfare by the

The Dalai Lama presenting Xuanzang's relic from Tianjin Dabei Temple to Jawaharlal Nehru at Nalanda in January 1957

foreign ministers of India and China but without the relic, which is still safely kept in a museum in Patna.

One day, a stupa should be built to house this relic in Nalanda University. It would mark the spiritual return of Xuanzang to his alma mater after more than a thousand years and be an inspiration to staff and students alike. The stupa should also be accessible to external visitors so that tourists can visit it without interrupting life on campus.

In January 2016, I was in Nalanda University with a delegation of visitors from Singapore. As it was Republic Day, a small flag raising ceremony was held by the students. Vice-Chancellor Gopa invited me to officiate. I demurred, explaining that I was not a citizen of India, but Gopa said that it was all right.

Among the students themselves, they had chosen one Indian and one non-Indian student from Myanmar to hoist the flag. The University believed that the future of a nation lies in the hands of its youth, and so rather than having the head of the institution unfurl the national flag on Republic Day and Independence Day, this responsibility was given to the students. They decided to draw lots for the honour. When the international students asked to be included, the Indian students agreed. After the ceremony, I gave a short speech complimenting the students for being big-hearted and broad-minded. That, I said, is the spirit of Nalanda.

A few years before, in 2012, I received an email from Jaishankar, who was then India's ambassador to China, congratulating me for being awarded the Padma Bhushan. I had not heard of the award before and only found out later that it was a high honour rarely given to foreigners. I am probably the only Singaporean who has received it to date. In my Hong Kong office, I hung a panoramic picture of the ceremony at the Rashtrapati Bhavan, which captured me receiving the award from the President of India, witnessed by members of the establishment and hundreds of other guests in the audience. I knew it would arouse the interest of Hong Kong visitors and give me an opportunity to talk about India.

Tianjin Dabei Temple Xuanzang Memorial Hall which once housed a relic of the great monk

Xuanzang Memorial in Nalanda finally completed in 2006

Flag raising ceremony at Nalanda University on Republic Day 26 January 2016

Receiving the Padma Bhushan from the President of India in 2012

❖

CHAPTER 10

The Homogeneity
of China

George Yeo reflects on the reasons for the homogeneity of the Han Chinese. Over thousands of years, China's 'operating system' has evolved to network many more human beings than any other social system in a single civilisational entity.

Q: How would you explain China's homogeneity?

China's homogeneity is unique. About 94% of its 1.4 billion people are Han Chinese. No other major ethnic group in the world comes close. Japan and Korea are homogeneous too but their populations are significantly smaller. They are also 'chopsticks people' whose history and culture are inseparably connected to China's. Vietnam is in the same category, but less homogeneous because of its southward movement into Southeast Asia.

China's homogeneity is not an accident of history. It came about by conscious choice. In the Great Learning (大学) (*da xue*), Confucius said: "Cultivate the individual, establish the family, govern the state and bring peace to the land" (修身齐家治国平天下). Chinese-ness is this both cultural and political. The state is viewed as an extended family. All citizens are members of this family, and its leaders are required to act morally.

Western and South Asian civilisations encompass comparable number of human beings but there is no similar political culture unifying them as there has been in China. After the fall of western Rome, Europe did not succeed in gathering itself into one political entity again. The current European Union (EU) is still an ongoing experiment.

Arnold Toynbee, who wrote *A Study of History*, is an important part of my intellectual formation. According to Toynbee, the inheritor of Rome is the Roman Catholic Church. Roman law has a direct successor in canon law. Meanwhile, South Asia had its greatest unity under the Mauryas. After the Kalinga War, Ashoka turned to Buddhism, which had a great influence on South Asian civilisation in the first millenium during which time Nalanda was a beacon for all of Asia.

I believe two aspects of Chinese civilisation contribute to its persistence: the digital nature of its written language and the enormous advantage it enjoyed with papermaking technology.

Language

Chinese characters are ideographic rather than alphabetic. When Qin Shi Huang unified the country, he standardised how they were written. Although their pronunciation changes across space and time, the characters are the same. This relatively fixed value of meaning gives written Chinese a digital quality. It is as if the same Classical Latin words and Classical Greek were still being used in Western Europe and Eastern Europe, respectively, today, or ancient Sanskrit words in all of South Asia.

Alphabetic languages are more convenient to use but they mutate constantly. Alphabetic words code for sound, not for meaning, although nothing is of course static. A student picking up an ancient Chinese text from more than 2,000 years ago will need some guidance, but he can, without too much effort, read it and access the first layer of meaning.

Checking the dictionary for the meaning or pronunciation of Chinese characters used to be a tiresome effort. With phonetic *pinyin*, it has become much easier. *Pinyin* has strengthened the digital nature of written Chinese by making it more convenient to use.

This said, Chinese characters are somehow able to convey more

At Taishan in October 1996. Chinese emperors have ascended Taishan from the earliest times. Here, Qin Shi Huang proclaimed the unity of China. Every generation leaves inscriptions to inspire future generations.

information than English words. At performances, pixel boards for surtitles near the stage are able to squeeze in more information in Chinese than in English for the same level of visibility from where one is sitting. I think this is because Chinese characters are ideographic and are often only fully understood in context.

Robin Hu uses the term 'encapsulation' to describe this. The frequent use of pithy idioms and proverbs where history, morality and wisdom are simultaneously referenced gives the language a high density of meaning. Without much training, one can as easily read Chinese characters left to right, right to left or top to bottom. Children who are dyslexic in English face less difficulty reading Chinese. Dyslexia seems to be less of a problem in China and may well require a different definition of what the condition means. Infants recognise Chinese characters earlier than they can recognise English words, which is not surprising since characters are pictorial. For adults, however, it is much harder to read and understand Chinese characters than alphabetic words. This has an important implication: it means that it is hard to become Chinese. It is much easier to be born into it.

In computing, there are different levels of programming languages. Machine language is the most basic, written in 1s and 0s. As an engineering undergraduate, I programmed in FORTRAN, which few young people today would have heard of. Today they learn languages like Python, C# and Scala, which are Greek to me. Just like programming languages, every human language has strengths and weaknesses. If we treat human society as a computational system, depending on society's conditions and needs, some languages may be more efficient than others.

The evolution of the Chinese language over thousands of years has networked more human beings within one deeply integrated computational system than any other language has been able to accomplish for other human groups in history. This is a fact. We can speculate about whether some other language system could have done the same for Chinese civilisation, but that would be an idle exercise. It is, however, unlikely that Chinese would be an efficient language for linking or hyperlinking different societies. The Chinese language is too highly evolved for such a purpose.

In Indonesia, Bahasa Indonesia was chosen as the common language when the young people of a vast archipelago pledged themselves to belong to one race and country in 1928 (*sumpah pemuda*). Even though roughly half the population spoke Javanese, Javanese was too evolved a language for non-Javanese to be able to learn easily.

In Singapore, we chose English. Had we remained in Malaysia, we would have stuck to Bahasa Melayu. Chinese and Tamil are both too difficult for those of other races to learn. In the same way, the Association of Southeast Asian Nations (ASEAN) chose English as its common language. In a world dominated first by the United Kingdom (UK), then the United States (US), English has become the most important international language. This used to be French, hence the phrase *lingua franca*. Whether English will still remain the primary international language in an increasingly multipolar world is hard to say. Chinese is unlikely to ever play this role. Perhaps, with artificial-intelligence-boosted translation enabling multiple languages to be simultaneously used like in the EU, English will be *primus inter pares*. Within China, however, the use of Chinese is deeply embedded in its culture and civilisation. *Pinyin* helps enormously for those who study Chinese as a second language, but it will not replace written Chinese as a digital language.

Data Storage

China invented paper 2,000 years ago. As a data storage medium, paper is orders of magnitude more advanced than other writing media like stone, clay, wood, papyrus, palm leaf, bamboo strips or parchment. During the Tang Dynasty, China invented printing (on paper). The Diamond Sutra is the earliest known printed scroll produced in 868. During the Northern Sung Dynasty, China invented movable type.

Alan Turing even reduced computational machines to pencil and paper. If the paper tape has no limit to its length, there is no limit to the amount of computation that can be done. In other words, the greater the ability to store data, the greater the ability to compute and build complex systems.

For centuries, China had a worldwide monopoly over paper technology. This enabled it to organise many more people in one system than anywhere else on Earth. Before the modern world, China was by far the most data-intensive civilisation. In a sense, human society is a computational system. How complex it is is an indicator of how advanced that society has grown.

Chinese ink has a much longer history, going back to Yangshao culture (仰韶文化) (*yang shao wen hua*) six to seven thousand years ago. The mass production of high-quality ink for use on paper was itself advanced technology, involving the incomplete combustion of pine wood down to nano-sized soot particles. Its collection and processing into the highest quality ink used for brush writing and painting is, till today, a craft secret in China and Japan.

Papermaking technology only left China in the 8th century. According to Arabic records, after the defeat of the Tang army by the Abbasids in the Battle of Talas in 751 AD (after which Chinese armies never crossed the Tianshan mountains again), the Islamic world learned how to make paper from Chinese prisoners of war. Paper mills were built in Baghdad and Damascus soon after. They would appear after 100 years in Egypt, 200 in Morocco and 300 in Muslim Spain.

Paper transformed the nature and quality of the Islamic civilisation. As it became data-intensive too, its repository of books grew to far exceed those of Europe. Like China, the Muslim world tried to keep paper making a secret. However, by the 13th century, paper mills were established in northern Italy and, not long afterwards, all over Europe. Without paper, the Renaissance could not have happened.

Imagine if one country alone had computers today and the advantage this would give it over other countries. That was the position China enjoyed for centuries. At the heart of Chinese civilisation is information storage and processing. Archive maintenance became a core function of government.

A Chinese minister once asked me for the notes of a meeting he had had with Lee Kuan Yew some years earlier. I was puzzled and asked why he had not kept his own. His reply was that his own notes had already been sent to the archives. In China, once documents are sent to the archives, accessing them requires high-level approval in order to protect data integrity. Even during the Long March, when Mao Zedong's army repeatedly came close to being wiped out by Chiang Kai-shek, securing the Communist Party's archives was a top priority.

China has the most extensive and accurate record of comets going back to the first millennium BCE. During the Covid-19 pandemic, the head of Chinese Medicine in China, Dr Zhang Boli, said that China had complete records of hundreds of epidemics going back over 2,000 years, including information on regions affected, pattern of spread, symptoms, durations and effective treatments. Although every epidemic is different, the same organs are affected. Chinese pharmacopeia contains abundant information on how inflammation of different organs and body systems can be treated. For Covid-19, some of the medicines being used to treat it in China contain herbs known since the Han Dynasty.

Careful monitoring of flood levels over long periods enabled huge hydraulic systems to be built and maintained over hundreds of years. Joseph Needham described how the Dujiangyan (都江堰) hydraulic system in Sichuan kept the Chengdu plains both continuously supplied with water and largely flood-free for over 2,000. North of Guilin, a canal was built by Qin Shi Huang along a contour line, roughly the width of Singapore, to connect the Li River flowing south to the Xiang River flowing north. This effectively connected the Yangtze River system in Central China to the Pearl River system in the south. A system of water separators, weirs and locks enabled boats to travel from one river system to the other. This canal, the Lingqu (灵渠), enabled supplies to reach the Qing army during its campaign to subdue the Baiyue people in the south and facilitated the spread of Han culture to the Pearl River Delta, also

over 2,000 years ago.

It was also Qin Shi Huang who established the Han settlement of Panyu (番禺) in the heart of the delta. Both these hydraulic projects were described in detail in Sima Qian's *Records of the Grand Historian* (史记). China's intricate canal system connecting different river systems helped it to facilitate a centralised system of timely grain distribution whenever the country was united and at peace.

Dujiangyan in September 2011. A hydraulic project in the Chengdu Plain commissioned by Qin Shi Huang.

Dujiangyan in September 2011. A hydraulic project in the Chengdu Plain commissioned by Qin Shi Huang.

Lingqu in 2015. Qin Shi Huang linked two major river systems to subdue the south.

Common Body of History and Literature

The unification of China and the Chinese people was greatly facilitated by a language which encoded for meaning rather than pronunciation and papermaking technology which provided huge data storage. The common standards imposed by Qin Shi Huang for the writing of characters, the width of axles, weights and measures, and other things are akin to the common language and protocols networking a large computer system today.

Scholars were the system managers and programmers of the imperial Chinese system. They were held in higher moral esteem than warriors and generals. Scholarship undergirded the entire system and remains a deep characteristic of Chinese culture today.

Unlike Europe, the Middle East and South Asia, Chinese civilisation was united by a single corpus of history and literature. Even if one masters many European languages, accessing all of Europe's laws and literature over the centuries requires translation because there are so many languages involved, and every European language has evolved over time. For example, an expert in modern English cannot easily read old English. William Shakespeare is comprehensible with effort and assistance. Geoffrey Chaucer requires separate study. Yet, according to Joseph Needham, China has a larger body of legislation in its history than all of Europe combined. China's literature is one, unlike Europe's, which is fragmented into different ones. All Chinese share the same historical romances and heroes, whereas Europe and South Asia have a vast pantheon. The Chinese even believe in the myth of a common ancestor. China would not be China without its collective memory.

One should therefore not be surprised that China has its own nature. China has to be comprehended with reference to its own history and traditions, not judged by external standards. Understanding China's rise today requires one to first study its history and civilisation.

Qin Shi Huang's great unification (terracotta soldiers).
The power of Qin expressed in the terracotta soldiers at Xi'an.

Q: How do non-Han minorities fit in?

There are gradations. Groups like the Mongols and Manchus, who have conquered China before, have been assimilated to a greater or lesser degree — not by force, but by a kind of osmotic process. The Chinese do not believe that you can 'become' Chinese by conversion if you were not born one. They certainly have no wish to 'convert' others. Over time, however, with intermarriage, assimilation over generations does take place.

The Han people are genetically diverse, but many of those who are considered Han today were not in the past. The local ancestors of Teochews and Hokkiens were non-Han 2,000 years ago. The northeast was largely made up of minority groups before the 20th century. Yunnan only became part of the Chinese realm in the last thousand years. In mountainous areas, including those in Hainan and Taiwan, minority groups are in various stages of assimilation. Current policies in China and Taiwan favour maintenance of minority status. Minorities are granted more privileges. In China, they were not subject to the old one-child policy.

Although Tibetans have been embroiled in Chinese history since the Tang Dynasty, they have been able to remain a separate entity because of geography and Tibetan Buddhism. It was very difficult to get to Tibet in the past and the high altitude posed a serious health challenge to those from the lowlands. Tibetan Buddhism fused religious and political leadership in the high lamas, unlike Chinese Mahayana, where the monks were eventually confined by the Mandarins to monasteries. Tibet is much more accessible today by road, rail and aircraft, and Tibetan Buddhism is also becoming more mixed with Chinese Mahayana. We see this even in Singapore. It is entirely possible that the Tibetans, over time, will be partially assimilated like Mongols and Manchus.

Muslim minorities are in a separate category. Islamic practices cannot easily be assimilated into Han culture, even though Han culture is constantly evolving itself. The Hui people speak Mandarin as their mother tongue. Historically, they are an intermediate group between

*Zhuge Liang's temple
in Chengdu in 2011*

Han Chinese and ethnic Muslim minority groups like the Uighurs, Kazakhs and Tajiks. For decades, the Chinese government left them be, not even requiring their children to learn *putonghua*. Quiet infiltration of Salafi ideas went unnoticed for many years until it led to a separatist movement and terror attacks.

The Han Chinese view themselves as being culturally superior to minority groups. When first the Khitans and Jurchens, and, later, the Mongols, took over north China from the Sung, the Southern Sung paid them off in exchange for peace. Although they feared them militarily, the Southern Sung were contemptuous of them culturally. The Han Chinese find it hard to govern non-Han people because they do not abide by the same behavioral norms (礼). There has therefore always been a reluctance to incorporate them.

There is a famous story in the *Romance of the Three Kingdoms* about how Zhuge Liang dealt with Meng Huo, the troublesome leader of a minority group in the south. Zhuge Liang captured and released him seven times before he finally accepted peaceful accommodation with Shu Han. Zhuge Liang could have killed him or occupied his land, but decided that that would lead to even more headaches. It is a moral tale for how Han Chinese should deal with non-Han people.

Q: The homogeneity of the Han Chinese may explain China's centralised system of governance. But isn't this concentration of power also a problem?

It is. When China is united and peaceful after a new dynasty is established, the internal division of labour makes the economy highly productive. I once read a tax history of China. At the beginning of a new dynasty, taxes might be light but the state coffers are full. At the end of a dynasty, taxes are crushing but the treasury is empty. Because of the size of the country, the cycles are long. Corruption is always the curse. Once rent-seeking behaviour gets embedded into the system, it is hard to eradicate and the spiral of decline begins.

In 1368, Zhu Yuanzhang established the Ming Dynasty in Nanjing. In 1405, the first of Zheng He's seven voyages was launched. That was only 37 years in between. Each voyage was an enormous undertaking, with 20 to 30 thousand men out at sea in hundreds of ships each time. The treasure ships themselves were over 100m long and 50m wide with nine masts and four decks. They carried soldiers, scientists, farmers, astronomers, cartographers, scholars and maintenance crews. The ships would dock at shipyards all over Southeast Asia and the Indian Ocean to be serviced. They had their supplies restocked and damage, including cracked masts, would be repaired.

Near Cirebon in West Java, there is a mountain called Gunung Jati or Teak Mountain. I was told by Tan Ta Sen, an expert on Zheng He's voyages, that at the base of the mountain by the sea was a shipyard which repaired Zheng He's ships. An old teak tree can grow so large, it takes six to seven men to circle its trunk with their arms. These teak trees make the best masts. After a few decades, Ming China's economy must have already grown very large to support these voyages, which did not yield a commensurate economic return. China's astonishing growth in the last few decades is a repeat of its history.

However, China is equally awesome in decline. The decline of the Han, Tang, Song, Ming and, most recently, Qing dynasties went on for decades before the final denouement. China has always been a gigantic drama. The ramifications of its rise and fall radiate far and wide. The history of a large part of Asia is only intelligible with reference to the flow and ebb of Chinese dynasties.

The current Belt and Road Initiative had its analogues in past cycles. The dual circulation economy is not new. For China, its internal circulation has always been much more important.

The Chinese take a philosophical view of their own history. At the beginning of the *Romance of the Three Kingdoms*, Luo Guanzhong wrote these famous words, which have been quoted by Xi Jinping: 天下大势, 分久必合,合久必分. In other words, long disunity leads to unity, and long unity leads to disunity.

According to Sima Qian's *Records of the Grand Historian* (史记), written during the Western Han, China has 24 official histories. Each dynasty has the responsibility of writing the history of the previous dynasty. These histories are treasure houses of information on wars and battles, political events, epidemics, astronomical phenomena, floods, famines, earthquakes, architecture, technology and foreign lands — just about every subject worth recording. The last official history of the Ming Dynasty was written during the Qing Dynasty. Mao Zedong read all the official histories and made annotations of his own, copies of which have been made available for sale (including explanations of the annotations).

By contrast, the history of the Qing Dynasty (1644–1911) is only now being written. China's Vice Premier, Li Lanqing, launched the project some 20 years ago. He asked the historians working on it not to rush to conclusions. At that time, they had collected a million documents. A priest at the Paris Foreign Missions Society responsible for evangelisation in Asia, often known by its French acronym MEP, told me that the history team was working on 99 volumes, including five on the Christian missions in China. Later, I heard that there could be as many as 250 volumes. In recent years, however, I have not seen any report on the work being done. Perhaps there is simply too much, as there is more material on the Qing Dynasty than on all of China's previous history.

China's obsession with collective memory is an important reason for the continuity of Chinese civilisation. There is constant reference to past experiences and reflections on factors that drove the rise and fall of previous dynasties. No judgment is final. Each period generates new interpretations. Qin Shi Huang was long criticised by Confucianist scholars, but is now deemed a great leader in today's China. Before China became a republic, Confucius had to be debunked or radically re-interpreted. Now a refreshed Confucius is re-emerging as an important philosopher in Chinese political discourse, with his name attached to China's cultural institutes around the world.

Within a framework of centralised bureaucratic government, China accommodates much internal diversity. Laws and regulations are often kept in draft form for years in order to assess their effects on the ground first. It is a huge country and there is much regional diversity. One size therefore cannot fit all. Adaptation to local conditions is always needed. China's internal space is not one big ocean. It is intricately subdivided. This cellularisation gives the larger polity resilience. In an emergency, the cell walls harden to prevent the spread of evil or pestilence. Even within cities, there are provisions to segment districts in case movement has to be controlled. China is governable despite its gargantuan size precisely because it has these sub-divisions. I describe it as One Country, Multiple Systems. It has always been this way.

You ask whether China represents too centralised a system of governance. Well, we have to understand China for what it is, not for what we want it to be. China has its own strengths and weaknesses.

Q: I was surprised by your quotation of Needham that China in history had a larger corpus of legislation than the West. Is China famous for its rule of law?

It is a simplification but, generally speaking, it is rule *by* law and not rule *of* law in China.

Recall *civis romanus sum*: I am a Roman citizen. Throughout the Roman Empire, Roman citizens were protected by certain rights. St Paul claimed this right when he was arrested and was brought to Rome to be tried. His execution was by beheading. As a Roman citizen, he could not be crucified, unlike Jesus Christ and St Peter.

In the Western tradition, the ruler is subject to law. If he is an absolute monarch, like the Pope, he can make the law but has to act within it. If the exercise of the law leads to a perverse outcome, that outcome stands until the law has been changed. Depending on the jurisdiction, laws can only be changed following a process which itself is defined in law. The conception of law in China is fundamentally different from that in the West.

China's first empire was based on a strict adherence to law (法) (*fa*).

The law of Qin was known to be unyielding and severe. Ironically, the system of Legalism adopted by Qin was developed by Han Feizi, who being from Han opposed the Qin during the Warring States period. Partly because of strict and rigid adherence to these severe laws, the dynasty did not extend beyond the son of Qin Shi Huang.

Under the succeeding Han dynasty, the rule of law was greatly softened by the acculturation of proper behaviour (礼) (*li*). Confucius (who came from Shandong) and his followers elaborated a system of proper behaviour, laying down clear expectations of how kings and ministers, rulers and people, husbands and wives, fathers and sons, brothers and friends should relate to each other. The entire nation is treated as a big family, with society composed of individual families; parents are required to teach their children the right way to behave. In recognition of this, John Fairbanks and Edwin Reischauer titled their classic text on the history of East Asia *The Great Tradition*.

I remember an occasion when one of my brothers criticised our father to our mother. Although father was not there to hear it, mother reproached my brother and told him never to do so again. Whatever wrong father had done to her was between husband and wife. We as children had to respect him as our father and had no right to criticise him, even behind his back.

By regulating behaviour, rituals made for stability in relationships. Manners are the expression of propriety (礼貌) (*li mao*), gifts the objects for the expression of proper relationships (礼物) (*li wu*). The imperial Chinese court used to have a minister for rituals. People who flouted them were criticised and punished. In Chinese society, people are expected to behave according to the nature of their relationship or standing. In a group photo, the centre positions are reserved for senior individuals. If you are Chinese, you should not have to be told this because you are expected to know it already, though some allowance is made for foreigners who are not expected to know this. The same protocols that govern international diplomacy govern all aspects of Chinese society.

Qufu, birthplace of Confucius, in 1995

Every Chinese New Year, billions of red envelopes are produced for the insertion of relatively small amounts of cash to be given to relatives and friends. It is a stressful period for women because the amount of money in each has to be carefully calibrated. What children receive are important information for the mother. Relativities are important. For example, one cannot give a smaller amount to someone considered more important. The latter may not know, but will be offended if they find out. If the objective of this annual exercise was merely to transfer money, it would be a big a waste of time, energy and envelopes. But the objective is not only the transfer of money; it is for the establishment or renewal of relationships.

I used to visit a wealthy Chinese matriarch at Chinese New Year with my family. She had a maid beside her carrying a big red box. In it were red envelopes of different sizes which were constantly replenished. Depending on who greeted her, she would dispense an appropriate red envelope. I whispered to my children that it is by such means that empires are governed.

Government leaders are supposed to behave like the heads of the nation-family. Leadership has to be moral even if it is hypocritical. With the ubiquity of cameras, microphones and social media, that hypocrisy is easily exposed nowadays, which can create a crisis in leadership. Official speeches are boring because they are supposed to be moral disquisitions. Important guests must often be addressed first, which is a tedious affair. Addressing them in the wrong sequence is embarrassing at the very least. A ruler's right to rule is governed by a moral mandate. If they are immoral, they lose the Mandate of Heaven.

The world of Confucius can be suffocating. An individual's place is often defined for him, leaving little room for spontaneity. Officials face this the worst.

The philosophical counterbalance to Confucianism is Taoism. Taoist philosophy, which is older than Confucianist philosophy, contains cycles within cycles. Cycles beyond our control have to be accepted for what they are; we have to move with them. Cycles within our control often involve a moral choice. The most well-known text is *Daodejing* (道德经). 道 (*dao*) is 'the way'. Only by knowing it can one achieve virtue (德) (*de*). Officials who are exiled or punished often find solace in Taoist philosophy. Taoism was founded by Lao Zi (老子). Tradition has it that even Confucius paid his respects to him.

An even older text is the Book of Change, *Yijing* (易经), which some scholars consider to be the most important text in the Chinese classics. Superficially, the text is used for divination, and I have friends in the financial industry who use the *Yijing* for this purpose. It is, however, a profound book about the nature of existence, binary division and cycles in the physical, biological and human worlds. The philosophy of the *Yijing* and the *Daodejing* suffuse Chinese governance and warcraft of all forms of Chinese art and martial art, Chinese spirituality and Chinese medicine. Within this philosophical framework, law finds its proper place. The equivalent idea in the western mind is that human law must ultimately conform to natural law.

Practising taiji in Chongqing in 2011

Top & centre: With my taijigong master Sim Pooh Ho and fellow disciples in a Taoist temple in Yilan, Taiwan in 2015. On the blackboard are his explanations of the trigrams from the Yijing which goes back more than 2000 years.

Bottom: Statue of Laozi in Yilan

Left: At the Great Wall in Badaling in 1986

Bottom: At the Great Wall near the Korean border in 2008. I was about to climb a steep flight of steps but was discouraged by my Second Permanent Secretary, Bilahari Kausikan (back left). Ambassador Chin Siat Yoon and wife (front, left) were also in the delegation.

Q: Will China change? Can China change?

Well, in light of Taoist philosophy, it must, but according to its own system of logic. If we see Chinese society as a computational system, it has many lines of code inherited from a long, unbroken history. The Chinese system is inherently conservative. Change has to be incremental and within what its legacy allows. China is a mystery only to those who do not dig into its history.

The system protects itself by building walls. Most of us are familiar with the Great Wall of China, which is actually a series of walls built all along its northern frontier. Depending on how the agricultural line shifted with climate change, the walls could be built further north or south. The current wall we see was mostly built during the Ming Dynasty. Generally speaking, Han culture was protected behind the wall even if the ruling house was non-Han, like the Manchus. In its national anthem, Chinese citizens declare that "with our flesh and blood, let us build a new Great Wall". Building walls runs deep in the Chinese psyche. They are not only physical; there are also walls for the capital markets, for cyberspace, for education and for culture. During the Covid-19 pandemic, China built the greatest wall of all against the coronavirus.

As China re-emerges on the global stage, many people worry that it might become expansionist like Western and Japanese imperialism in the 19th and 20th centuries. However, when seen against China's own interests, this is unlikely.

This does not mean that China will never intervene militarily outside its borders. It might. During the Ming voyages, Zheng He's ships carried soldiers who fought battles in foreign lands. However, China's strategic objectives never extend to incorporating non-Han people into its own realm because it values its own homogeneity too much. It would be unimaginable for China to have its own version of Emma Lazarus' poem welcoming foreigners to its shores.

❖

CHAPTER 11

The People's Republic

> *China has a long history, but its history as a republic is relatively short. To paraphrase Deng Xiaoping, China advances by feeling the rocks beneath its feet.*

Q: How do you see today's China against its long history?

Before becoming a republic, China had to overturn rule by royal or imperial families, which was a tradition going back thousands of years. For as long as he had the Mandate of Heaven, the legitimacy of a ruler was derived from his family line. The Inner Palace (内宫) (*nei gong*) was not merely the harem kept for the ruler's pleasure; its purpose was to produce male successors. The Inner Palace was the preserve of the Empress, of secondary wives and concubines, of eunuchs and servant girls. It was here that the continuity of a dynasty was maintained.

Although the Inner Palace was not to interfere in affairs of the state, which were reserved for the Emperor and his Mandarins, concerns of state and its conflicts invariably reverberated within the Inner Palace. Today, the intrigues of the Inner Palace provide material for an endless supply of historical drama series on television.

This system of imperial rule was preserved by tradition, by *li* (礼) and by force (力) (*li*). Dynastic change was invariably a violent affair with bloody battles fought across a vast land. Transitions could take decades and involve millions of deaths. For this reason, ordinary people fear political instability because it could lead to generations of hardship.

Chinese people have a high threshold for pain. They know the alternative is often much worse.

The 1911 Revolution was much more than dynastic change. It replaced imperial rule with a democratic republic, the Republic of China. Transforming the world's longest, largest and most conservative civilisation created the greatest revolution the world had ever witnessed. This said, 1911 itself was only one act in a long play. The full play started much earlier with the Opium Wars and the Taiping Rebellion.

In 1839, the Opium Wars began a series of western and Japanese incursions into the Chinese mainland which eventually turned China into a semi-colony. The Taiping Rebellion, which began in 1850, was led by Hong Xiuquan, who believed he was the younger brother of Jesus Christ. The movement was led by a Christian cult. Taiping marked the start of western incursions into the Chinese mind. The Taiping Rebellion was a serious threat to the Manchu Qing Dynasty, fought all the way from Guangxi to Tianjin along the waterways. It was Han generals like Zeng Guofan and Zuo Zongtang who put an end to things. Till today, the Communist Party of China (CPC) sees the Taiping Rebellion as a precursor inspiration. Marxism and Leninism are also western ideas which adapted to Chinese conditions. The most important revolution takes place in the mind.

Without the series of western humiliations in the 19th century, the Qing Dynasty might have continued, though not for too long because the entire world was in ferment. In Europe and elsewhere, absolute monarchies were coming to an end. The idea of China as a republic was novel. Chinese rulers and mandarins had always relied on historical precedents, but now there were none. Instead, China now had to learn from foreigners.

Adapting foreign ideas like Western liberal democracy to China was, however, difficult. The Constitution of the Republic of China drawn up by Dr Sun Yat-sen provides for five branches of government. In addition to the Western three — the executive, legislative and judiciary — Dr Sun added two more for inspection and examinations. If only it were so

Visiting Wuchang at the end of 2011, the centennial celebration of the 1911 Revolution. The revolution established China as a republic for which it had no experience in its long history to draw on.

simple. Dr Sun's writ ran only in the south and, even there, only partially. In the north, there was a separate Beiyang government. Elsewhere, regional warlords held sway.

Chinese intellectuals knew that the most important change must take place in the mind. When the victors of the First World War gave in to Japan's demands and, instead of returning German concessions to China, gave them to Japan, there was outrage. Peking University was the epicentre of the May Fourth Movement, which quickly spread to all parts of China.

In 1921, inspired by the October Revolution in Russia, the CPC was established in Shanghai. It allied with Dr Sun's Kuomintang (KMT) to unify China. In 1927, Chiang Kai-shek turned against the Communists, slaughtering many of them in Shanghai with the help of the Green Gang. Zhou Enlai escaped by the skin of his teeth. When Chiang's forces encircled the Communist base in Jinggangshan, the Red Army narrowly escaped and moved south and west before turning north in an epic Long March which ended in Yan'an. During the Long March in Zunyi, Guizhou, Mao Zedong assumed leadership. Before that, the Communist leadership took orders from the Soviet Union through the Communist International (Comintern), which led to bad mistakes on the ground.

In the midst of this civil war, Japan steadily expanded its presence on the Chinese mainland. Japan's ambitions had started much earlier, when it joined the Western imperial powers in carving up China. In 1894, Japan sank the Qing fleet. Under the Treaty of Shimonoseki, China gave Taiwan to Japan and its rights to Korea, which was a tributary state. Although it viewed Qing China with contempt, Japan feared Russia's advance to the Pacific.

In 1905, Japan sank the Tsar's fleet in the Battle of Tsushima. In 1910, it annexed Korea. On 19 September 1931, Japan manufactured the Manchurian Incident and moved into Manchuria. The last Qing emperor, Puyi, was installed as emperor of Manchukuo in 1934. In China, people clamoured for the KMT and CPC to unite against Japan. The warlord, Zhang Xueliang, kidnapped Chiang in Xi'an in December

Left & right pages: Visiting Zunyi in 2015. The Zunyi conference held during the Long March established Mao as leader of the CPC. It was a key event in the history of the People's Republic of China.

1936. Chiang then agreed to work with Mao against Japan.

On 7 July 1937, following the Marco Polo Bridge Incident, Japanese forces invaded China proper. Japan's expansion into the Asian mainland eventually led to the American oil embargo against Japan and the Second World War in the Pacific. After the Second World War ended in Europe in May 1945, Joseph Stalin, keeping the promise he made to Franklin D. Roosevelt and Winston Churchill in Yalta, moved 1.6 million Soviet soldiers to the Pacific. On 8 August, after the United States (US) dropped the atomic bomb on Hiroshima, the Soviet Union declared war on Japan. Its armies, which were already massed on the border, rapidly swept into Manchuria, Korea and the Kuril Islands. On 9 August, the US dropped the second atomic bomb on Nagasaki. On 15 August, Japan surrendered.

The US was anxious to end the war quickly. If it did not, Soviet forces would have landed on the main islands of Japan within weeks. Without the atomic bombs, Japan, like Germany, would have been divided after the Second World War.

On the Chinese mainland, American Ambassador Patrick Hurley accompanied Mao to Chongqing on 28 August 1945. It was Mao's first flight in an aeroplane. He and Chiang agreed in principle to work on a united government. Serious fighting between the two sides broke out not long afterwards. When Soviet forces pulled out from Manchuria, both sides scrambled to occupy vacated territory.

Over the next two years, the Americans intervened repeatedly to try brokering peace between them, but every agreement, every truce, lasted only a short while. By December 1947, Mao announced that a turning point had been reached. The tide was now flowing in the Red Army's favour despite increasing US support for Chiang. The People's Republic was proclaimed in Tiananmen Square on 1 October 1949.

The founding of the People's Republic was the last act but not the end of the long play which was the Chinese Revolution. The ideological basis of the People's Republic was fundamentally different from that of the Republic of China. The method of governance changed, and the minds of the Chinese people also had to change as well. Scarcely a year after its establishment, the People's Republic was dragged into the Korean War when Douglas MacArthur's forces moved to the Yalu River. The terrible war on the Korean Peninsula was eventually fought to a standstill. An armistice was agreed in July 1953. In 1958, Mao tried to accelerate the Chinese Revolution during the Great Leap Forward. It was a disaster made much worse by the great famine of 1959–61. Millions perished. Mao was forced to retreat to the second line, but not for long. In 1966, he launched the Great Proletarian Cultural Revolution which created chaos.

As he grew older, after years in power, Mao lost touch with reality on the ground and became subjective. The People's Liberation Army (PLA) had to be called in to restore law and order. Mao died in 1976. In 1978, Deng Xiaoping became the paramount leader and moved China on a new trajectory of reform and opening up, which was briefly derailed by the Tiananmen Incident in 1989. Deng brought things back on track during his Southern Tour of February 1992 shortly before becoming incapacitated himself. China's explosive growth after that shocked the world.

The period from the Opium War to the end of the Cultural Revolution spanned almost 14 decades, the lifetimes of many generations. During that time, the Chinese mind was transformed. The title of later editions of Fairbanks and Reischauer's book was changed from *The Great Tradition* to *Tradition and Transformation*.

When I was a student in Cambridge, I pasted a part of Mao's poem in reply to Guo Moruo about so many things crying out to be done on my wall. I found it inspiring. On my first visit to China, in Queshi Park outside Shantou, I saw the poem etched onto a large boulder in Mao's calligraphy. Mao was a romantic, but became subjective in the end. While it is important to be hard-headed and practical in affairs of the state, it is also necessary to infuse people with a certain idealism, a dream of a better future. This is what President Xi Jinping has been attempting to do.

Chongqing in 2011. Chongqing was Chiang's wartime capital. In the war against Japan, the US was an ally. After the end of the Second World War, the US arranged for Mao to meet Chiang in Chongqing.

Q: What were the most important changes in the Chinese mind?

I would list three — attitudes to land, the position of women and the role of the Communist Party.

Attitudes to Land

At one level, the entire revolution was about land. Land concentration had always been the bane of Chinese feudal society, causing the immiserisation of the peasantry. When officials and generals performed well, they were rewarded with land and households. When there was flood or famine, peasants were forced to sell their land for food and medicine. Over time, the pattern of land ownership became evil, leading to the impoverishment of the majority. The Mandate of Heaven would be withdrawn and a new cycle would begin again.

Most of the land in China today is collectively owned. For economic activities, land is leased out for periods of 30, 50 or 70 years, but never in perpetuity. Because private land rights are relatively weak, the principle of eminent domain is much easier to invoke in China than in other countries. In many countries, acquiring land to build a highway, tunnel or new town is tedious. Litigation is common and the process is often politicised. Without this collective ownership of much of China's land, the transformation of its landscape and the development of its infrastructure in the last few decades would have been much more difficult to achieve.

This even extends to leasehold properties, with the Chinese government growing concerned about speculation and acting to dampen it. Inflation of property prices is a source of social injustice. Those who enter a rapidly rising market later simply because they happened to be born later are severely disadvantaged. It affects their sense of hope for the future. Politics in many Asian countries is soured by land speculation. While we need the market to allocate resources sensibly, an unregulated market often leads to perverse outcomes. Among many Chinese business families outside China, there is greater faith in land than any other asset

1983 at Queshi Park near Shantou. The first Mao poem I learned as a student in Cambridge.

class. The CPC does not want this attitude to take fresh root in China and often reminds the Chinese people of the Revolution's origins in land reform.

It is interesting that the Taiwanese economy took off only after land reform was carried out by Chiang Kai-shek. In a sense, Hong Kong will only be fully part of one country after land reform has been carried out, providing decent housing for the great majority of its people.

Position of Women

The change in women's position in Chinese society is possibly the greatest achievement of the Chinese Revolution. The practice of binding of women's feet for male pleasure, which went on for centuries, represented the extent to which women were subordinated to men in the old society. Chinese women are probably the most 'liberated' amongst Asian women today, compared to Korean, Japanese, Thai, Malay or Indian women. I use inverted commas because being liberated may be considered positive or negative depending on one's values. In a sense, Chinese women have been more 'liberated' than Chinese men. A new equilibrium has yet to be found. The plummeting birth rate of Chinese communities within and outside China reflects an imbalance in the attitudes of men and women. In Singapore, various measures to increase the birth rate have been tried without success. We make up for this by 'topping up' with new migrants. China can't do this.

Chinese girls now enjoy the same educational opportunities as Chinese boys. In university exams, girls generally do better than boys. In many professions, women are beginning to outnumber men at the entry level. However, when one looks at the composition of China's top leadership at the centres of power and in the provinces, it is still overwhelmingly male. Could China have a female leader one day? One is reminded of the response to Wu Zetian becoming emperor during the Tang period, that the hen cannot call the dawn (牝鸡不司晨).

China is determined to reverse the decline in its birth rate, which requires a complex system to be adjusted. It will not be easy but it is imperative. It is right that members of the CPC are asked to take the lead in having larger families. After the 20th Congress of the CPC in the fall of 2022, we can expect a massive campaign to be launched to encourage families to have more children. The revolution might be over, but the nature of the Chinese family is still evolving. Confucius might have been a 'male chauvinist', but he has not become irrelevant. A Chinese solution is needed.

Role of the Communist Party

China is China because it has always been centrally governed. When it became a republic, the question of political succession came to the fore. There was no longer an imperial family to confer legitimacy. Direct elections, which are the norm in Western liberal democracies, cannot work in China because it is too big and diverse a country. One-man-one-vote means I favour my family, clan, town or province's interests over outsiders. Indeed, Confucius teaches us to act according to the degree of our relationships. Were the Chinese people to vote according to the tenets of Confucius, China must break up. China has no precedent in its past to look to. Neither is there a model in the West it can follow.

From 1911 to 1949, China tried different paths to the future without success. The evolution of the Communist Party was a response to a life-and-death challenge. Despite making many mistakes and suffering many failures, the CPC was somehow able to right and renew itself again and again. Before Xi Jinping took over in 2013, corruption had become so bad it threatened to destroy the CPC and China itself. Credit, however, cannot go to Xi alone. Without the support of millions of Party members, Xi could not have turned the situation around. Hu Jintao also cleared the way for Xi. For many Chinese people, faith in the CPC has become inseparable from faith in China's future. The political legitimacy of the CPC has replaced the legitimacy of the imperial family. Like the old imperial family, the CPC views all of China as its responsibility, treating all of China as one nation-family. It draws talent from all of China in a way the imperial examination system never could.

Although they both use the term 'party', the CPC bears little

Calling on Vice Premier Zhu Rongji in 1994 together with DPM Ong Teng Cheong

resemblance to political parties in Western liberal democracies. In the latter, democratic will is exercised through competition among political parties. In China, democratic will is exercised through the Party's internal processes. Whether it is Western liberal democracy or the internal democracy of the Communist Party, the key is controlling corruption.

In Chinese, 'democracy' is translated as 民主 *(min zhu)* based on the root words in Greek, *demos* and *kratos*. Whether a system of governance is democratic depends on how much it establishes the people as masters of their own destiny. The CPC establishes its democratic ideal when it proclaims that the party has no interests beyond that of the Chinese people.

Around 1993, I used the phrase 'democracy with Chinese characteristics' in a speech I made on China. The CPC's Secretary of Shanghai, Zhu Rongji, was visiting Singapore at that time and read what I said. At the dinner I hosted for him, he expressed neither approval nor disapproval about the phrase I used.

Q: What are the most important challenges facing China and the CPC today?

Corruption

I put control of corruption at the top. Confucian values are fertile ground for corruption. Gifts express relationships but they also impose obligations. It is easy for gifts to become bribes.

The most trusted institution in China is probably the examination system, because it is free from *guanxi*. China invented examinations as a way to sift out merit without bias. We can argue over what should be examined and the extent to which examinations should depend on book knowledge. Whatever the criteria, however, it is key that no *guanxi* should be involved in the assessment of a person's academic merit.

China's government is finding ways to reduce the stress of examinations on students and parents. That is a good thing, but national examinations should never be dispensed with. Every year, some 10 million Chinese kids take the *gaokao* (university entrance examinations). During this period, even their families and friends are all stressed out because the examinations determine which universities students will go to. The stakes are high. The system should be improved and wastage ought to be reduced. But if the *gaokao* is abolished one day, as examinations were during the Cultural Revolution, both China and the world should be alarmed.

China's size requires its system of administration to be broken up into many levels. It is difficult for those at the top to know what takes place many layers down. Bad behaviour at the lower levels may be covered up by complicit officials at higher levels. There is a common saying that "the mountains are high, the emperor is far away". Every court creates a system of inspection that can sift through the layers so that wrongdoings can be exposed. This is a recurrent theme in Chinese opera precisely because such exposés are so rare. Justice Bao Zheng is a legendary figure because there are not many like him. Zhang Yimou's *The Story of Qiu Ju* describes how difficult it is for someone at the bottom to seek redress.

Xi Jinping has been unrelenting in his crackdown on corruption from top to bottom, from tigers to flies. Many people wonder how long this can continue before the system goes back to its old ways. Even in a small city-state like Singapore, the fight against corruption never ceases because of the social propensity to make use of *guanxi*. Xi is dredging up a younger generation of leaders who are not tainted by the corruption of a previous era. Official salaries are gradually being raised, but this will take time.

Artificial intelligence (AI)-powered data analytics may provide a technical solution to an age-old problem. The Chinese government collects a huge volume of data using multi-dimensional matrices. The same data is picked up from different sources, making it difficult for an official or a department to lie. For example, a town might understate its energy consumption, but the actual amount of energy used can also be determined by its population, the number and type of factories it has, the number of cars on the road, pollution levels and so on. Inconsistent data will naturally be flagged for higher scrutiny. Knowing that fake data is easily picked up, officials become more careful. With data analytics, it is possible to construct what constitutes a healthy data profile for a town or province or university. When strange patterns emerge, the centre zooms in to check. In this way, administrative corruption can be detected early.

Corruption at the top is harder to catch, but this may become easier as a wider range of information is captured. In all systems, the greatest fear is the anti-corruption system becoming corrupt itself. In theory, this problem can be resolved by two anti-corruption systems acting independently. There is therefore hope that China can ameliorate (not eliminate) a problem that is intrinsic in its social design. All that is fine, provided the CPC remains vital and its General Secretary a good leader. China has a 'key man' risk, and has always had this throughout its long history. When the system works well, the economy becomes highly productive and the internal market ginormous.

In Western liberal democracies, the notion of such data collection by a single centralised authority is anathema. With increasing intrusion by information technology companies into the lives of ordinary people, new laws are passed to prevent governments and private corporations from knowing too much. While the Chinese people are also concerned, they are less hung up about this because China has long been governed that way. Compared to Western society, privacy is less of a concern among Chinese people.

China's Relations with the World

Much of the world is still grappling with China's rapid rise and trying to make sense of it. The West has been unsettled by this and increasingly sees China's rise as a threat to its long dominance of the world. For a while, it thought it could manage China the way it did Japan in the 1980s. Japan was easier to pressure because it depended on the US nuclear umbrella and the post-war Constitution imposed by the US prevented it from becoming a normal country. Japan's competitiveness was also severely blunted when the Plaza Accord in 1985 forced a sharp increase in the Yen–USD exchange rate. When major issues are discussed at the Group of Seven, Japan, as the only non-western power, has to go along with the Western view. China is proving to be a completely different kettle of fish.

China joined the World Trade Organization in November 2001 on tough terms. No one, not even the Chinese themselves, anticipated that its economy would grow so rapidly. From the end of 2001 to the end of 2019, before the Covid-19 pandemic swept the world, China's economy expanded seven times in terms of purchasing power parity (PPP), nine times in terms of RMB and 11 times in terms of USD with its surplus already exceeding US$650 billion. China's economy is already bigger than the US' in PPP terms. In nominal terms, China's economy is likely to overtake the US within 10 years.

China's share of global trade has grown steadily. It is now the most important trading partner of all countries in the Association of Southeast Asian Nations (ASEAN) and of many countries in the world. China's economy was also the least damaged by Covid-19. It is the principal manufacturer for the world in many product categories. Ships leave China full and come back empty, which has caused freight rates to soar. In 2021, China's imports and exports rose 30%. Its trade surplus exceeded US$600 billion. Today, China accounts for more than a quarter of world trade.

In the last 10 years, the US has shifted its primary focus to China as a strategic challenge, beginning with then President Barack Obama's so-called 'pivot to the East'. Bilateral relations got much worse under former President Donald Trump and have not improved under the Biden Administration. In 2021, the US, Australia and the United Kingdom (UK) signed the AUKUS agreement, the purpose being to work together to contain China at sea. Among the Five Eyes, policy on China is being driven by intelligence and security concerns. A concerted move against Huawei has produced mixed results, with these countries paying a price for it via delays in rolling out 5G technology. By contrast, China had over 1.3 million 5G base stations by the end of 2021. This increase in bandwidth has spawned a dazzling range of new products and services.

On many issues concerning western values, the EU is aligned with the US against China. On hard economic interests, however, the EU pursues its own agenda. China supports the European Union (EU) and the Euro because it wants Europe to be a separate pole in the world. It wants a multipolar world because this will give it more flexibility in dealing with the US. China's trial of strength with the US will go on for many years, maybe 20 or 30.

But while China cannot afford to show weakness, because weakness only invites more pressure from the US, it does not want to escalate. With its economy growing faster than the US', time is on its side. China might repeatedly declare that it does not want to fight but is not afraid to fight. This makes sense according to conventional game theory. China prefers the win-win quadrant, but if the US pushes China to a win-lose quadrant, China is prepared to move into lose-lose. However, domestic

With Hong Kong businessman, Raymond Kwok, in an empty Forbidden City before the big parade

The 70ᵗʰ anniversary celebration of the victory of the World Anti-Fascist War at Tiananmen Square. It was a proud display of China's re-emergence on the global stage.

politics in the US can be driven to emotional swings and is not always rational. If, for example, there is an incident at sea which causes the death of dozens of US servicemen, the White House may not be able to hold back pressure from Congress and the media to go to war. Taiwan is particularly dangerous because China has little flexibility regarding it. US pressure on both China and Russia has brought them much closer together. In Eastern Europe and the Middle East, China will generally back Russia, but in the Pacific, Russia will generally back China.

The Belt and Road Initiative, which began in 2013, helps to build a co-prosperity sphere around China. Countries which find their accounts with China growing naturally seek diversification. The US, instead of seeing economic advantage for itself by providing such diversification, has set a policy to disrupt the Belt and Road wherever possible. China expects its external economy in different continents to be disrupted from time to time. It sees the US systematically cutting off its access to advanced technology in strategic sectors. China's dual-circulation economy helps it to manage such disruption. It already has the most vertically integrated economy in the world and is investing huge efforts in overcoming strategic vulnerabilities.

This tension between the US and China is a protracted struggle affecting every region and country on earth. China has to manage it well, for which it needs to combine hard and soft responses. Although Western domination of the international media makes China's communication efforts more difficult, the Chinese have been learning from mistakes and making adjustments. They treat Europe differently from the US. Within Europe, they tweak their policies to the requirements of individual countries, causing some Europeans to accuse China of dividing them. Even among the Five Eyes, China makes distinctions. It knows the City of London needs the RMB. What it does not buy from Australia, it gets from the US and New Zealand.

The prevailing Western view is that China's diplomacy has been too reliant on wolf warriors and crude. I am not so sure. In ASEAN, China's moves on the whole have been deft. Despite US efforts at spoiling the

2022 Winter Olympics in Beijing, many heads of states and governments attended, including Singapore's.

Humility

I hope China will stay humble and continue to learn from others. When Lord George Macartney attempted to see the Qianlong Emperor in 1793, he was told that China had nothing to learn from England. There was nothing in the gifts he brought from George III which China desired or did not already have itself. China then was at the height of its arrogance, which precipitated its rapid decline in the 19th century.

Macartney did not waste his time in China. He decided to return overland via the Grand Canal to Hangzhou, and from there by carriage to Guangzhou. The notes of his observations became useful when England fought the Opium Wars decades later. After the Second Opium War in 1860, any ship landing on the Chinese coast or up the Yangtze had to deal with Western customs officers who collected duties, deducted their share and passed the rest to Qing officials.

After China opened up in 1978, its people scoured the world for information and knowledge. Countries big and small alike interested them. Once on a free morning in Reykjavik, I chanced upon its modest-looking Parliament building. Iceland's Althingi is the oldest Parliaments in the world. The Speaker invited me in to view the chamber and for a chat. He told me that many Chinese delegations had visited and he was wondering why. I was intrigued too. For a while, I wondered whether it was because of Iceland's strategic location; the US has a naval air station at Keflavik. I even checked my globe on the great circle trajectories of intercontinental ballistic missiles.

I was probably too suspicious. By and by, I came to the realisation that China is in a learning mode and happy to learn from anyone and everyone. No major project in China is undertaken without first learning from the experiences of others. Singapore does the same, but we are a small country.

Singapore became of particular interest to China because of our

China in Iceland. As I was desultorily walking the streets of Reykjavik, the Speaker invited me into the Parliament House and told me of frequent visits by Chinese delegations.

Chineseness. Deng's visit to Singapore in December 1978 left an indelible impression on him. In 1985, China's State Council appointed Dr Goh Keng Swee as Economic Adviser on Coastal Development and Tourism. I will discuss Singapore's relations with China in a later chapter, but let me first describe a visit by a high-level delegation to Singapore in 1996 as an illustration of China's willingness to learn from others.

The delegation, which included three ministerial-level officials, was led by Ding Guangen, a politburo member and bridge partner of Deng Xiaoping. My cousin in Shantou told me later that "he (Ding) is in charge of our brains (管我们头脑)". The delegation spent a week studying and dissecting our laws and regulations on every aspect of mass communication, including radio, TV, cinemas, bookshops, libraries, museums and the Internet, which was then still in its infancy. I wondered what was behind this intense interest and had the uncomfortable feeling that on some matters, they knew more than I did as Minister for Information and the Arts. They took no time off for shopping or sightseeing and called on Lee Kuan Yew and Goh Chok Tong.

With Ding Guangen whose visit to Singapore in 1996 preceded China's Internet policy

Lianhe Zaobao report of my comments about Ding Guangen's visit to Singapore in 1966. Article from Lianhe Zaobao, *reproduced courtesy of SPH Media.*

On the morning before they flew off, Ding requested for a briefing on Changi Airport, not wanting to waste even a minute. With regard to the Internet, I remember telling Ding that we could always exercise control through the portals. In fact, at any one time, we made it a point to block 100 sites — mostly pornography and hate sites.

I only found out the purpose of Ding's visit a few months later when China released its policy on the Internet. It had decided to open up its internal cyberspace universe. Connections with the world outside would go through state-controlled portals. Without making that decisive move, China's economy would not be what it is today, with companies like Alibaba, Baidu, Tencent, Huawei and many others.

Before finalising their policy position, Ding's team wanted to make final checks against Singapore's experience. We were a scaled-down model for them. Without knowing it, we played a tiny role in the construction of the great internet wall of China. On my next visit to Beijing, Ding gave me a small private dinner at Zhongnanhai. I knew it was to show appreciation. Since then, China's cyberspace has become the liveliest in the world, but it is a cyber universe unto itself. Xi Jiping's comment that developing cyberspace is part of overall national development takes an approach which many countries are increasingly adopting — or wish they could.

As China grows in self-confidence, it is perhaps only natural that they should increasingly behave like a great power, but it is important for China to stay humble. In an ironic reversal of the state of affairs in 1793, it is the West today which feels it

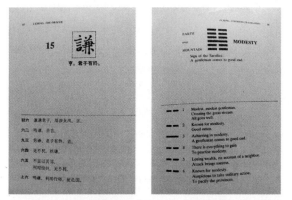

According to Massachusetts Institute of Technology Prof Kerson Huang, the hexagram qian is "unique in that all six lines are good"

has nothing to learn from the East. Everything China does is criticised, based only on superficial knowledge. This is not good for the West. Of the 64 hexagrams in the *Yijing*, only one contains no negative possibilities. All the other 63 have both positives and negatives. That single unique hexagram is *qian* (谦), for modesty.

Q: When will the trial of strength between China and the US end?

American President Joe Biden has said that America's greatest long-term challenge overseas comes from China. He added that confronting China is the work of generations, a battle that this generation's grandchildren will study in college. It is a question of whether democracy or autocracy will prevail across the globe. In recent years, the Five Eyes has surfaced because of the perceived need to confront a rising China. AUKUS is an expression of it. The Quadrilateral Security Dialogue (Quad) has a more limited role because India has its own independent agenda and Japan has a deep wish to be less dependent on the US and become a more normal country.

A nuclear exchange between the US and China will destroy the world. I think both sides understand this, but limited war or proxy war is possible. It is necessary for both sides to engage each other in deep conversation so that in the event of conflict, there are firebreaks. Both are high-tech powers which means that conflict may break out in new domains like space and cyberspace. The use of AI to kill can lead to unintended escalation. Such conversation requires the US to respect China's point of view. Respect requires understanding, which is currently lacking.

I think the trial of strength will only ameliorate when US leaders develop a deeper understanding of China and the nature of its society. Today, China's understanding of the US is significantly greater than the US' understanding of China. Wang Huning, a member of China's Politburo Standing Committee, studied in the US and has written an insightful book called *America Against America*. Provided China does not make serious mistakes, the US will eventually exhaust itself on its current course. During the Vietnam War, an exhausted US improved relations with China in order to create better conditions for the withdrawal of its forces from Southeast Asia. When the US is exhausted again, relations with China will stabilise. The US will become less anxious when it realises that China is not expansionist. It should not be a Manichaean struggle.

Q: What about China's attitude towards religion?

Actually, its policy on religion is little different from that of Imperial China. Religion must not interfere with affairs of the state. When Buddhism intruded into the political sphere, the Mandarins opposed it. The great scholar-mandarin who uplifted the Teochew people, Han Yu, was banished to Chaozhou because he memorialised the Emperor against excessive devotion to a Buddha relic. The Mandarins succeeded in confining Buddhist monks to monasteries and in the private sphere. Unlike Theravada monks in Sri Lanka and Southeast Asia, Mahayana monks in East Asia have generally been depoliticised. The Sinicization of Buddhism has made it a Chinese religion.

In Chinese civilisation, *tian* (天), or heaven, is always acknowledged. The emperor is the Son of Heaven (天子) (*tian zi*). He needs the Mandate of Heaven (天命) (*tian ming*). Human existence is 天下 (*tian xia*), in recognition of a higher moral authority over human beings. Unlike Europe before the Enlightenment, the moral order in China is never derived from organised religion. The Jesuits who entered Ming China were astonished to see this. Their observations of China influenced French intellectuals like Joseph Needham wrote about China's contribution to the philosophical underpinnings of the French Revolution and the Enlightenment. Matteo Ricci knew that Christianity had to be sinicized before it could take root in China. Blessed with a photographic memory and a brilliant mind, he mastered the Chinese classics and interpreted Christianity in a way which the Chinese could accept philosophically. He did for Christianity what Xuanzang had done for Buddhism 900 years earlier.

Ricci's translation of Deus into Chinese was profound. God is 天主 (*tian zhu*), the Lord of Heaven. The Catholic religion became the religion of the God of Heaven (天主教) *(tian zhu jiao)*. Jesus Christ instructed his followers to give to Caesar what is Caesar's and to God what is God's. Using this precept, Ricci inserted Christianity into a space (天) which was not the Emperor's main domain (天下).

The Christianity that entered China in the 19th century was assisted by gunboats and guns. It entered as a foreign religion. Jesus Christ, the Virgin Mary and the saints were foreign 'gods'. Chinese intellectuals saw Christianity as an instrument of imperialism. If the Chinese people accepted that their 'gods' are European, their subjection would be complete. An important reason why Hernán Cortés was able to subdue the great Mexican empire despite his meagre forces was because the Aztecs believed in a powerful white god, Quetzalcoatl, whom Cortés deliberately made himself out to be. Dr Sun Yat-sen and Chiang Kai-shek were Christians, at least nominally, and associated with the West. Their wives, who were sisters, were educated at Wellesley College in Massachusetts. The Communists viewed Christianity in a different light. After Mao took over, white Catholic bishops opposed him, which led to their expulsion from China.

China's policy on foreign religions is that they must be sinicized. What does this mean? To some Christians, this sounds like heresy. Whether it is or not depends on the religion's response to state policy. Intellectually, the Chinese know that Buddha and Guanyin were Indian but, spiritually and emotionally, they are Chinese. Europeans know that Jesus and Mary were Jews but, spiritually and emotionally, they are European. For Christianity to take root in China, Jesus and Mary must be Chinese, spiritually and emotionally.

Pope Francis talks about how God reveals Himself in our deepest identity. In Guadalupe, he reflected that the Virgin Mary appeared to Juan Diego as a *mestiza*. When he visited Rohingya refugees in

Bangladesh, he proclaimed God to be Rohingya. In this way, God is Chinese, too. When I said that God is Chinese at a centennial celebration of the May Fourth Movement in Singapore organised by Peking University alumni, some in the audience were startled.

China is particularly sensitive about religious influence over Han Chinese because this affects national coherence. With minority groups, the concerns have to do with security, rather than culture. As Tibetan Buddhism fuses spiritual and political leadership in high lamas, the reincarnation of high monks has always been of political concern in Beijing since the Ming Dynasty and requires state approval. The appointment of the 14th Dalai Lama needed Chiang Kai-shek's approval.

Islam is in a separate category. Allah spoke in Arabic and translations of the Quran are not the Quran. In contrast, translations of the Bible are still the Bible. I doubt if Islam can ever be sinicized the way Buddhism was and Christianity can be. The Huis speak Chinese and are half-Han, but they cannot be fully Han because of Islam. They often mediate between Han Chinese and Muslims belonging to ethnic minorities, like the Uyghurs. So long as Muslims are not a significant minority in China, this will not be a grave concern. Those who convert to Islam are treated as members of minority groups. It is interesting that Chinese who convert to Islam in Singapore are treated in a similar way.

Sinicization of Christianity in China. The holy picture of Mary and Jesus as Chinese was given to me by the Prelate of Opus Dei Bishop Javier Echevarria.

❖

CHAPTER 12

Singapore's Chineseness

George Yeo discusses Singapore's Chineseness and how it has affected our relations with China and other countries.

Q: Some of your former colleagues in the Ministry of Foreign Affairs (MFA) have said that Singapore should strive to have a normal relationship with China, the same way we do with other countries. Is that possible?

I think that underlying that comment is a concern that Singapore might be overly emotional in our dealings with China. It is a valid concern. Emotions are inseparable from both our foreign and domestic policies. The feelings are real. Our Chineseness matters in our relationship with China and affects our relationship with other countries.

Singapore has a unique relationship with China because it is the only country outside China that has a large majority Chinese population. It is impossible for Singapore to have a normal relationship with China because China is in our DNA. This of course presents both opportunities and challenges.

Diaspora Chinese are often self-consciously Chinese even when they are citizens of other countries. China's history goes through long cycles. During periods of disunity and disorder, Chinese culture still gets transmitted through the extended family, including the political ideal of a united Chinese nation. Chinese culture is tenacious because of its long history and the depth of its civilisation.

On a flight from Auckland to Tahiti in 2001, I chatted with an air hostess whose father was Chinese Hakka. She looked to be of mixed heritage. I was thrilled when she referred to a book published in Singapore which included a chapter on the Chinese in the South Pacific. That was the *Encyclopedia of the Chinese Overseas,* published by the Chinese Heritage Centre (housed in the old

Recording the living heritage of ethnic Chinese communities outside China from a non-Mainland perspective

Nanyang University Administration Building). I was directly involved in that project; Pan Lynn was the Centre's first Director.

The Chinese diaspora continues to grow and evolve. There are now growing communities on all the continents, including Africa and Latin America.

For diaspora Chinese, split loyalty can be a political problem. When their country of citizenship has good relations with China, diaspora Chinese play useful bridging roles. But when relations are bad, they come under suspicion.

Realising that potential split loyalty can cause problems in bilateral relations, Zhou Enlai made clear in Bandung in 1955 that Chinese should be loyal to the country of their citizenship. Only overseas Chinese would retain the right to Chinese citizenship. However, the reality is not so clear-cut. Around 1974, as the secretary of the Cambridge University Malaysia Singapore Association, I asked to borrow a Chinese movie from the Chinese Embassy in London. The lady at the service counter asked me to go to the Overseas Chinese section in a different part of the building even though she knew I was Singaporean.

In all my visits to China (and Taiwan), I am treated as both a Singaporean and a fellow Chinese. Ethnic ties matter. While neither China nor Singapore recognises dual nationality, many European countries do. For some, like Ireland or Spain, you can claim citizenship if you can prove that one of your grandparents came from there. Ethnic Chinese like Robert Kuok hold firm to both his identities as Malaysian and as Chinese. He proudly proclaims that he is a patriotic overseas Chinese (爱国华侨) (*ai guo hua qiao*).

I saw the same affection for China in my own parents. For my mother, that was to be expected since she grew up in China. My father however was English-educated, spoke no Mandarin and could not read Chinese. During the Los Angeles Olympics Games in 1984, there was a keen contest between the United States (US) and China for the men's gymnastics gold medal. My father watched the event live and lamented that 'we' lost.

While in government, I said that I would consider myself a failure as a father if my children did not consider themselves to be Chinese. It might have been impolitic for me to be so frank but it was the truth. Singaporeans of other races feel the same way about their identity too. When my kids were young, my wife and I bought a small house on the shore of Lake Tai in Jiangsu developed by CapitaLand, intending to go there every year so that they could be more acquainted with China and Chinese culture. As it turned out, my youngest son had to battle leukaemia for many years and we hardly made use of the house before it was sold to make way for redevelopment of the entire area. Man proposes, God disposes.

We do not begin with a blank slate. Each of us is a book with many chapters already written. What we write in subsequent pages proceeds from what we are now.

Q: How will this connection with China affect our relationship with other countries?

As China moves to centre stage in global politics and economics, the relationship between China and diaspora Chinese will naturally grow stronger. Chinese communities which lost their connection to China (like the Peranakans of Indonesia, Malaysia and Singapore) are finding renewed interest in Chinese heritage and language.

For generations, the Peranakans of Singapore and Malaya developed their own sub-culture. They were self-consciously Chinese but looked down on new Chinese migrants, whom they called the *sinkeh* (新客). Peranakan food is a favourite cuisine among Singaporeans and Malaysians. The fastidiousness of their womenfolk is expressed not only in their food and dressing

A delightful exhibition of Peranakan jewelry in 1993 called "Gilding the Phoenix"

but also, and especially, in their jewellery. When in mourning, the women wear only silver jewellery as gold was reserved for celebrations.

In 1993, Edmond Chin put together a delightful exhibition called *Gilding the Phoenix* at the old Tao Nan School, which became a part of the Asian Civilisations Museum. Many of Singapore's first generation of leaders including Lee Kuan Yew, Goh Keng Swee and Lim Kim San were Peranakans. With the rise of China, Peranakans are reconnecting to their mother culture. This creates new tensions.

In the US today, American Chinese working in science, technology, engineering and mathematics (STEM) have suddenly found themselves under surveillance or suspicion by the Federal Bureau of Investigation (FBI) because of worsening relations between the US and China. In 2018, the Director of the FBI, Christopher Wray, said that the US was concerned with "the China threat as not just a whole-of-government threat, but a whole-of-society threat on their end", which requires "... a whole-of-society response by us". In a speech at the Ronald Reagan Presidential Library in January 2022, Wray stressed again, "I want to focus on it here tonight because it's reached a new level — more brazen, more damaging, than ever before, and it's vital, vital that all of us focus on that threat together."

In Southeast Asia, ethnic Chinese have gone through difficult

Visiting Ee Hoe Hean Club with Lim Chin Joo and Dr K. K. Phua of World Scientific

Tan Kah Kee remembered in the Pioneers' Memorial Hall of Ee Hoe Hean Club

Lee Kong Chian and his family remembered in the Pioneers' Memorial Hall at the Ee Hoe Hean Club

periods in the past. After South Vietnam fell to the North in 1975, the first waves of boat people were mostly Chinese. Under Suharto, Indonesia banned Chinese language and literature, probably the only country in the world to do such a thing. I remember reading with disgust customs forms which stated that, along with drugs and firearms, Chinese-language material was also considered contraband. In Thailand, those of Chinese descent were not allowed to join the Army (although many still did).

The main cause of anti-Chinese sentiment in Southeast Asia is the disproportionate role ethnic Chinese play in business. Among the very wealthy, many are ethnic Chinese. Some are known for their philanthropic work like Lee Kong Chian's family, but a few behave badly and live ostentatiously. Thailand's King Rama VI criticised the ethnic Chinese as the 'Jews of the East' even though his own ancestor, Rama I, had Chinese blood.

They are also seen as being disloyal or not loyal enough. Overseas Chinese supported China's resistance against increasing Japanese encroachment into the Chinese mainland from the early 1930s. Tan Kah Kee organised the Nanyang Federation of China Relief Fund Technicians. From 1939 to 1942, over 3,000 overseas Chinese volunteered as truck drivers and mechanics in China along the Rangoon–Yunnan Road. About 1,800 technicians died from bombing, disease and exhaustion. His nephew, Tan Keong Choon, raised money to build a memorial by Dian Lake near Kunming to remember their sacrifice. At the Ee Hoe Hean Club in Singapore, there is an interesting memorial hall to Tan Kah Kee and other Singapore Chinese leaders.

Japan viewed overseas Chinese communities in Southeast Asia as extensions of China. Japan's invasion of Southeast Asia was carefully planned for years before it was executed in December 1941.

Plans for the Malayan Campaign were made in Taiwan (which Japan took from Qing China in 1895). In his book *The Killer They Called a God*, Ian Ward writes about how Lieutenant Colonel Masanobu Tsuji drew up a detailed plan to eliminate many overseas Chinese once the Japanese Army had occupied Singapore. Post-war sources revealed that the order was to kill 50,000. The Japanese referred to the Sook Ching as the Kakyō Shukusei (華僑粛清), meaning purging of overseas Chinese.

Sook Ching was second only to Nanjing in the cruelty inflicted on a civilian population.

During the Japanese occupation of Malaya, the Malayan Peoples' Anti-Japanese Army (MPAJA), led by the Communist Party of Malaya (CPM), fought a guerilla war against the Japanese in the jungle. They were mostly Chinese. Between the Japanese surrender on 15 August 1945 and the return of British forces

"The Japanese referred to the Sook Ching as the Kakyō Shukusei (華僑粛清, 'purging of Overseas Chinese')" (Wikipedia). It was the result of decades of Chinese nationalism which supported the republican revolution and the resistance against Japan on the Chinese Mainland.

in September that year, the MPAJA took action against Japanese collaborators, many of whom were Malay. Ultimately, the failure of the CPM struggle in Malaya was due to their inability to win over the Malays, who expressed their nationalism through the United Malays National Organisation (UMNO).

The Malayan Emergency will eventually be seen in the historical context as a nationalist struggle which failed because of racial division which the British exploited. Many young men lost their lives in pursuit of a righteous cause. Robert Kuok burns a joss stick everyday for his second brother, who was killed by the British during the Emergency and whom he admired for his good heartedness, brilliance and eloquence. *The Straits Times* had a photographer, Sim Chi Yin, who accompanied me on a number of overseas trips when I was a minister. On one such trip to Hong Kong, I bumped into her in Stanley one evening. She told me that she had an exhibition on the Emergency. When I asked her about the reason for her interest, she said that it was the story of her grandfather, who had been banished to China during the Emergency and killed by the Kuomintang (KMT). The exhibition was titled *One Day We'll Understand*.

In both Malaya and Singapore, the British were determined to hand power over to credible nationalist groups who were less unfriendly to them. In Malaya, the proposal for a Malayan Union was changed to one for the Malayan Federation, enshrining the position of the Sultans and Malay rights. In Singapore, the British favoured Lee Kuan Yew and his faction in the People's Action Party (PAP). Both direct and indirect British interventions at critical moments were decisive. The British did not want an independent Singapore because it could become a satellite of China. They manoeuvred for Singapore to gain independence through the merger with Malaysia.

Lee Kuan Yew later said that Sarawak and Sabah were the dowry the British gave to the Tunku to admit Singapore into Malaysia. When the Tunku agreed two years later that Singapore could go free, Lee Kuan Yew wrote that he kept it a closely-guarded secret from the British until it was irreversible because they would have thwarted it.

Although many ethnic Chinese in Southeast Asia threw themselves into nationalist struggles against the colonial enemy, like the Philippines' José Rizal, as a group they were sometimes seen to be less supportive, as in Indonesia, or too aligned with China-backed communist movements, as in Thailand and Malaya. When, for whatever reason, countries in Southeast Asia are unhappy with their indigenous Chinese populations, they project their unhappiness on Singapore as a headquarters for Southeast Asian Chinese.

Whatever we say or do, the fact is that many countries factor Singapore's Chineseness into their planning and calculations. For this reason, Lee Kuan Yew held back diplomatic relations with China until Indonesia had done so. To some extent, we have succeeded in convincing other countries that while Singapore has close cultural ties to China, on political matters, we calculate in our own self-interest.

One day in the mid-1990s, Singapore's relations with China went through a bad patch. Indonesian Foreign Minister Ali Alatas expressed his concern about the state of Singapore–China relations to me, and indirectly offered his assistance. I was pleasantly surprised that here was Indonesia worried that we were having bad relations with China.

For a period, Vietnam viewed us with suspicion too. After Vietnamese divisions moved into Cambodia in 1978, Singapore, together with other Association of Southeast Asian Nations (ASEAN) countries, worked with China to support anti-Vietnam forces in Cambodia. (Unlike China and Thailand, Singapore kept a distance from the Khmer Rouge but supported all other factions.) At the United Nations and other international gatherings, we combined efforts to deny legitimacy to the government in Phnom Penh installed by Vietnam. After 10 years, Vietnam withdrew from Cambodia. They then decided to follow China in gradually opening up its economy.

Prime Minister (PM) Vo Van Kiet visited Singapore in 1991. At the end of a dinner hosted by Lee Kuan Yew at the Istana, Kiet asked Lee Kuan Yew to be an adviser to Vietnam. Although he was taken aback

Lee Kuan Yew and Vietnam Communist Party General Secretary Vo Van Kiet at a dinner in the Istana in 1991, after which he asked Lee Kuan Yew to be Vietnam's adviser

and promised to visit Vietnam regularly, he did not agree to become an adviser.

I accompanied Lee Kuan Yew on his first three trips to Vietnam. Relations steadily improved. The first Vietnam Singapore Industrial Project (VSIP), was a mini-Suzhou, established near Ho Chi Minh City in 1996. (Since then many VSIPs have sprouted across the length of Vietnam.) When I was Minister for Trade and Industry, I co-chaired a bilateral commission with the Vietnam Minister for Planning as my counterpart. Whenever meetings were held in Hanoi, I called on PM Phan Van Khai. He was always polite but somewhat formal until, one year, he spoke to me as if I was his minister and started giving me 'homework'.

Something had happened. My belief was that Vietnam had come to the conclusion that Singapore was not an agent of China and could become a strategic partner. On Khai's next visit to Singapore in 2004, the two countries launched the Connectivity Initiative, which I helped put together for Goh Chok Tong.

Q: Will the suspicion go away eventually?

I doubt so. Chineseness is an inseparable part of Singapore. Others believe and expect that so long as Singapore's core interests are not affected, Chinese Singaporeans are likely to view China with greater sympathy. Some of my Chinese Singaporean friends who are critical of China nonetheless get upset when they see Western countries finding fault with China.

Singapore's One China policy is not merely a decision. The position that Taiwan is part of China and only separated because of Japan up to 1945 and the US after that is widely held by older Chinese Singaporeans. A Singapore government that departs from this policy is likely to face strong opposition from the majority of older Chinese Singaporeans.

In 1989, I was asked by Lee Kuan Yew to announce in Parliament that Singapore would allow US military forces in the Pacific to use our base facilities after the closure of Clark Air Base and Subic Bay. Without the US, Singapore could not be sure that the Straits of Malacca and Singapore Strait, which are our lifelines, would always be kept open. Lee Kuan Yew was, however, very clear that should there be conflict between the US and China over Taiwan, Singapore would not be involved. I don't believe that position has changed despite close defence links between Singapore and the US.

Chinese communities everywhere in Southeast Asia are conscious of their 'Jewish' status. Anti-Chinese sentiments have generally subsided but they are still there in the soil. In countries where bad experiences are more recent, a certain sense of insecurity is pervasive, like background music. Singapore is a safe harbour they know they can turn to in a crisis. In Singapore, they can celebrate their Chineseness without worrying that some may take offence. However, there are a few who worry that if Singapore emphasises its Chineseness too much, they might be negatively affected. In my years as minister, I was conscious of this dynamic.

During my time at the Ministry of Information and the Arts (MITA), one of my missions was to promote Singapore's diverse heritage,

Establishment of the Chinese Heritage Centre at the old Nanyang University Administration Block in 1995

including our Chinese heritage. An Indonesian scholar of Chinese descent whom I know well whispered to a Singaporean friend of mine that he was uncomfortable with what I was doing. That was during the Suharto years when Chinese language and culture were suppressed in Indonesia. At the launch of the Chinese Heritage Centre in 1995, Mochtar Riady, an Indonesian Chinese tycoon and a member of the Advisory Board, came for the first meeting chaired by Wee Cho Yaw. He told the meeting that he received a phone call the day before from the Indonesian Home Minister asking him why he was going to Singapore for the meeting. It was a hint which he happily brushed aside.

In 1998, Indonesia was shaken to its core by the Asian Financial Crisis. Shadowy figures orchestrated racist attacks on Chinese Indonesians. Many fled to Singapore and stayed here for months. I used to go running along East Coast Park and I remember seeing many of them taking evening strolls — women with their children and maids in tow looking out to the sea. Two years later, at Ministry of Trade and Industry event, we invited the Indonesian scholar who had been uncomfortable with my promotion of Chinese heritage to give an in-house talk on the Indonesian economy. Before he began, he expressed his gratitude to Singapore for our assistance to Indonesian Chinese in their darkest hour of need, choking on his tears.

Who we are is not only who we think we are, but also how others see us. We have to be aware of the games which big powers play, whether to influence us or to sow seeds of suspicion here.

Q: How then do we establish our own identity as Singaporeans?

My old friend and political colleague, Zainul Abidin Rasheed, once described Singapore to me as a nation of minorities. Seeing the puzzled look on my face, he explained that even the Chinese in Singapore feel themselves a minority because of the position of Chinese in the region. I never forgot this profound insight. To a certain extent, Singapore Chinese have internalised a cultural self-restraint in order not to cause others discomfort. However, taken too far, this restraint is felt as suppression and leads to resentment.

When the British were here, the majority of Chinese were seen as pro-China. After 1911, reflecting the situation in China, many were inclined to the Left and supported the anti-Japanese resistance. When the Japanese occupied Malaya and Singapore, they viewed overseas Chinese as supporters of the anti-Japanese resistance in China and put them down harshly.

After the war, during the Malayan Emergency, Chinese-educated Singaporeans were generally suspected by the British of either being Communists or supportive of their cause. In a Zoom conference on his latest book, *Home is Where We Are*, Professor Wang Gungwu reflected on this period, observing that the British thought that Communists were under every bed. They easily labelled the Chinese-educated as either Communists or chauvinists, continuing even after merger with Malaya and after Separation.

An entire generation of Chinese-educated Singaporeans was scarred by this period of history. Not long after I entered politics, I made a speech on Chinese culture in which I remarked that we should not be chauvinistic. It was covered by *Lianhe Zaobao,* which emphasised that remark in their headline. Within a few days, Dr Ow Chin Hock, a Chinese-educated PAP Member of Parliament, put me down in a speech, saying that I should not have equated cultural promotion with chauvinism. Though I had not, I realised that I had touched a raw nerve and was more careful thereafter.

At the bicentennial exhibition of Singapore's founding by Sir Stamford Raffles in 1819, the narrative was carefully constructed to take into account Singapore's history before Raffles, going back 700 years. This was the right perspective to take as there was indeed a Singapore before Raffles. When Admiral Zheng He's ships sailed through these waters, Singapore was an important navigation point called the Dragon's Gate (龙牙门) (*long ya men*) because of a prominent tooth-shaped boulder which could be seen from far away. In the 16th century, St Francis Xavier wrote letters from Kallang Basin, where there must have been a Jesuit station.

In the exhibition, however, Singapore's history was presented as a series of exogenous events which impinged on us. Missing was how Singapore was always affected by the ebb and flow of trade with China, which accompanied the fall and rise of Chinese dynasties. I wondered whether that explanation had been deliberately omitted or was just missing due to ignorance.

Modern Singapore cannot be explained without reference to the arrival of the European powers eager for their share of Chinese trade. The story cannot be told without the backdrop of the Qing Dynasty's long decline, the humiliation felt by the Chinese (including the overseas Chinese), the violent struggle to establish a modern republic and the determination to expel Western and Japanese imperialists. In the same way, Singapore's future will be greatly affected by the re-emergence of China on the global stage and the rise of new Chinese trade along the Belt and Road.

Two medals presented by Dr Sun Yat-sen to Ho Sum Tin. I showed this to Ma Ying-jeou, then KMT Chairman, when he was at my house for dinner. He immediately had his assistant take pictures of them.

Grandma Mary's grandfather Ho Sum Tin who helped Dr Sun Yat-sen established Tongmenghui

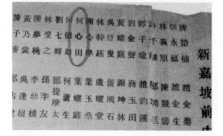

Founders of Tongmenghui in Singapore in 1906. Ho Sum Tin's name circled.

The Chinese who migrated to Singapore during China's troubles stayed connected emotionally to the great drama on the mainland. Many supported Dr Sun Yat-sen, who set up a Singapore branch of the Tongmenghui (同盟会) in 1906 to serve Southeast Asia. My wife's great-grandfather, Ho Sum Tin (何心田), was one of the co-founders and was subsequently awarded two medals by Dr Sun. An early republican, he refused to close his shop when the Guangxu Emperor died in 1908, which infuriated pro-Qing supporters. His shop was stoned by Qing loyalists. In this period, many Chinese cities, business chambers and trade associations concerned themselves with national renewal. Newspapers carried supplements with serious commentaries on the state of Chinese society. School curricula were reformed.

Frustration and anger with China's weakness and its degradation by imperial powers swept across Chinese communities in Southeast Asia. (Many failed revolts against the Qing were organised in Singapore and Penang. Till today, the tradition of Chinese business chambers and newspapers concerning themselves with larger social issues continues. *Zaobao's* Fukan, which is qualitatively different from *The Straits Times'* Life Supplement, is directly descended from that period.

Wan Qing Yuan (晚晴园), a bungalow which was used as the Tongmenghui's headquarters in Singapore, was only declared a national monument in 1994. It was owned by Teo Chee Hean's grand-uncle, who let Dr Sun use it whenever he was in Singapore (a total of nine visits). It then passed through many hands until Lee Kong Chian and a few other Chinese businessmen bought over it in order to preserve it. In 1938, they donated it to the Chinese Chamber of Commerce, which took its responsibility seriously.

On a visit there some years ago with Chinese leaders, I said that we should prepare for the centennial celebration of the 1911 Revolution in 2011. I heard Tan Keong Choon, nephew of Tan Kah Kee, mutter under his breath whether he would live to see it. He did. In 1996, I was invited to launch Wan Qing Yuan as the Sun Yat Sen Nanyang Memorial Hall. In 2001, on the 90th anniversary of the 1911 Revolution, Lee Kuan Yew

Opening of Sun Yat Sen Nanyang Memorial Hall in 1996 in conjunction with
130ᵗʰ birth anniversary of Dr Sun Yat-sen

*Opening of the refurbished Sun Yat Sen Nanyang Memorial Hall by Lee Kuan Yew in 2001.
Right pictures shows Foong Choon Hong who worked with passion on the exhibits
painstakingly gleaned from sources in Singapore, Malaysia and China (including Taiwan).*

Centennial celebration of the 1911 Revolution

opened it as a heritage museum. For years, it was preserved by the Chinese business community because of its association with Dr Sun Yat-sen and the 1911 Revolution.

Since its establishment as the Sun Yat Sen Nanyang Memorial Hall, Wan Qing Yuan has become a place of pilgrimage for Chinese leaders on both sides of the Taiwan Straits. On the grounds, there is a boulder cleft in two, with calligraphy written by Wang Daohan on one face and by Koo Chen-fu on the other. They were the representatives of China and Taiwan who held a historic meeting in Singapore in 1993 following the 1992 Consensus on One China. The divided boulder expresses the hope that China will be whole again one day.

In preparation for the centennial celebration of 1911, I made a request to the land authorities to allocate a nearby piece of empty land for a Dr Sun Yat-sen Park, the only one outside China. They bargained me down to a smaller piece but it was sufficient. It was a narrow strip of land that Dr Sun Yat-sen had walked many times between Balestier Road and the bungalow. The banyan trees which shaded him are still thriving today.

In May 2011, I lost my seat in the General Election and left the government. I came back from Beijing, where I was a visiting scholar at Peking University, specially to attend the centennial celebration at Wan Qing Yuan and to give my reflections on the occasion.

A few years after, I was invited to give a speech at Hwa Chong Institution 100th anniversary celebration in 2019. Upon my arrival, I asked the Principal whether Hwa Chong celebrated the centennial of May Fourth. He hesitated for a moment and said no, then asked: should we have? The New Culture Movement, which led to May Fourth, also resulted in the reform of Chinese education in China and in overseas Chinese communities like Singapore. Hwa Chong's founding was intimately connected to this historic movement, which also engulfed the Chinese community in Singapore. If I were a Hwa Chong student and familiar with this history, I would feel prouder of my alma mater's heritage.

Speech to Peking University alumni in Singapore at the 100th anniversary of the May Fourth Movement

Speaking at Hwa Chong's 100th anniversary in 2019

Penang's top Chinese school, Chung Ling High School, also suppressed an important part of its history. I first knew of the role Chung Ling played in China's war against Japan from former Penang Minister Dr Lim Chong Eu. During Lee Kuan Yew's last visit to Malaysia as PM, he went to Penang to call on the Tunku and took time off to meet old friends. At one of the gatherings, Lim recounted his time serving as personal physician to Chen Cheng, who was one of Chiang Kai-Shek's top generals. Lim

History of Penang's Chung Ling High School

remembered heroes from Chung Ling flying rickety Chinese planes over Chongqing against better and more numerous Japanese aircraft. Many lost their lives.

The Chinese Heritage Centre wrote up a history of Chung Ling. Khaw Boon Wan, a proud alumni, was pleased to receive a copy. I also persuaded Lim Chong Eu to have his oral history recorded by our Oral History Unit. At his funeral, I presented the complete transcript to his family. It was for them to decide what to do with it. Many years later, I got to know Captain Ho Weng Toh, who flew with the Flying Tigers as a bomber pilot. I encouraged him to write his memoirs and wrote the foreword to it. Recently, to my delight, a friend agreed to sponsor the Chinese translation. As I write this, Captain Ho is now 102 years old and remarkably alert.

Lee Kuan Yew struggled for many years to achieve dominance in the PAP and in Singapore. To use the metaphor in Dennis Bloodworth's *The Tiger and the Trojan Horse* and Khor Eng Lee's *Riding the Tiger*, the tiger which Lee Kuan Yew rode was the Chinese-educated Left. With the help of the British and the Malaysians, he was able to dismount safely. After Singapore became independent, he finally tamed the tiger by radically revamping Chinese education in Singapore. The issue of Chinese education in Singapore is bound up with Singapore's identity as well as its future.

Flying Tiger Captain Ho Weng Toh at a sprightly hundred years of age

✥

CHAPTER 13

Chinese Education

> *George Yeo discusses how Singapore's identity and future are bound up with Chinese education. Singapore cannot return to the past when each ethnic group had its own separate school system. He suggests that Nanyang University be restored not for the past, but for the future.*

Q: How did Lee Kuan Yew tame the tiger — the Chinese-educated Left — by radically revamping Chinese education?

It is important to briefly recount the history of Chinese education in Singapore.

The early Chinese in Singapore had to bury their dead and educate their young. During the colonial period, the Chinese community provided for its own cultural and educational needs. They acquired private land burial plots as the colonial government only provided Christian cemeteries. The Hokkiens bought large tracts of land in the west. As an officer cadet, I remember hiking through Bulim Cemetery in Jurong many times. The Teochews were lucky to acquire land near the city, along today's Orchard Road. Ngee Ann Kongsi was created by an ordinance of the Legislative Assembly in 1933 principally to meet burial needs. Non-Christian Teochew members of the Legislative Assembly automatically became members of its Management Committee.

Not long after Stamford Raffles' arrival, private Chinese schools were established and financed by businessmen and clan associations. Apart from those set up by Christian missionaries, Chinese schools followed the system in China. The late Qing modernised China's education system by learning from Japan, which had modelled theirs on Germany's. The

*Opening of Nanyang University. When the new plan for the campus was drawn up,
the old gate was left stranded at a road intersection.*

military-like uniforms of Chinese schools in Singapore, with their pocket flaps and metal buttons, had their origins in that lineage.

Teachers and students alike were affected by the winds of change in China. Politically, they supported Dr Sun Yat-sen and the republican movement and were swept up by the New Culture Movement (新文化运动). When the May Fourth Movement spread to Malaya and Singapore, the British were concerned by the politicisation of schools and began a system of grants-in-aid, motivated partly by the need to monitor and influence school activities. Alliances and splits between the Kuomintang (KMT) and the Chinese Communist Party (CPC) were reflected in Singapore. They were united in the war against Japan. For the Chinese community, nationalism began as Chinese nationalism.

During the Japanese Occupation, Chinese nationalism morphed into Malayan nationalism, which was mostly Chinese-led and strongly supportive of China. After the war, Malayan nationalism hit a wall with the rise of Malay nationalism on the Peninsula. The original British proposal for a Malayan Union was changed to a federal structure protecting the special position of the rulers and the Malay race.

In Singapore, it was the Chinese-educated Left who posed the greatest threat to British rule. It was on that tiger that, Lee Kuan Yew, an English-educated Peranakan, rode to power. When the split between the People's Action Party (PAP) and the Barisan Sosialis took place in 1961 over the use of the Internal Security Council and the proposal for merger with Malaya, Lee Kuan Yew dismounted the tiger and the Chinese-educated Left became his principal opponents. He first had the British government to help him, followed by the Malaysian government. After Singapore became independent, revamping Chinese education in Singapore became part of his political consolidation and nation-building priority.

The founding of Nanyang University, or Nantah (南大), in 1955 marked the high point of Chinese education in Singapore. It was the first Chinese-medium university to be built outside China. Nantah would serve as the tertiary institution for Chinese high school graduates in Southeast Asia who were no longer able to go to China for university.

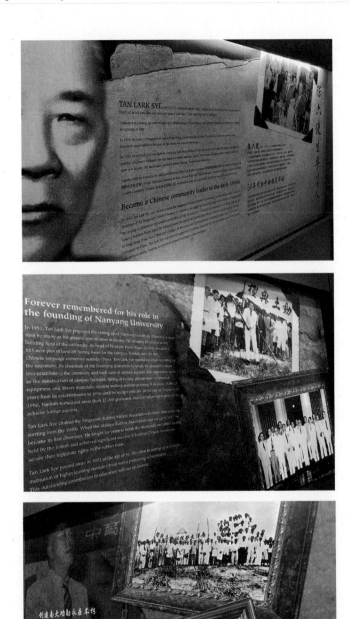

*Tribute to Tan Lark Sye for the leading role he played in establishing
Nanyang University at the Ee Hoe Ean Pioneers Memorial Hall*

Support for its establishment was widely felt as an affirmation of Chinese self-identity.

The proposal to set up Nantah was first made by Tan Lark Sye who played the most important role in its formation. The land it was situated on, originally intended for burial purposes, was donated by the Singapore Hokkien Huay Kuan. Big donations came from the business community and clan associations. Small donations came from everywhere including hawkers, trishaw riders and cabaret girls. Money also flowed in from the surrounding region, especially British Malaya. The donations from those who were ordinarily looked down upon counted the most.

Nantah was not only a tertiary institution; it was a symbol, one of anti-colonial politicals. Notwithstanding this, Governor William Goode carried out the official opening in 1958. In 1964, when Singapore was still part of Malaysia, Tan Lark Sye was accused of supporting communist activities and had his citizenship revoked.

With the growing importance of English to business and the economy, enrollment in Chinese-medium schools had been falling. At the time of Singapore's internal self-government in 1959, these schools made up slightly less than half of total student enrollment. After Singapore became independent in 1965, English became our common language, which encouraged even more Chinese parents to send their children to English-medium schools. Graduates of Nantah were not as employable as graduates of the University of Singapore and commanded generally lower salaries. By 1978, enrollment in Chinese-medium schools had fallen to 11% of total enrollment. Lee Kuan Yew's call for Nantah to switch to English as its medium of instruction was met with cynicism. His reasons were economic and practical. Many, however, saw in the proposal an additional political motive to root out his opposition.

In 1979, Lee Kuan Yew invited Professor Frederick Dainton, the Chancellor of The University of Sheffield, to study what was fast becoming an unsustainable position and make his recommendations. Dainton's proposal to merge Nantah and the University of Singapore into the National University of Singapore, with English as the principal language of instruction, was accepted. Nantah's last convocation, its 21st, was held on 16 August 1980. Low Thia Khiang was in one of the last Nantah classes that switched over. He has cited Nantah's closure as one of the reasons he entered politics. The last Chinese-medium high school shut in 1984, followed by the last Chinese-medium primary school in 1987.

For an entire generation of Chinese-educated Singaporeans, the end of Chinese-medium education was agonising. Many were not persuaded by Lee Kuan Yew's argument. They countered that it was the way the playing field had been tilted against the Chinese-educated that caused the decline in enrollment. However, had Singapore not made English the dominant language of administration then, it is unlikely our economy could have taken off the way it did.

Parents tended to be practical when it came to choosing the medium of instruction for their children. I think of my late mother, who chose Malay as my second language, because of the impending merger with Malaya. Had Singapore remained in Malaysia, Chinese-medium schools would have continued as private schools and remained an integral part of race-based politics. Singapore, after separation, was at a crossroads. Switching to Chinese as Singapore's dominant language after independence would have created a different Singapore and made our position in Southeast Asia untenable. China was then in the throes of the Cultural Revolution and supported Communist insurgencies in Southeast Asia. In 1966, Singapore adopted a bilingual policy, with English as the common language and language of administration. Malay remained the national language and the language for parade commands in the Singapore Armed Forces (SAF) and the Police.

Frustrated, the Barisan Sosialis boycotted the 1968 General Election, enabling the PAP to win all 51 parliamentary seats. It failed to win any seat when it returned to contest in 1972 and subsequent elections. In 1988, it dissolved and was absorbed into the Workers' Party. The charismatic leader of the Chinese-educated Left and founding leader of Barisan Sosialis, Lim Chin Siong, was arrested during Operation

Lee Kuan Yew and Lim Chin Siong

Coldstore in 1963. He suffered from depression during his detention and attempted suicide in 1969. He was then then released to further his studies in England. When he died in 1996, Lee Kuan Yew wrote:

> *"He and many of his comrades, graduates from the Chinese middle schools, taught my colleagues and me the meaning of dedication to a cause. They were prepared to sacrifice everything for their cause, and many did. Some lost their lives in the jungles, many were banished to China. Because of the standards of dedication they set, we, the English educated PAP leaders, had to set high standards of personal integrity and spartan lifestyles to withstand their political attacks."*

Lee Kuan Yew ended with these words:

> *"Like thousands of idealistic bright and promising young men and women of his generation, he has expended the best years of his life in the Malayan Communist Party's futile bid to overthrow the system in Malaya, including Singapore, and create a communist state — their ideal society where no man will exploit his fellow man, and each will give what he can, and receive what he needs. The tragedy was that they believed that communism as practised in the Soviet Union and China was then on their way towards this ideal state."*

Lee Kuan Yew's obituary note was carefully crafted to give his side of the story. Others have given theirs, as he knew they would. It will take time for this painful period in Singapore's history to be seen in perspective. Singapore's history of that period is bound up with the evolution of its Chineseness, even Lee Kuan Yew's own sense of being Chinese himself. The saga of Nantah is emblematic of this evolution.

Q: During and after your time in government, you talked about Nantah and the Nantah spirit. Is all this history now or, like Singapore's Chineseness, part of an evolving story?

It is important for Singapore's future that some closure should be brought to the history of that period. Some Nantah alumni have bitterly said that "our mother has died, there's no point talking about her any more". When Nantah and the Chinese schools were shut down, many teachers could not find good jobs. My calligraphy teacher, Tan Siah Kwee, from the 13th batch of Nantah graduates, told me how bookshops stopped selling writing brushes because the market had evaporated. For a period, he taught calligraphy with fountain pens.

Tan Siah Kwee was close to Pan Shou, the Secretary-General of Nantah, and edited his works after his death. He shared with me heartrending stories of Pan Shou's sadness and anger with me, including how, in 1958, the colonial government revoked his citizenship.

Legally speaking, Nantah was not shut down but merged with the University of Singapore into the National University of Singapore (NUS). However, Nantah alumni have no feelings for NUS. Nor do NUS students have any feeling for the old Nantah. Very few NUS students know that the three rings on their university crest came from the crest of the old Nanyang University. The attachment to the old Nantah is in the 'Nanyang' name and in its physical location, not to NUS. As a sop to leaders of the Chinese community, the Nanyang name was attached to a new teaching institution called Nanyang Technological Institute (NTI), which took over the old campus. In 1991, NTI became what is now Nanyang Technological University (NTU). In Chinese, the shortened name of the university became Lida (理大). It was an unusual abbreviation, made necessary because Nantah was by then no more.

Nanyang University

南洋大学

The crest of NUS is a fusion of the old Nanyang University and University of Singapore crests

As Minister for Information and the Arts, I understood the depth of feeling on the closure of Nantah and got the old Adminstration Block gazetted as a national monument. When Kenzō Tange redesigned the campus for NTI/U, the entrance was shifted to Jalan Bahar, leaving the old entrance arch as an island in a road intersection as a standalone relic. That, too, was gazetted a monument. The original characters for 南洋大學 were taken down in 1979. We did an extensive search but could not find them. I was dismayed to find out that someone from the National Arts Council took the liberty of writing new characters on the arch and insisted that the old ones be expunged. It seemed sacrilegious to me.

Replica of the old gate built near the Yunnan Garden in the current campus

Around that time, I had Lee Kuan Yew's agreement to have the abbreviated name, Lida, changed to Nantah. It was a delicate matter which I broached delicately with him over lunch. Once he indicated that he had no objections, I worked with Minister of State Dr Ker Sin Tze, NTU President Cham Tao Soon, Wee Cho Yaw, members of the Singapore Chamber of Commerce and Industry and Singapore Federation of Chinese Clan Associations, the Nantah Alumni Association headed by Chia Ban Seng and the Chinese newspapers to prepare the ground for the name change. Changing the abbreviated name of NTU to Nantah immediately associated it with Nanyang University and raised expectations that NTU would be re-named Nanyang University. That was my hope too, but it would need time. Just changing the abbreviated name was a sensitive matter which involved many parties and could have easily misfired. Chia Ban Seng played the critical role and persuaded Nantah alumni — not only in Singapore, but also those in Malaysia and elsewhere — to support it.

The name change took place in 1995 without too much controversy, although a few members of Parliament who were Nantah graduates, including Low Thia Khiang stated in Parliament that they did not see the point in making the change. In 1996, the alumni name roll of the old Nanyang University was transferred to NTU. Many saw that transfer as a return.

In 1997, Pan Shou requested to call on me. His citizenship had been restored by the PAP government in 1983. According to Tan Siah Kwee, Home Minister Chua Sian Chin played the critical role in arranging this. Tan Siah Kwee was awarded the Cultural Medallion in 1986 and the Meritorious Service Medal in 1994, becoming the first artist to receive it. In 1995, I launched a collection of his poetry at the Singapore Calligraphy Centre and met him for the first time.

When we met in 1997, Pan Shou wanted to see me over a proposal by NTU to confer him with an honorary doctorate. Should he agree? He was torn and wanted my guidance. He said that his contribution had been to Nanyang University, where he was Secretary-General, not to NTU. He had nothing to do with NTU. With tears streaming down his cheeks, he asked why we could not restore the old name. His only concern was over the name, for restoring it would mean that the old university did not die. Without the restoration of the name, there could be no continuity.

I listened with a heavy heart and said that his acceptance of the honorary degree would help in the process of eventually restoring the name. However, it could not be rushed and we had to establish consensus after careful preparation. I recalled how even shortening the name to Nantah took much effort. With some reluctance, he finally accepted NTU's conferment. At the ceremony in 1998, he called for the name restoration 'to quieten the hearts of many'.

Pan Shou passed away shortly after in February 1999. Hanging in the Singapore Calligraphy Centre is a 1985 painting by four famous artists. Pan Shou contributed a poem with poignant words about the future of Chinese language and culture in Singapore: 不死之蛇忽化龙. It meant the snake that would not die suddenly becomes a dragon.

葆芳落笔画寒松
不死之蛇忽化龙
关老竹枝黎老柏
双禽偕老雪霜冬
乙丑新粤诗人节雅集纪念　潘受题

The Nantah spirit is part of the spirit which created Singapore and made it what it is today. Remembering this in our education and culture gives us strength. For the Chinese-educated, to use the words of the former *Lianhe Zaobao* Editor-in-Chief Lim Jim Koon, it also means "silent endurance and perseverance in the face of difficulties (sometimes humiliation), the struggle for rightful status and due recognition in society, and a more enterprising spirit forced mainly by circumstances". The Nantah spirit has morphed into the Singapore spirit.

This painting in the Singapore Calligraphy Centre was executed by four artists in 1985. Pan Shou contributed the words 不死之蛇, meaning that the snake that would not die suddenly becomes a dragon. It was his hope that Chinese language and culture in Singapore would be revived.

In 2005, I launched Pan Shou's collection of poems at the Singapore Calligraphy Centre

Two pieces of calligraphy presented by Pan Shou to me

Q: Do you think that Nanyang University should be restored?

Yes. There are two aspects to this. One is the restoration of the name, which is important for a sense of continuity. It is emotionally necessary, as Pan Shou argued before he died. Doing so will help our society reconcile. Many families were caught up in the political struggles of Singapore's early history. Some suffered unjustly. Whether they were misguided is for history to judge eventually, but their motives were honourable. The other aspect is what Nanyang University should stand for looking forward.

Before Lee Hsien Loong assumed the premiership in 2004, he asked me for ideas to mark the change. I suggested the restoration of the Nanyang University name. I said that it would heal old wounds and open a new period of reconciliation under his leadership. His reaction was positive. The university leadership under President Su Guaning was enthusiastic, but did not prepare sufficiently for it. At an event in NTU to which Lee Kuan Yew was invited to speak, a couple of non-Singaporeans in the audience criticised him for the closure of the old university without taking into account the historical circumstances of that period. When Lee Kuan Yew subsequently heard of the proposal to restore the name of the university, he objected. I do not know if Lee Hsien Loong had informed Lee Kuan Yew of it beforehand. The name restoration could not be seen to be done out of pressure or weakness. It should not be interpreted as a reversal of historical verdict in a Chinese cultural context.

Lee Kuan Yew's memoirs went through many drafts before they were published. In some versions, he opposed the restoration of Nanyang University's name. When that section was finalized for printing, Cham Tao Soon, who had to run through the drafts on Nanyang University, told me excitedly that Lee Kuan Yew remained open to the name change.

Lee Kuan Yew never doubted the importance of Singapore's Chineseness or the critical role of the Chinese language. The challenge posed to him by the Chinese-educated Left was not a matter of culture or language per se, but the political activism of that segment of

Singapore's population which was pulled to China and Chinese communism and, of course, their opposition to him. When the decision to shut down Nanyang University and, with it, the eventual cessation of Chinese-medium education was made, he introduced Special Assistance Plan (SAP) schools to ensure that Chinese language and culture would be preserved. The first nine SAP schools had all been Chinese-medium schools previously. In the same year, he launched the first Speak Mandarin campaign. He pushed for Chinese Singaporeans to be bi-cultural and became the Founding Patron of Business China. Lee Kuan Yew persisted with his study of Chinese till his last days.

Without a continuing supply of graduates from Nanyang University, Singapore faced a growing shortage of younger Singaporeans with mastery of not only spoken and written Chinese, but also of Chinese history, literature and culture. This is already affecting leadership succession in many institutions, including political parties, government ministries, statutory boards, schools, newspapers, television, museums and the private sector. It has become too convenient to use English as the default language. Using Chinese for professional or business purposes has become arduous for many of our institutions.

Not many people can master two unrelated languages to the level of a university graduate. It requires huge effort to try, and for most people, it is either not possible or unnecessary. Our brains have not evolved for such a purpose. Mastery is more than fluency. Some of us are able to pick up other languages relatively easily, which is very useful for building bridges. From an evolutionary point of view, it is a useful ability. Fluency, however, is not enough for cultural transmission. There is a hard trade-off. If we want to master Chinese, this will come at the expense of English, and vice versa: if we want all Chinese Singaporeans to master English, it will be at the expense of Chinese.

Among younger Singaporean graduates, even those who went to SAP schools, their mastery of Chinese is significantly below that of graduates in China. As older generations of Chinese-educated Singaporeans retire, they willl leave a void in many institutions that is not being adequately filled. Immigrants can supplement our supply of local workers but they cannot replace them. The core must be Singaporean. Where there has been an over-dependence on foreigners to make up for a shortfall of local Chinese writers, new distortions arise because of a lack of an indigenous Singaporean perspective. National security agencies also worry that these institutions may be captured, wittingly or unwittingly, by China.

Looking 30 years ahead, China will be far the biggest economy in the world and among the most advanced technologically. China will be a very important part of our future. Naturally, a growing number of younger Singaporeans will study and work in China. We must expect some of our children to spend much of their school years in China with their parents. Singapore has also become an attractive home away from home for many Chinese (from mainland China, Hong Kong and Taiwan) because of Singapore's independence *and* Chineseness. Some of them will become our citizens. Their children will both have a strong command of spoken and written Chinese and be steeped in China's history and culture.

Chinese education in Singapore has to adjust to the emergence of a new and different world. The decline in enrollment in Chinese-medium schools was principally caused by the diminishing economic utility of the Chinese language in the past. As this trend is reversed, our education system needs to be revamped once again.

The level at which SAP schools have maintained Chinese education is insufficient for our future needs. We have no means today to replace the current Chinese cultural elite who are getting old. We cannot rely on imported talent because their sense of Singapore will not be deep. We need a Singapore core around which to accrete them. We should therefore consider making one of our polytechnics a 'SAP poly' and one of our universities a 'SAP university'. The mix of languages will evolve as has been happening in SAP schools. In this way, we will raise the bar for Chinese education in Singapore. Nonetheless, this will still not be enough. We need to send many more students to China for further

Chinese Literary Camp in 1998 co-organised by NTU and National Arts Council.
Bottom picture with NTU President Cham Tao Soon.

studies, as many as those going to the United States, United Kingdom and Australia.

Ngee Ann Polytechnic is a possible candidate for the SAP polytechnic. Ngee Ann College was established by Ngee Ann Kongsi at the Teochew Building along Tank Road in 1963, partly to compete with Nanyang University, which some Teochew community leaders like Lien Ying Chow saw as mainly a Hokkien initiative. The Kongsi was not wealthy at that time and could not keep Ngee Ann College going. A deal was then struck with the Ministry of Education (MOE) to take over it in return for which 75% of the Kongsi's annual surplus would be paid to the college. Its name was changed to Ngee Ann Polytechnic in 1982.

With the development of Ngee Ann City, the shopping mall and commercial development, the Kongsi's surplus soared. Only a part of the 75% now goes to the polytechnic, with the remainder allocated according to the Ministry's discretion. The Kongsi owns other land along Orchard Road, which will revert to it when the current tenants' leases expire, such as the Mandarin Hotel (whose leasehold will end in 40 years' time). Converting Ngee Ann Polytechnic into a SAP polytechnic is financially very doable. It will complement Hwa Chong Institution as a SAP junior college.

Singapore now has many universities. Making one of them a SAP university will enrich Singapore and enhance our connections with China and the Chinese world. The natural candidate for this is NTU. Restoring the old Nanyang University name when it is turned into a SAP university will help resolve a historical problem in a way which positions us for the future. Such a change has to be carefully managed. The support of stakeholders for the main direction is essential. Many details will have to be debated. A university which uses two languages as the mediums of instruction will not be easy to achieve, but it can be done. There are many examples in the world that can be studied.

Great universities have difficult beginnings. Peking University was established in 1898 during the 100-day reform period of the late Qing. However, it celebrates its anniversary on 4 May to align with the

Speaking at Madrasah Aljunied. I hope it will one day be the nucleus of our own Islamic college. Its historical links to Al-Azhar in Cairo are invaluable.

movement in 1919 because of the critical role the latter played in mobilising the spirit of an entire nation. As China grows, Peking University will become one of the world's top universities.

The establishment of Nanyang University in 1955 was part of a great movement which created an independent Singapore. The Nantah spirit should be recaptured for Singapore's future. It is much better for the bulk of Singapore's future Chinese-language elite to be educated in Nanyang University than in universities in mainland China or Taiwan.

Q: How will Singapore's other racial groups react to this?

There are bound to be misunderstandings, as there were over SAP schools. We should, however, be able to persuade the great majority that having greater internal diversity is in our collective interest. Singapore is stronger if we are more diverse, but only provided that there is strong team spirit. Within the team, we should have experts in different languages and cultures, not just in Chinese. Depending on need, we can alter the composition of our team to achieve the best result.

For example, Singapore needs an Islamic college which can provide higher training for the bulk of our imams. We should send some overseas, like to Al-Azhar University, but not all, which is the current situation. Madrasah Aljunied is a good candidate to be turned into a college because of its existing links to Al-Azhar. Singapore's Hadhrami community has been holding classes in Arabic. We should also consider establishing a West Asian department in one of our universities to complement the Middle East Institute and help revive our historical connections to that part of the world. Arabic should not only be taught in madrasahs.

When I was Minister for Information and the Arts, the Nanyang Academy of Fine Arts (NAFA) and LASALLE College of the Arts were private institutions which constantly suffered from lack of funding. NAFA was established in 1938 by Chinese artists who were determined to create Nanyang-style Chinese art with Nanyang characteristics. That remains as NAFA's ethos today and it retains its strong links to China.

I was a strong supporter of Brother McNally from the start, becoming a Patron of LASALLE since 1988. He had me officiate at one of the graduation ceremonies before MOE recognised its educational status.

The award-winning LASALLE campus at Queen Street. The Street and Building Names Board only agreed to having a road named after Brother McNally after I appealed to Prime Minister Lee Hsien Loong.

However, it also attracts many non-Chinese students and teaching is carried out in both English and Chinese.

LASALLE, which was founded by Brother Joseph McNally, has a different character. Its orientation is more Western. Many students are Malay, whom Brother told me have a gift for design. I was involved in LASALLE's development over many years and remain a Patron of the college today. When Tan Chin Nam informed me of the good news that MOE was prepared to subvent students for qualifying courses at the same level as polytechnic students, I was overjoyed, but also cautioned him that this funding arrangement should not cause both institutions to be homogenised. I was conscious of the bureaucratic instinct to standardise and rationalise. Public funding should not snuff out the creative spirit of both colleges. The incorporation of NAFA and LASALLE into a new arts university should be based on the principle of 'unity in diversity', not 'from many, one'.

Q: What about security concerns?

As a small city-state in the heart of Southeast Asia, there will always be security concerns. We must expect that all the major powers will want to have agents of influence in Singapore. We should worry if they have no interest in us. Our worry is not foreigners wanting to influence us openly — those we can manage — but activities which are covert. Our security agencies play an important role in ensuring that we are not played without our knowing.

Our deeper resilience comes from our own unity as Singaporeans. Here, the role played by educational institutions in the formation of young minds is critical. It is the same role that Chinese-medium schools once played in shaping young minds in the last century. Switzerland is an inspiration to us in this. Language diversity is embedded in their system of education. During the Second World War, Nazi Germany surrounded Switzerland on all sides. Despite being majority German themselves, the Swiss stayed neutral and were armed to the teeth. But, of course, Switzerland has a much longer history than we do.

I know Singaporeans who have lived and worked for many years in China. Despite their familiarity with China, they remain Singaporean at heart. For people who grow up here, Singapore will always have a special place in their hearts. Most ethnic Chinese in Southeast Asia who returned to China because they had to flee or because they were banished were never fully accepted in China. They were never fully trusted and never felt completely at home there. Some relocated from the mainland to Hong Kong. There will always be a few who sell their loyalty for money, but that should not taint the many. Let the security agencies deal with them.

Among ex-political detainees and their families in Singapore's history, deep grievances still linger. Many do acknowledge Singapore's progress under Lee Kuan Yew. While still in government, I got to know Lim Chin Joo, Lim Chin Siong's younger brother. He was detained for many years under the Internal Security Act but did well as a lawyer after his release. When retaining Aljunied looked shaky during the 2011 election, I asked for his support. He replied with some pain that he could not because of what had been done to him. Later, when I was preparing to stand for Presidency, he agreed to help, which touched me greatly. Reconciliation with the Old Left in Singapore will make Singapore a better and stronger society.

Chineseness in Singapore has to be Chineseness with Singaporean characteristics, which internalises, first, the instinct to embrace non-Chinese members of the Singapore family and, second, the understanding that we are politically sovereign in our relations with China. This is not a slogan; it is a matter of life and death. While in the SAF, I read *The 6th Overseas*

An old book describing Singapore as the 6th overseas Chinese state. Such a conception of Singapore will lead to tragedy.

Chinese State, written by Sie Hok Tjwan, an Indonesian Chinese. He identified five overseas Chinese states in Southeast Asian history — Palembang (at the end of Srivijaya), Demak (Central Java), Thaikong and Lara Sin-ta-kiou (West Kalimantan) Lanfang (West Kalimantan), and Singapore. The first five did not last more than one to two hundred years.

For Singapore to endure and to be an inspiration to others, we cannot just be another overseas Chinese state which appears and disappears, but one which represents much more than just being Chinese. Chinese education in Singapore must reflect our position in Southeast Asia.

CHAPTER 14

Managing Singapore's Political Relations with China

George Yeo recounts his involvement in managing Singapore's political relations with China during his term as Minister for Foreign Affairs.

Q: Under your watch as Minister for Foreign Affairs from 2004–2011, Singapore's political relations with China were good. How was the crisis in bilateral relations which followed Deputy Prime Minister (DPM) Lee Hsien Loong's visit to Taiwan in 2004 overcome?

When I became Minister for Foreign Affairs in August 2004, Singapore's relations with China were bad.

In July of that year, Lee Hsien Loong, who was then DPM, visited Taiwan. It was to be his last visit to Taiwan before becoming Prime Minister (PM). Despite assurances by Taipei that publicity would be kept low-key, Taiwanese television and newspapers carried extensive reports about the visit. Beijing was shocked and furious, and put a freeze on bilateral contact. Although Beijing did note Singapore's military relationship with Taiwan — albeit without explicitly agreeing to it — when diplomatic relations were established in 1990, that relationship was supposed to be kept discreet and confidential. Otherwise, it would undermine conditions that China placed on other countries with regard to Taiwan. Bilateral relations took a sudden nosedive and reached their lowest point in years.

This was the first issue I had to deal with as Minister for Foreign Affairs. It could not have come at a worse time for me personally because my youngest son, Frederick, had had a second relapse of his leukaemia just a month earlier. As a result of two rounds of chemotherapy he had previously received, each lasting two years, he developed a second kind of leukaemia in addition to his original condition. It could only be treated with a bone marrow transplant. The prognosis was poor. None of his three siblings was a bone marrow match, and there was no good match in Singapore or Hong Kong either. Finally, we found a match through the Tzu Chi Foundation in Taiwan.

My entire family uprooted ourselves to be with him in Memphis, Tennessee, where St Jude Children's Research Hospital is located. The hospital required that children be accompanied by their mothers throughout because the transplant process is tough. In one phase of treatment, Fred was awakened every hour to pee so that the drug did not damage his bladder. During another, my wife had to bathe him every few hours to prevent another drug from hurting his skin. Family support was critical. I stayed alone at home to supervise an extension of our house in Changi so that if or when Fred came back, there would be enough space for everyone. His immunity was expected to be low for a while and needed the air to be HEPA-filtered.

About two weeks after becoming Minister for Foreign Affairs, I remember receiving a curious dispatch from Minister Tharman Shanmugaratnam, who was then in Liaoning for a bilateral meeting — one of the few meetings the Chinese did not cancel or postpone. In order to facilitate business development, Singapore maintained bilateral economic and business councils with some Chinese provinces. The Singapore side would normally be represented by an ethnic Chinese minister. Tharman was my deputy for a short while when I was Minister for Trade and Industry. When a council was established for Liaoning, I persuaded Tharman to represent Singapore. It was good for him, and good for Singapore, to field a non-Chinese as co-chairman.

After the bilateral council meeting concluded, the Chinese side asked Tharman for a party-to-party meeting. This was most unusual. Unlike China, the People's Action Party (PAP), as a party, was never involved in official foreign relations. Something was afoot. The Ministry of Foreign Affairs (MFA) asked Tharman to proceed. Trade officials on both sides excused themselves when Tharman, now representing the PAP, met Minister Wang Jiarui from the Communist Party of China (CPC) International Liaison Department. Nothing substantive was discussed. What *was* significant was a message which was conveyed that China's Foreign Minister Li Zhaoxing sent his good wishes to Professor S. Jayakumar, my predecessor, and to me. China was sending a signal that it wanted a resolution. In their thinking, since we tied the knot, we would have to untie it.

I then made a request to meet Li Zhaoxing in New York on the sideline of the United Nations General Assembly (UNGA). We said that the meeting could be confidential if the Chinese side wished. Their Foreign Ministry agreed to the meeting and confirmed that they wanted it kept confidential. Unfortunately, we could not find an early date for a meeting in New York. In the end, I made my speech at the UNGA, flew to Memphis to see Fred and my family, and then returned to New York for the meeting.

To signal that there was absolutely no shift in Singapore's One-China policy, I incorporated a paragraph on Taiwan in my UNGA speech. I did not say anything new, merely reaffirmed an old position, but it was the first time that we had stated it at the UNGA. Although Taiwan could not be in the UN compound, it always had a large delegation in New York during the UNGA to lobby for its cause.

The Taiwanese Foreign Minister took great umbrage at my speech and criticised Singapore. He used a crude Hokkien phrase to dismiss Singapore as being small and insignificant. As for me, he reserved a vulgar choice of words, also in Hokkien. I was interviewed by Singapore media on my reaction to his graphic remarks. In sorrow, rather than anger, I replied that his words were unfortunate and in no way reflected

*Taiwan Foreign Minister
Mark Chen dismissing
Singapore as a little piece
of booger*

the good unofficial relations between the people of Singapore and Taiwan. His strong reaction in fact strengthened Singapore's position before my meeting with Li Zhaoxing. My signal to China was subtle; Taiwan's Foreign Minister had amplified it for me.

In Memphis, I put up a brave front before Fred, my wife, mother-in-law and children. Inside, I was devastated. Fred told me innocently that before he had total body irradiation, Mummy had signed a form. It affirmed she knew that, despite the irradiation, the statistical chances of survival were only 20%. Doctors subsequently told us that his chances were more like 10%. Returning to New York, I blanked out all that and concentrated on the task at hand.

At the meeting, Li Zhaoxing insisted that Singapore adhere to the One-China policy. Singapore had to respect China's core interests regarding Taiwan. I affirmed that there was absolutely no change in our policy and stated that Singapore also had a core interest in military training in Taiwan, which I hoped China would also respect. He neither agreed nor disagreed with my statement, which was enough. By not disagreeing, he was implicitly saying that China did not require our discontinuing military ties with Taiwan as a condition for reconciliation.

The meeting went on for half an hour. It got less tense as we went along, with the both of us making the same points in different ways. It ended well with Li Zhaoxing proposing a toast with Evian in place of alcohol. As we left the room, he held me by the elbow. He repeated that Singapore must respect China's core interests. My parting words were that if China also respected Singapore's core interests, we would find a way out. My security officer, Anthony Tan, who knew about the importance of the meeting, was waiting anxiously outside the meeting room. Observing the light banter on our way out, as we walked to our next meeting, he asked, "Good meeting, sir?".

The negotiations took many months in Beijing. Ambassador Chin Siat-Yoon worked doggedly with the Chinese. China did not want a repeat of what had happened during DPM Lee's visit. On our part, we were determined not to agree to any weakening of our unofficial military relations with Taiwan. I knew that China's concern was not our military training in Taiwan per se, which had gone on for many years, but how publicity of that relationship affected its position on Taiwan vis-à-vis the rest of the world. Gradually and painfully, we reached a settlement.

The Chinese did not let up on the pressure they put on us during the negotiations. When Lee Kuan Yew visited Shanghai for a meeting of an international advisory board, the Chinese did not extend the usual courtesies to him. Ambassador Chin did not let it pass. He told the Chinese Foreign Ministry that like in Sichuan opera, China had suddenly 'changed faces' in their dealings with Lee Kuan Yew, whom they knew had gone out of his way to be helpful to China in the past.

Till his last days, Lee Kuan Yew never forgot how the Chinese acted. Ambassador Chin was an excellent negotiator and played a critical role in putting bilateral relations back on track. Second Permanent Secretary Bilahari Kausikan was pleased with the way negotiations were conducted and, in his inimitable way, commented that Ambassador Chin was born for this task.

The settlement was due to be confirmed in a meeting between Lee Hsien Loong (who was by then Prime Minister) and Hu Jintao at the 2004 meeting of Asia-Pacific Economic Cooperation (APEC) leaders in Santiago. I had a preparatory meeting with Li Zhaoxing before that to finalise little details. When PM Lee and Hu sat down facing each other, the former reiterated the reasons for his visit to Taiwan.

The Chinese side had not expected him to do this. I saw Hu Jintao's normally expressionless face tighten. He countered that there was a larger picture which Singapore ought to be aware of. For a brief moment, I thought that the carefully-crafted settlement would be undone. Happily, neither side pressed things further, and both sides quickly adjourned to take photographs. That photo was to announce to the world that bilateral relations were good again.

I learned a lot from this entire episode: both how China conducts its diplomacy, and how Singapore should conduct its own with China. Years later, over the Terrex issue, I saw this state of affairs play out all over again when Hong Kong (obviously under China's instruction) impounded Singapore Armed Forces (SAF) armored cars carried by a ship from Kaohsiung. Things were not as serious, but the principles involved were the same.

I thought it significant that China chose not to impound the vehicles in Xiamen or Shenzhen — the ship being a coastal tramp — but in Hong Kong instead. China's core concern was the South China Sea; ours was international maritime law governing freedom of movement. Professor Tommy Koh played a major role in putting the United Nations Convention on the Law of the Sea (UNCLOS) together in the 1970s. There was no need for a clash. A more careful reiteration of positions enabled a way out to be found eventually. Playing on Singapore's Chineseness, Hong Kong, no doubt on Beijing's instructions, released the Terrex armoured cars in time for them to return home for Chinese New Year.

Q: How did you view our relations with China? What were your interactions with your Chinese counterparts like?

Over my years in government, I interacted with counterparts from different Chinese ministries. As it was obvious that China would become more important to our future, I prioritised that relationship in every ministry I headed.

In my early years in government, Lee Kuan Yew often took me along for his visits to China. I saw how he developed intimate relations with Chinese leaders while maintaining the separateness and dignity of Singapore's own position.

Before he handed over the premiership to Goh Chok Tong in November 1990, Lee Kuan Yew made his last visit to China as Singapore's Prime Minister. That visit included a side trip to Xinjiang. Our Ürümqi itinerary included a visit to a shopping centre. Xinjiang was relatively underdeveloped at the time and the visit must have been included to give a boost to the local economy, or perhaps there was Singaporean investment in it. However, Mr and Mrs Lee wanted to rest instead and asked the rest of us to go ahead for the visit. With us in the delegation was fellow Member of Parliament Davinder Singh, tall and distinguished-looking with his full beard and turban. As he stood in front of big banners welcoming the Singapore Prime Minister, local onlookers at the shopping centre thought that Davinder was the Prime Minister, since he looked the most distinguished. We chuckled merrily to ourselves, but I am not sure if Davinder relished the sudden attention.

I was surprised that the road signs in Xinjiang were in Chinese, Roman and Arabic characters. A local official explained that the restoration of Uighur names and the use of Arabic characters took place after the CPC took over Xinjiang from the Kuomintang government. China is a big and complicated country.

In January 1991, Lee Kuan Yew asked me to be his notetaker for two private meetings which took place in quick succession at the Istana. The first was with United States (US) President George Bush Senior and

In January 1992, within a few days, Lee Kuan Yew saw first US President George Bush Senior and then Chinese President Yang Shangkun. I was the notetaker for both meetings.

the second was with Chinese President Yang Shangkun.

It was not long after the Tiananmen Incident in June 1989. That incident was greatly exaggerated and misrepresented by the international media as a 'massacre'. It was only years later that I learned that in fact no one was killed on Tiananmen Square itself, that the tank did not roll over the protester who stood in front of it and that some demonstrators had acted violently before the People's Liberation Army (PLA) cracked down. That said, many hundreds of demonstrators were killed. A Taiwanese reporter was shot with a handgun in the back of his neck. The bullet came out through his mouth, knocking out some teeth, but miraculously missed his spinal column and major blood vessels. Who shot him remains unknown. Miraculously, he survived and became a friend; I later arranged for him to interview Lee Kuan Yew twice.

Deng Xiaoping had ordered the crackdown, but was determined that China's reform and opening up should get back on track after two years. Among developed countries, Japan was the first to advocate re-engagement with China. Bush Senior, too, was sympathetic, but Congress was not easily persuaded. He asked Lee Kuan Yew to pass a message to Yang Shangkun: he needed China's help to convince Congress that China's most-favoured-nation status should be renewed. Yang Shangkun, who was completely at ease with himself, listened carefully. Lee Kuan Yew advised China to get onto the General Agreement on Trade and Tariffs (GATT), the precursor to the World Trade Organization (WTO), as early as possible. At that time, there was probably no one else in the world who could have acted as an intermediary between the top leaders of those two great powers.

As Minister for Foreign Affairs, I worked with Li Zhaoxing, Yang Jiechi and Dai Bingguo. I was able to develop some degree of a personal relationship with them because of Lee Kuan Yew's reputation and what Singapore represented in China's eyes.

Li Zhaoxing was warm, with a firm handshake that sometimes threatened to dislocate my arm. He could be blunt but was never rude. I remember once calling on him in Beijing and finding him very upset, as the Japanese government had announced the day before that it would be charging some Chinese fishermen in a Japanese court for intruding into the Diaoyu (Senkaku) waters. After repeated protests by the Chinese, Japan relented and let the fishermen go. Not long afterwards, Japan nationalised the little group of islands, giving the reason that it was to

With Foreign Minister Li Zhaoxing at Pulau Ubin

prevent right-wingers, led by Shintaro Ishihara, from buying them over. The current tension over those islands can be traced back to this.

China was outraged, claiming that Japan had changed the status quo agreed upon between Deng Xiaoping and then-Japanese Prime Minster Kakuei Tanaka back in 1972, when the two countries established diplomatic relations. Taiwan, too, was outraged, and several boatloads of Taiwanese landed on the islands in protest.

Li was also keenly interested in how Singapore remembered its experience of the Japanese Occupation during the Second World War. On a visit to Singapore after he stepped down as Foreign Minister, I invited him and his wife to Pulau Ubin for a hike. My wife and two of my boys came along. Li liked climbing trees and invited my boys and me to join him in clambering up some mangrove roots. He must have thought poorly of my feeble attempt.

I first met Yang Jiechi at a three-day forum in Pebble Beach hosted by Senator Bill Bradley. He was then China's Ambassador to the US and spoke fluent English. I met him from time to time as he rose up the ranks of China's foreign policy establishment. As Vice Minister, he spent a few days in Singapore under MFA's Distinguished Visitor Programme. At a lunch I hosted just for the two of us, we had a relaxed discussion in which we exchanged views on many issues. I can never forget his remark to me that both countries shared considerable mutual affection for each other. It was not something I could say to him without coming across as presumptuous.

One or two weeks after that meeting, it was announced that he would become China's next Foreign Minister. The diplomatic community in Singapore thought that MFA had inside knowledge of his appointment. We did not. The timing was a pleasant surprise to us too, but everyone knew that he was in the running to take over from Li.

At one Association of Southeast Asian Nations (ASEAN) Regional Foreign Ministers Meeting, there was a sharp altercation between Secretary of State Hillary Clinton and Yang. This was at the time when the US announced its 'Pivot to Asia' strategy. The American newspapers

Foreign Minister now State Councillor Yang Jiechi. I first met him at Senator Bill Bradley's gathering in Pebble Beach when he was China's Ambassador to the US.

reported that Yang had remarked, apropos of China's relationship with ASEAN countries in the South China Sea, that while China was big, other countries were small, and that was just how it was — all the while glaring at me. Yang was accused of browbeating me. If he were, I would have felt it — which I did not in the slightest. In fact, the day before, I had a bilateral meeting with him during which he might have been rehearsing some of the points he was going to make the following day, including flinging a pencil onto the table.

Foreign Minister Dai Bingguo was Li's deputy during the latter's term as Foreign Minister, although Dai, being party secretary of the Foreign Ministry, was senior to Li in the party hierarchy. When Yang Jiechi took

With State Councillor Dai Bingguo at EFC. Dai chairs the International Advisory Council of which I am a member.

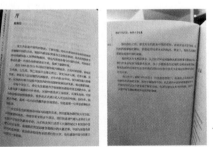

Dai Bingguo's foreword for the Chinese edition of my book

Dai Bingguo inscribing his book for me

At Peking University's annual North Pavilion Dialogue

over as Foreign Minister, Dai became State Councillor for Foreign Affairs. I had met him many times and liked his modesty and his informal, even self-deprecatory, style. After I left office, he got me involved in two activities: the Northern Pavilion Dialogue at Peking University, which meets every year to discuss strategic affairs, and the annual Eco Forum Global (EFG) at Guiyang as a member of the International Advisory Council he chairs.

Dai himself is a Tujia minority from Guizhou. When the mainland Chinese edition of my book, *George Yeo on Bonsai, Banyan, and the Tao*, was published in China, I requested him to write a special foreword for it. He agreed even though he had never done this before.

The Secretary-General of EFG is my old friend from Suzhou, Zhang Xinsheng. China has written the objective of creating an ecological civilisation into its Constitution. It is an unprecedented commitment by a fifth of humanity to live in harmony with nature. Much of the world is still unaware of this.

Wang–Koo talks in 1993

Xi–Ma talks in 2015
Photo credit: 總統府, https://www.flickr.com/photos/presidentialoffice/22655287560/.

Q: How should we manage the Taiwan issue in our relations with the mainland?

We have always had a clear position on Taiwan. Chiang Ching-kuo knew Singapore's stand when he allowed the Singapore Armed Forces to train there in the 1970s. Lee Kuan Yew told him that we had a One-China policy, and when diplomatic relations were established with Beijing in 1990, the flag and crest of the Republic of China in Singapore would have to be taken down. As Singapore's relations with Taiwan, including defence links, are unofficial, form has to reflect the substance. While there were misunderstandings with the mainland from time to time, as our core position never changed, it was always possible to bring relations back on track. Singapore's special relationship with Taiwan has to be managed with great discipline and we must be mindful of the larger picture and the ups and downs of cross-straits relations.

Singapore's Chineseness places us in a unique position vis-à-vis cross-straits relations. It is not for us to seek a role as cross-straits relations are a family matter, and we are not part of said family. We are, however, a well-intentioned relative, and cannot refuse to play a helpful role when requested to by both sides. Both the People's Republic of China and Taiwan acknowledge the historic role played by Dr Sun Yat-sen and are fully aware of Singapore's role in helping him bring about the 1911 Revolution and supporting the anti-Japanese resistance on the mainland. The latter led to the slaughter of tens of thousands of young Chinese men in Singapore during the Japanese Occupation. The Sun Yat Sen Nanyang Memorial Hall — what was for years called the Sun Yat Sen Villa — is visited by leaders from both sides of the Taiwan Straits.

After the 1992 Consensus, Wang Daohan and Koo Chen-fu met in Singapore. It was a historic moment for cross-straits relations. In November 2015, Xi Jinping met Ma Ying-jeou in Singapore as an equal, the first time Beijing had done so with a leader of Taiwan. One brought Guizhou Maotai, the other Kinmen Kaoliang — both equally strong spirits. (I later heard from Shangri-La's Kay Kuok that the bill was split 50-50.)

Xi's bold move was to pave a road for Tsai Ing-wen's ascent to office. Ma was already stepping down and China knew that Tsai was going to be the next President. That road is not a superhighway but nor is it bad for Taiwan's future. That the Wang–Koo talks and, more significantly, the Xi–Ma talks, were held in Singapore and not anywhere else in the world is because of the special relationship which Singapore has with both Mainland China and Taiwan.

At the June 2001 APEC Trade Ministers' Meeting in Shanghai, I tried to launch bilateral free trade negotiations on the side with Taiwan, which is a member of APEC. I drafted a few sentences which carefully avoided politics and stuck to the WTO provisions, which allowed for separate customs territories to enter into free trade arrangements. Taipei wanted to politicise the launch and counterproposed a lengthy statement, which was a non-starter.

Later, when cross-straits relations had significantly improved under Ma Ying-jeou, we began negotiations with China's acquiescence. The agreement took effect in 2014 under a carefully-agreed name which took the mainland's concerns into account: the Agreement between Singapore and the Separate Customs Territory of Taiwan, Penghu, Kinmen and Matsu on Economic Partnership (ASTEP). Recalling Confucius' dictum: if names are not correct, language is not in accordance with the truth of things; if language is not in accordance with the truth of things, affairs cannot be carried on to success (名不正，则言不顺，言不顺，则事不成).

When APEC was launched in Canberra in 1989, China did not join as a member because of the Tiananmen Incident. Lee Hsien Loong, who was then the Minster for Trade and Industry, led the Singapore delegation. I attended as Minister of State representing the Ministry of Foreign Affairs. The APEC member countries knew that China's inclusion was necessary, but also wanted Hong Kong and Taiwan to participate. This was called 'the three-China problem'.

A solution was found by making APEC a meeting of economies in the Asia-Pacific without any mention of countries. Details were

APEC Ministerial Meeting in Singapore in 1990. On my right is US Secretary of State Jim Baker. Next to him is my old friend, Under Secretary of State Robert Zoellick.

hammered out the following year in Seoul on Hong Kong's and Taiwan's representation. There would be no state insignia displayed, no flags flown. Taiwan was to be referred to as Chinese Taipei. If political matters needed to be discussed, the members would have to do so separately outside the APEC umbrella without Taiwan. It was during these early few years of APEC that I got to know Indonesia's Ali Alatas, the US' Robert Zoellick (Secretary Jim Baker's deputy) and Australia's Gareth Evans, who was a strong proponent of APEC. US leadership was indispensable to the endeavour. Unlike US policy today, which sees China as a strategic rival, US policy then was to keep the Asia-Pacific united (under its leadership).

At the third APEC meeting in Bangkok, China was represented by Li Lanqing, Taiwan by Vincent Siew and Hong Kong by Brian Chau. I sat down with all three at an open lunch which had not been specially planned; things just flowed that way. The atmosphere was amiable. For me, it was a moment for the history books: the three Chinas sitting together for the first time, members of one Chinese family, and I, a relative, joining in. All three also became good friends.

Unveiling of the Berlin Wall with Chancellor Helmut Kohl's message in December 2009. China objected to it being part of the APEC Leaders' Meeting.

Q: How do we maintain our independence from China?

Friedrich Engels said that freedom is the recognition of necessity. As a small country, we have to deal with the world as it is, not what we want it to be. China has its own nature. Understanding that nature gives us more freedom of manoeuvre; ignorance of that nature causes self-injury. Let me illustrate with two examples.

In 2009, Singapore hosted the APEC Leaders' Summit. Apart from the usual agenda, I was working on a side project. APEC had been launched some 20 years ago by then, at the same time when the Berlin Wall came down. An American friend of mine had loaned me a piece of the Berlin Wall, which the National Parks Board (NParks) installed in a small enclosure at one end of Bedok Reservoir in my constituency. Through my officials, we proposed that the APEC leaders assemble for a side event at Bedok Reservoir to launch the Berlin Wall enclosure and mark the end of the Cold War.

I was rather pleased with my own proposal and thought that no one could possibly object to it. It had the further advantage of helping me politically in Aljunied GRC. However, the Chinese Foreign Ministry was aghast. For them, the fall of the Berlin Wall had led to the collapse of Communism in the Soviet Union, which was not cause for celebration. A senior Chinese foreign official threatened that if this event was part of the APEC agenda, President Hu Jintao would not come to Singapore.

My staff reported the threat to me sheepishly, afraid I would be disappointed. My reply was immediate: this Berlin Wall idea was not essential at all. Just drop it. PM Lee learned of my disappointment and, as a consolation, agreed to be the guest of honour for the opening of the enclosure.

Around 1997, the Cabinet was informed that China had launched a communications satellite into orbit, next to a slot belonging to us, without prior consultation. Under Intelsat regulations, we had to de-conflict frequencies so that the satellites would not interfere with each other's transmissions. China refused to discuss the matter. We decided

Lee Kuan Yew bowing before Deng Xiaoping

Lee Kuan Yew and Xi Jinping unveiling Deng Xiaoping's bust by the Singapore River

to launch ours anyway and accept severe mutual interference. China understood our message: if they tried to force a win–lose outcome on us, everyone would end up in the lose–lose quadrant. After a while, they disciplined their own transmissions so that our satellites stopped interfering with each other. It is sometimes easier to manage a problem discreetly without media publicity.

When Deng Xiaoping died, Hong Kong Chief Executive Tung Chee-hwa bowed deeply before Deng's portrait. In Singapore, Lee Kuan Yew also bowed but not as deeply. Although he thought highly of Deng, he was conscious that respect should not be mistaken for subservience or subordination. At China's 40th anniversary of reform and opening up in 2018, Lee Kuan Yew was listed as one of the 10 foreign friends who contributed most to China's development.

Q: Can Singapore be an intermediary between China and the US?

We cannot ask to play this role, but as we are friends with both, it is natural that our views will be sought from time to time. We should always try to be a peacemaker.

When I was a visiting scholar at Peking University in 2011 after leaving office, I was invited to speak at the PLA National Defence University. I did not know it was a closed campus and the students, all fairly senior officers, wore military uniform. I was in jeans and carrying a backpack and was discomfited by the students saluting me.

I had been asked to speak on US–China relations from a Singapore perspective, which I was happy to do. I remember being asked about our air and naval bases being used by the US military: would Singapore welcome China to use them too? Of course, I said, which elicited loud applause. I was also asked about Obama's 'Pivot to the East' strategy and the stationing of US marines in Darwin. My reply was that, while Australia is increasingly dependent on trade with China, when core strategic interests are affected, China must always assume that Australia will be with the US. A visit to the war museum in Canberra would make this clear; both countries had shed much blood together. It was a good session and I was flattered that many students came up to take pictures with me.

I have also been involved in an initiative called "Understanding China", organised by Zheng Bijian from the China Institute for Innovation and Development Strategy and Nicolas Berggruen and Nathan Gardels from the Berggruen Institute in the US. Many former

Lecture to PLA officers at China's National Defence University in Beijing in December 2011

leaders of various countries like Ernesto Zedillo of Mexico, Gordon Brown from the UK and Gerhard Schröder from Germany are also involved. China gives it top-level attention and there is usually a meeting with either Xi Jinping or Li Keqiang.

Zheng Bijian of China Institute for Innovation and Development Strategy

Zheng Bijian in 1999
Photo credit: Ministry of Information, Communications and the Arts Collection, courtesy of National Archives of Singapore.

Nicolas Berggruen of Berggruen Institute working for a better understanding between China and the US

Q: You must have met Xi Jinping. What was your impression of him?

I saw him a number of times at bilateral and multilateral meetings in Singapore and China. On an official visit to China in 2009, I called on him when he was Vice President. He was pleased with my visiting Tibet after Beijing.

When he became General Secretary of the CPC in 2012, he identified growing corruption as the greatest threat to both the CPC and China. No one expected him to be able to reverse the trend. Chinese society has a tendency towards corruption because of Confucian values that an individual should make distinctions in relationships. Gift-giving as an expression of *li* (礼) can easily become bribery.

Shortly after Standing Committee member Zhou Yongkang was arrrested in 2014, I spoke about the significance of what Xi was doing at the Singapore Summit, which was jointly sponsored by the Economic Development Board, Monetary Authority of Singapore, Temasek and GIC. I had been asked by PM Lee to chair the Summit, which was launched in 2012, after I left government the year before. I did this for five years.

In my opening address in September 2014, I said that China was doing surgery on a cancer in its own brain. I was perhaps too blunt and mentioned too many names. Chinese delegates at the gathering protested to Ho Ching, who fed their reactions back to me. Some also complained to Robert Kuok, who pleaded with me to stop talking about China. When the official transcript of my unscripted speech was released, I removed the more offending bits.

To me, Xi Jinping's move to reduce corruption in China is his greatest achievement thus far. After cleaning up the public security apparatus at the top, he focused his attention on the PLA and other institutions with a relentlessness which shocked the Chinese establishment. The opening lines of *Romance of the Three Kingdoms* talk about the cycles of empire. Xi has prolonged the current cycle through his actions. Without

With Xi Jinping in 2009

his predecessor, Hu Jintao, clearing the way for Xi's early consolidation of power by refusing to hang on to the Chairmanship of the Central Military Commission, Xi might not have succeeded.

❖

CHAPTER 15

Singapore's Economic and Cultural Relations with China

In this chapter, George Yeo recounts his role in improving economic and cultural relations with China.

Q: What was the backdrop to our cooperation with China on the Suzhou Industrial Park?

After the Tiananmen Incident, Deng Xiaoping wanted China to get back on track with reform and opening up. He was not happy when this was not done by the fall of 1991, two years after that. He was then already 88 years old. Sensing he had to make a final push before he grew too frail, Deng went on his famous southern tour in early 1992.

In Zhuhai, he called Hong Kong business leaders over for meetings. In one of his speeches, he was reported to have said that when it comes to social management, China should strive to overtake Singapore. When we received news of what Deng said, we wondered whether they were casual mutterings from an old man. We did not realise then that his words had the same effect as the Pope speaking *ex cathedra*. A few hundred delegations visited Singapore that year.

China's system is centralised. By the time an instruction from the centre reaches small towns, the original signal has been amplified many times. The old slogans were "In agriculture, learn from Dazhai" and

苏州工业园区是一项宏大和史无前例的
两国政府合作计划。

——李光耀，2004年6月9日

Suzhou Industrial Park is a grand, unprecedented
cooperation plan between the governments of the
two countries.

Lee Kwan Yew, Jun. 9, 2004

新加坡的社会秩序算是好的，他们管得
严，我们应当借鉴他们的经验，而且比
他们管得更好。

——邓小平．1992年春

"The social order in Singapore can be reckoned
good because they enforce strict administration.
We should draw upon their experience and do an
even better job."

Deng Xiaoping, Spring of 1992

Suzhou project

"In industry, learn from Daqing". Now, it was "In social management, learn from Singapore".

Deng's visit to Singapore in December 1978 left a deep impression on him. While we should not overstate the role Singapore played in China's transformation, there is no denying that Singapore's success was an inspiration to China that they too could succeed — and on a much grander scale. In 1985, China's state council appointed Dr Goh Keng Swee as an adviser to the coastal regions and for tourism.

While we were flattered by China's sudden interest in us, all those visits were also a burden to our officials. We are after all a small city-state. Lee Kuan Yew decided that if China was sincere in wanting to learn from Singapore, we should work on a joint project together. That was the origin of the Suzhou Industrial Park. Lee Kuan Yew had been receiving reports about China's rapid growth in the early 1990s and knew that the country would one day be very important to Singapore. By helping China when it needed us most, we built up goodwill for the future.

Two months after Deng's southern tour, I led a delegation on a visit to the Pearl River Delta. It was put together with the help of Sino Land's Robert Ng, a Singaporean. Also in the delegation were Philip Yeo and Ho Ching. We took a ferry from Hong Kong to Humen, where Lin Zexu destroyed British opium in 1839, and from there, we travelled by road to Guangzhou, Foshan, Zhongshan and Zhuhai. Everywhere we went, we saw development taking place helter-skelter.

The officials who briefed us were in high spirits. I was impressed to see the way Ho Ching gamely downed half a glass of brandy in one toast. At night, our sleep would be interrupted by the sound of explosions in nearby quarries. Someone mentioned that over a few years, a thousand bridges, big and small, were built to cross waterways in the delta. Lee Kuan Yew listened with great interest when I reported what we had seen to the Cabinet. It was still very early days then, but we already had intimations of China's future. During that period, ethnic Chinese businessmen from Southeast Asia were largely responsible for the first post-Tiananmen wave of investment in the delta.

After I lost the election, Gong Xueping wrote this piece for me

Gong Xueping launched my book in Shanghai in August 2018

The Shanghai Oriental Pearl Tower was built at incredible speed and remains highly profitable

In 1993, I made my first official visit to China as Minister for Information and the Arts. I was not yet 40 years old. My avuncular host Ai Zhisheng, the Minister for Radio, Film and Television, received me with extraordinary kindness. Most unusually, after I called on him in Beijing, he accompanied me to Shanghai and Suzhou. I still wonder why. Perhaps he was cultivating me, but it was not necessary to go to such lengths. Ai Zhisheng never asked anything of me. He passed away many years ago.

In Shanghai, we were hosted by the director of Shanghai TV Station, Gong Xueping. In Suzhou, I met the Mayor, Zhang Xinsheng, who spoke excellent English. Both became lifelong friends.

In Shanghai, Gong briefed us on the Pearl Tower project, together with the Hakka engineer from Meixian who was overseeing it. The scale of its ambition was breathtaking. Its name came from the line in the Tang poem, 大珠小珠落玉盘, meaning 'big pearls and little pearls tumbling onto the jade tray', represented by the big and small spheres on the tower.

Gong, whose resourcefulness reminded me of Philip Yeo, told me the project was self-financing. The TV station ran a taxi company which made lots of money. I ended up calling on Gong, who became Vice Mayor of the city, on each of my subsequent visits to Shanghai. A year later, he brought me to the Pudong site at the time when concrete was being continuously poured into the foundation for three whole days and nights. A couple of years later, he hosted me for dinner at the Peace Hotel and sat me by the window, where I could see the resplendent Pearl Tower across the river changing colours every few minutes. I found out later that the colour change was normally not as frequent. He had arranged it specially for my delight.

Gong was responsible for several gigantic projects in Shanghai, including the Shanghai Museum, the Shanghai Library, the Shanghai Sports Stadium, the Shanghai Conservatory of Music and the Shanghai International Convention Center, which was completed in less than a year. He personally showed me all of them. The scale of these projects reflected the self-conception and ambition of Shanghai city leaders. By the mid-1990s, I was convinced that Shanghai would become the world's greatest city and said so publicly. After all, it had been Asia's greatest city before the Second World War.

Gong has since retired, as have I, but we still keep in touch. He loves Shanghai and declined offers to work in Beijing. In his youth, he spent seven years in Tibet and once wrote calligraphy in blood to express his patriotism. When he retired, Zhu Rongji advised him to pick up an art form. Gong chose *jingxi* (Peking opera) and would sometimes sing a few lines for my wife and me after dinner. He told me that Zhu himself had picked up the *erhu*. I am an admirer of Zhu, who is the reason I am also attempting to learn the *erhu* myself.

When Zhu Rongji was the Party Committee Secretary of Shanghai, he wanted Singapore involved in the development of Pudong, which was still far off at that time. Goh Keng Swee was sceptical and advised Lee Kuan Yew against it. Later when Singapore was deciding between Suzhou and Shandong as the site for our joint project with China, Zhu, by that time the Premier, advised Lee Kuan Yew to choose Suzhou. When I heard him utter those words, I knew he must have felt secretly rueful that we had not chosen Pudong earlier. That would have taken us down a different pathway, but we lacked a sense of China's rapid development then.

Around 1993, I met Robert Kuok in Hong Kong. He told me that the Yangtze Delta was starting to take off. Compared to Singapore, the business community in Hong Kong has its fingers much more on the pulse of China.

Our choice of Suzhou was due to Ong Teng Cheong. He had been to Suzhou before and envisaged the old city being conserved and infused with new life. However, the redevelopment of the old city required existing activities to be moved out to a new urban area. As I had been in Suzhou just a few months earlier, I understood the reasons behind his vision.

When he mentioned to Lee Kuan Yew that the mayor, Zhang Xinsheng, was enthusiastic, I chimed in. However, we had to go through a formal selection process between Shandong and Suzhou before coming to a decision. I accompanied Ong Teng Cheong to Suzhou and Lee Kuan Yew to Shandong. As the former had been Chinese-educated, his background enabled him to communicate with the Chinese officials in a more personal way.

Q: Why did you lead a Young People's Action Party (PAP) delegation to China in 1995?

I had two objectives. The first was to build up party-to-party links. It was easier to start with the Young PAP. Remember, it was not long before this that communism was a dirty word in Singapore. The second was to expose young party members, a number of whom were already Members of Parliament (MPs) or likely to be fielded as election candidates afterwards, to China. It was important for them to have a sense of China's transformation and its implications for us in Singapore.

We were hosted by the Communist Youth League of China, then headed by Li Keqiang. We made a call on Politburo Member Ding Guangen and took a group photo with him at the Great Hall of the People. (A year later, he visited me in Singapore with an important delegation, a visit I recounted at some length in an earlier chapter). We were warmly received everywhere we went. I knew from the way we were treated that China was giving some importance to our visit. It was the first by the Young PAP, and possibly the first time the PAP itself had made a study visit to China.

It was an eye-opening experience for the Young PAP members. In Chongqing, the Party Secretary rushed back from another town in order to host us for dinner. Another particularly memorable component was our cruise down the Yangtze from Chongqing to Yichang. The Three Gorges Dam was still being built at the time. Many of us were familiar with the stories from *Romance of the Three Kingdoms* and took countless photographs when our boat passed the Red Cliff. A few of the towns we alighted to visit would soon be submerged by the rising water. The countryside on both sides of the Yangtze looked impoverished.

Meeting Vice Minister Xu Weicheng in July 1992. He was sent to study Singapore's after Deng Xiaoping's remarks about Singapore a few months earlier and wrote a book about our politics.

Photo credit: Ministry of Information, Communications and the Arts Collection, courtesy of National Archives of Singapore.

Calling on Secretary for the Communist Party of China Youth League Li Keqiang in 1995

Calling on Politburo Member Ding Guangen in 1995. A year later, I hosted his visit to Singapore.

Dinner hosted by Li Keqiang. On my left is Xu Weicheng.

Young PAP goodwill visit to China in 1995

Cruise along the Yangtze at the Three Gorges Dam

Q: During your time as Minister for Trade and Industry, Singapore's trade relations grew strongly. China joined the World Trade Organization (WTO) and the Association of Southeast Asian Nations (ASEAN) launched free trade agreement (FTA) negotiations with China during this time. What role did Singapore play? What were our considerations?

We worked closely with China to liberalise trade bilaterally, regionally and internationally. China had to move step by step from a centrally-planned economy to a mixed economy, with the market playing a growing role in resource allocation. Its accession to the WTO was the toughest any country had to face.The United States (US), Europe and Japan all collaborated to squeeze maximum concessions from China, which had to negotiate with all the existing WTO members. When it came to Singapore, China asked for a pass. I agreed because Singapore's needs were more than fully met by the demands others were making on China.

China's chief negotiator, Long Yongtu, did a fantastic job patiently explaining to the Chinese people what WTO accession would mean for Chinese companies and Chinese consumers in their daily lives. He appeared regularly on Chinese TV to explain the economics of trade in simple terms. I told my staff no other country had a citizenry better educated on trade matters than China's. Finally, in November 2001 in Doha, both China and Taiwan acceded to the WTO one after the other, with Taiwan acceding as a separate customs territory.

Singapore's trade liberalisation strategy had two prongs. While we were an ardent supporter of the WTO, we were also worried that it might not be able to progress as much as our economy needed. Thus our second prong was to negotiate as many FTAs as possible. Singapore's general approach was to initiate a bilateral FTA first and then work to bring ASEAN in subsequently, except in the case of China, which we approached in reverse order. For China, we decided to work on an ASEAN–China FTA first before negotiating a bilateral one with higher standards. This was to minimise suspicion that we were somehow conspiring with China to flood Southeast Asia with cheap Chinese products. As it turned out, it was China which initiated the FTA with ASEAN.

During the Asian Financial Crisis, one ASEAN economy after another took a hit, beginning with the sharp fall in the value of the Thai Baht on 1 July 1997. During this period, Zhu Rongji increased public spending, which also stimulated the private economy. China's economy streaked ahead of ASEAN during those few years. Financially, China was also less exposed to the international financial markets. By the end of the 1990s, China was so far ahead that many countries in ASEAN saw China as an economic threat.

At the ASEAN–China summit held in Singapore in December 2000, Zhu Rongji proposed an FTA between ASEAN and China. He said that the economies of both China and ASEAN were intertwined; both shared a connected future. ASEAN leaders were shocked by the proposal and had no immediate response. In the usual ASEAN way, the bloc's trade ministers were asked to study the idea and make their recommendations.

Singapore was keen to launch negotiations, but we were acutely aware that our ASEAN partners were less enthusiastic. At the Trade Ministers meeting in Hanoi the following year, the views were mixed. There was not going to be a consensus. I then suggested asking China for an early harvest for agricultural and mineral products, giving special access to ASEAN countries for these products without reciprocity for a period of time. Except for Singapore, all the other nine ASEAN members stood to benefit significantly. I argued that China, much as it wanted the FTA for political reasons, also sought ASEAN's friendship, which the bloc ought to parley to our own benefit. Since Singapore itself would not benefit from the early harvest, I was able to make the argument without coming across as being self-serving in a narrow way. We were self-serving in an enlightened way. Good ASEAN–China relations would of course benefit Singapore eventually, one way or another.

It was an intense evening and my ASEAN colleagues were finally persuaded. I cannot forget the date: it was 11 September 2001. All of us were receiving messages on our mobile phones about the events taking place in New York City at the time. I was so focused on the discussion that when the news flashed that the World Trade Centre tower had collapsed, I thought it was referring to the TV tower on top of the building. It was only after the meeting ended that I was fully aware of the audacious attack which altered the course of American history.

At the subsequent ASEAN–China Summit, ASEAN leaders gave their positive replies to Zhu Rongji. As I expected, China readily agreed to ASEAN's request for an early harvest. The framework agreement was signed the following year in Phnom Penh. I remember two remarks Zhu made at that event: one, that if after 10 years, the FTA leads to an imbalance in China's favour, China would agree to its re-negotiation. No other major power would make such a commitment. Two, that China was not seeking an exclusive position in ASEAN for itself. Zhu's statesmanship was impressive and spoke well of China. Long Yongtu told me some years later that Zhu told his officials at the time to give ASEAN what it wanted. They wanted ASEAN's goodwill for the long term.

We then embarked on bilateral FTA negotiations with China. My counterpart, Shi Guangsheng, took a friendly approach. He said that it

Chinese Premier Zhu Rongji and ASEAN leaders signing the ASEAN–China Framework Agreement on Comprehensive Economic Cooperation in Phnom Penh on 4 November 2002

was much easier to negotiate with Singapore than with ASEAN, though he did, however, issue a threat on one occasion. China had learned of our intention to negotiate an FTA with Taiwan, which, as a separate customs area, was allowed under the rules of the WTO. One day, after a multilateral meeting, he pulled me aside to say that if Singapore proceeded to negotiate with Taiwan, there would be no FTA with China. It was clear to me he was speaking under instruction.

He chose a time when we were walking together along a corridor to deliver the message. As it turned out, a journalist overheard Shi issuing the threat and informed my staff that he had to report it, but would like a response from me first. I issued a response in writing that it was within Singapore's rights under the WTO to negotiate a trade deal with Taiwan as a separate customs area, but declined to comment on a private conversation. As it was clear that the Chen Shui-bian administration was more interested in politicising free trade negotiations than in the substance of it, we stopped pushing for a deal. In any case, the Mainland market was much larger than Taiwan's. Some years later, when cross-Straits relations were much better, it was China which suggested we proceed to negotiate an FTA with Taiwan.

Q: How important was personal diplomacy as opposed to official diplomacy in your dealings with China?

To me, you can't differentiate cleanly between the two. Countries have interests which are important. Negotiations are, however, between human beings, and human beings have minds and hearts. An intelligent officer who lacks an understanding of the heart cannot be a good diplomat or negotiator.

Getting our two pandas from China involved both the mind and the heart. Our zoo was keen to have a pair, but pandas are a protected species and can only be loaned out, for which a donation is expected in return. The Ministry of Foreign Affairs (MFA) had asked Deputy Prime Minister Teo Chee Hean to raise this request with Vice Premier Liu Yandong, who nodded politely in reply, but there was no follow-up from the Chinese side.

In 2009, Singapore hosted the APEC Leaders' Meeting. President Hu Jintao was also scheduled to make a state visit at the same time. MFA thought this would be a good time to remind China of our panda request. I suggested to my counterpart that if China was considering loaning two pandas to Singapore, announcing this during Hu's visit would make the headlines. The Chinese Foreign Ministry immediately understood what I meant and worked to make it happen.

Explaining our objective to the zoo management, however, was not easy. CapitaLand agreed to make the million-dollar donation and wanted to make the announcement. MFA said, no, the pandas were an expression of friendship, not an occasion for corporate publicity. In the end, China asked for the announcement to be made at the highest level, after Hu Jintao formally informed President S. R. Nathan of it at their meeting in the Istana. That announcement made the headlines.

During my time as a visiting scholar at Peking University at the end of 2011, I made a visit to Chengdu and was brought by CapitaLand to see the two pandas in the panda park before they were sent to their new home in Singapore. Though they were only a few months old, they already had sharp claws and we had to keep a safe distance. The keepers assured me that the pair were chosen to maximise chances of bearing offspring. For many years, there was no good news, until Jia Jia, the female, delivered a baby panda in September 2021 during the Covid-19 pandemic. The announcement lifted Singaporeans' morale, who voted to name the cub Le Le (叻叻).

On a working visit to China in 2010, I asked to visit Tibet. Tibet had become an international issue in the run-up to the 2008 Beijing Olympics and foreign visits were severely curtailed. Some monks immolated themselves to draw international attention. I intended my visit as a friendly gesture, which Beijing recognised as such.

I was the first minister from a foreign country to go up. I say 'up' because the high altitude made me sick. We took the train from Xining.

Meeting our pandas in Chengdu in 2011 before they came to Singapore.
After 10 years, they have become proud parents of Le Le.

After we passed Golmud, the train climbed rapidly. The rails were mostly built on permafrost, which posed an engineering challenge for years. The cabins were pressurised and supplemented with extra oxygen. A special kitchen wagon was hooked up to ensure our delegation had good food. However, after we had climbed above 4,000m, I developed a headache and nausea. I had no appetite at all.

When we crossed the Tanggu La Pass into Tibet, the train stopped briefly for photograph taking. By this time, we had reached an altitude of over 5,000m. I tottered out slowly because of the lack of oxygen. I had taken a course of *hongjingtian* (红景天) capsules a week before my trip as a prophylactic against altitude sickness, but it did not help.

My first night in Lhasa was tough. I had a pounding headache and woke up frequently. The centre of my brain felt as if it might explode. When I staggered out of bed in the morning, I did not feel able to go through the day's programme, which was meant to begin with a tour of the imposing Potala Palace. When I arrived at the breakfast hall, the Tibetan doctor assigned to me took my pulse and asked me to inhale oxygen from a canister. I felt better. As my body became more active, the headache lessened, which enabled me to function quite normally.

Visit to Tibet in 2009. Travelled by train from Xining to Lhasa mostly on permafrost.

Fortunately, we were brought up by car right up to the top level of the Potala Palace, which meant that we only had to walk down.

On the second night, the doctor asked me to inhale oxygen for a few minutes before I slept, which helped. Every time I woke up to go to the toilet, I drank lots of water, which meant I woke up more often and took the chance to breathe in some oxygen each time. My body gradually began to adapt, and the nights became manageable.

Tibet was fascinating and had incredible scenery. Sim Chi Yin, the photographer from *The Straits Times*, took beautiful shots of me. Some were published in the paper, which led to snide comments that I was taking a holiday in Tibet. Bilahari Kausikan sent a message to alert me of this. I took care after that to explain to the media my deeper objective in visiting Tibet, which made possible a subsequent call on the Panchen Lama in Beijing.

The Panchen Lama happened to be resident in Shigatse when I was visiting the city. I asked to call him knowing that it was highly unlikely that permission would be given. My guide told me apologetically that this required approval from Beijing. This gave me a reason to write to him when I returned to Singapore. In 2010, I called on him at the Donghuang Temple outside Beijing. It was his first meeting with a foreign dignitary. Flanking him on his left were three teachers — two high Tibetan lamas and a Chinese monk. I had with me Venerable Kwang Sheng from Por Kark See Temple, Lee Bock Guan from the Buddhist Lodge and fellow Aljunied MP Yeo Guat Kwang. I extended two invitations to the Panchen Lama to visit Singapore, one to him in his capacity as an official from the Singapore government and the other to him in his capacity as a Buddhist monk from the Singapore Buddhist community.

The visit went well and was given extensive news coverage in China. At my other appointments in Beijing the following day, everyone I met knew that I had called on the Panchen Lama. Unfortunately, to date, the Panchen Lama has not yet visited Singapore even though he indicated a wish to do so when he visited Hong Kong in 2012.

Calling on the Panchen Lama at the Donghuang Temple outside Beijing in 2010

The Dalai Lama and the Panchen Lama are the two highest lamas of the dominant Yellow Hat sect in Tibet. The Dalai Lama is believed to be the reincarnation of Avalokiteshvara and the Panchen Lama the reincarnation of Amitabha. The Dalai Lama's seat in Lhasa is the Potala Palace while the Panchen Lama's is at the Tashilhunpo Monastery in Shigatse. Miniatures of both were built at the Qing summer capital of Chengde by the Qianlong Emperor, one to mark his 60th birthday, the other to mark his 70th birthday.

After returning to Singapore, I wrote an op-ed in *The Straits Times* on Tibet, which pointed to the fact that the appointment of the Dalai Lama and the Panchen Lama had always required Beijng's approval since the time of the Ming and Qing Dynasties. High lamas were not only spiritual leaders, they were also political leaders. Their reincarnations had to be sanctioned by the Emperor. The appointment of the current Dalai Lama was approved by Chiang Kai-shek. I heard that there was some unhappiness over what I wrote among those close to the Dalai Lama. As my op-ed was carefully written, stating only facts, I did not think much about it.

After I left government, I received a request from Rinpoche Lodi Gyari to meet. This came as a pleasant surprise. I knew Lodi was a friend of Tommy Koh. We arranged to meet for breakfast at Casa Verde in the Botanic Gardens. Poor Lodi got lost and arrived, flustered, half an hour late. We had a friendly conversation and got to like each other. He told me interesting stories of his meetings with Chinese negotiators. I also learned that the Dalai Lama had once given a Swiss watch to Xi Zhongxun, Xi Jinping's father. China has a positive view of Lodi, who showed me an article written by a Chinese vice minister praising him.

In 2014, I received an invitation by Lodi to attend his daughter's wedding in Sikkim. I accepted immediately. My wife and I looked forward to an exotic experience and booked our air tickets and hotels. As it turned out, we had to cancel our trip and forfeit the money we had paid because one of our sons fell seriously ill.

At a subsequent meeting in Singapore, Lodi told me that he was

Dalai Lama's special envoy for negotiations with China, Lodi Gyari

writing a book on his negotiations with China. He said that both sides had assessed each other wrongly and made mistakes. He hoped that his book would help improve relations between China and Tibet. He was living with his wife in Washington D.C. by that time. In the 1950s, the Central Intelligence Agency was very involved in Tibet and had a base in Mustang on the Indian side of the Himalayas. Although Lodi was now a US citizen, he said that he did not want to write his book in Washington D.C. and worked on it in Bangkok instead. At his request, I also arranged for him to do a stint at Singapore's Lee Kuan Yew School of Public Policy.

When the book was ready, he asked me to recommend a publisher. I got in touch with my old friend Dr K. K. Phua of World Scientific, who had published my book earlier. Dr Phua agreed immediately but later changed his mind when World Scientific staff in China fed back to him that the book was too politically sensitive. Lodi wrote to me a day before his surgery in San Francisco in September 2018, again expressing his respect for the Chinese leaders he dealt with. After his death in October, his daughter, Tenzing, asked me to write an endorsement for Lodi's book.

This is what I wrote:

> *For all those who wish for reconciliation between the Dalai Lama and China, this is a most important book to read. Lodi Gyari wrote it in order for both sides to learn from the mistakes and misunderstandings of the past. He rushed to complete it when he found out that he was ill and did not have much time left. Lodi Gyari described himself as radical in his youth. As Special Envoy for many years, he was a realist. He kept true his loyalty to the Dalai Lama. He was an enlightened individual who always strove to find good in others. Over nine rounds of formal talks, Lodi Gyari earned the respect of his Chinese interlocutors. Till his last breath, he believed that, with goodwill and persistence, a solution could be found between the Dalai Lama and Beijing to safeguard fully Tibetan identity and autonomy within the framework of the People's Republic of China. The Tibetan contribution to the culture and philosophy of the Chinese nation is profound. All the placards on buildings in Beijing's Forbidden City include Tibetan as an integral language. Tibetan threads greatly enrich the Chinese tapestry.*

Personal relationships can make a decisive difference in diplomacy. My long years in government enabled me to build up a network of friendships which proved helpful at critical moments.

Before going to bed one night, my wife passed me a folder from Jackie Chan's agent in Singapore. She asked me whether Singapore might be interested in some old houses. Old houses? I leafed through the pages and saw that the 'old houses' were not ordinary dwellings, but houses in Anhui from the late Ming and Qing periods. They were older than any house in Singapore would be.

Jackie, who is a friendship ambassador for VIVA Foundation, the foundation my wife established for children with cancer, had purchased

Jackie Chan's old houses from Anhui incorporated into SUTD's campus

many of these old houses. They were dismantled and the parts repaired and reconditioned so that they could be reassembled anywhere. He offered them to the Hong Kong authorities, but there was no taker because land is scarce there and probably too valuable for such use. The folder was full of these houses, maybe 10. I was fascinated and wondered who in Singapore might be interested in them.

I suddenly thought of the Singapore University of Technology and Design (SUTD). The campus was being built at the time and Philip Ng, as Chairman of the university's Council, had a lively interest in architecture. Philip was as enthusiastic as I was and we worked to make it happen. However, I had niggling concerns that China might object. China was increasingly protective of its heritage buildings and had forbidden any of such buildings from being taken out of China and, later, even to be taken out of a province. What if China took issue with Singapore over Jackie's gift?

On one visit to China, I was with PM Lee Hsien Loong. At a lunch hosted by Li Keqiang, the conversation drifted to his own province of Anhui and his own hometown of Fengyang. After Zhu Yuanzhang established the Ming Dynasty in Nanjing, he built a huge palace for his mother in Fengyang, where he grew up. According to Li Keqiang, the foundations remain there to this day. I decided at that point to raise the matter of Jackie's houses with him and to ask for his blessing. I was also worried that Jackie might get into trouble, which would not be good for Singapore, SUTD or VIVA.

I explained that SUTD had been established in cooperation with Zhejiang University. Li Keqiang, whom I first got to know when he was leader of the Communist Youth League and called on when he was the Provincial Governor of Henan and Provincial Party Secretary of Liaoning, smiled and said that it was a difficult request. However, there was no follow-up, which meant that there were no objections. The architects of SUTD did a good job in integrating the old wooden structures into a modern campus. They have become a talking point whenever Chinese officials visit SUTD.

Q: Tell us about your involvement in China's effort to develop an ecological civilisation.

The invitation came through former Suzhou Mayor Zhang Xinsheng, whom I first met in 1993. I am a member of the International Advisory Council chaired by Dai Bingguo. Before the Covid-19 pandemic, we met every year in Guiyang. Guizhou was for the longest time the most backward province in China — which, happily, also meant that it had the most pristine environment. With communications no longer a problem, Guizhou now has the best of both worlds.

China has codified the objective to establish an ecological civilisation in its constitution, which strikes me as being remarkably far-sighted. China's planners see the green economy as a key engine of growth for

Eco Forum Global, annual meeting of the International Advisory Council chaired by State Councillor Dai Bingguo

Meetings and activities at Guiyang during Eco Forum Global

the future. China now has the most advanced electrical car market in the world and is a leading force in developing alternative energy sources.

One humble area where China has made great progress is the provision of better toilets. In 2011, while I was a visiting scholar in Peking University, Jack Sim, the founder of the World Toilet Organization, asked me to be a keynote speaker at the World Toilet Summit he was involved in organising in Haikou. When replied that I had left office, he said that in China, retired ministers are still ministers.

I invited my old comrade Chin Harn Tong to accompany me. He was born in Wenchang and I thought it would be fun to visit Hainan with him. At a new public toilet, he bantered with the service workers in Hainanese. Down in Sanya, I saw a notice in a public toilet that there are two WTOs in the world, one headquartered in Geneva and one in Singapore. Jack Sim has even succeeded with the help of MFA to get the

United Nations to approve 19 November as World Toilet Day.

The whole of Hainan island has become a free trade port and there will soon be movement controls between the mainland and Hainan. Singapore should explore opportunities for cooperation here. The Hainanese component of our society is a plus. I hope that the area between the Raffles Hotel and Middle Road, bounded by Beach Road and North Bridge Road, will be designated Hainan Town one day. It would add an additional point of interest to Singapore and will facilitate contact with Hainan.

Keynote speaker at the World Toilet Summit in Haikou in 2011

Signboard above a urinal at a public toilet in Sanya

Wenchang, where the ancestors of many Hainanese in Singapore came from, has historically produced men of talent

At Chin Harn Tong's birthplace

Wenchang chicken from which Singapore chicken rice is derived

Q: What role did our Chinese chamber and clan associations play in furthering bilateral relations?

Both the Singapore Federation of Chambers of Commerce and Industry (SCCI) and the Singapore Federation of Chinese Clan Associations (SFCCA) play a critical role. Their members are generally in touch with ground conditions in China. They are careful not to appear too enthusiastic in the eyes of the government and check themselves in order not to come across as being emotional or somehow having been captured by China. This tension is perhaps unavoidable given Singapore's nature.

In 1991, SFCCI, under the leadership of Tan Eng Joo, organised the first World Chinese Entrepreneurs Convention. It was a great success and Singapore, Hong Kong and Bangkok quickly became important nodes for a global network that had great potential. Lee Kuan Yew was the guest of honour for the event and I remember being asked by him to draft his speech. He knew that I was an enthusiastic supporter. Twenty years later, I was asked to address the convention myself, which by that time had grown wings.

The first World Chinese Entrepreneurs Convention held in Singapore in 1991, opened by Lee Kuan Yew

Receiving banner from Manila before Singapore played host again

World Chinese Entrepreneurs Convention returned to Singapore after 20 years in 2011

CHAPTER 16

❖

Love China, Love Hong Kong

In this chapter, George Yeo recalls his involvement with Hong Kong after the Tiananmen Incident, the return of Hong Kong to China in 1997 and the events which led to the introduction of the National Security Law in 2021.

Q: You were in charge of the Approval-in-Principle scheme which enabled Hong Kongers to come to Singapore in the run-up to 1997. What were the considerations and results?

The Tiananmen crackdown on 4 June 1989 created panic in Hong Kong. Uncertainty over Hong Kong's future had been looming for some time. The Treaty of Nanjing in 1842 ceded Hong Kong Island in perpetuity to the British. The Convention of Peking in 1860 ceded a small part of Kowloon (old Kowloon), also in perpetuity. The rest of Kowloon (new Kowloon) and the New Territories were leased to the British for 99 years under the Second Convention of Peking in 1898. China considered all these treaties to be unequal treaties but left them be. In any case, 1997 would end British rule because the return of new Kowloon and the New Territories would make British rule over Hong Kong Island and old Kowloon unviable anyway.

In 1982, Margaret Thatcher, who was badly advised, suggested to Deng Xiaoping that British rule be extended over the whole of Hong Kong for 50 years. Apparently, Deng spat into the spittoon in response. A shaken Thatcher tripped as she came down the steps of the Great Hall

Commemorative envelope in 1997 recalling the meeting between Deng Xiaoping and Margaret Thatcher in 1982

of the People. Two years later, London and Beijing issued the Joint Declaration, which would provide for a through-train in 1997.

The Joint Declaration was not a new treaty governing the future of Hong Kong because China never accepted the legality of British rule in the first place. China would never have agreed to an agreement which gave Britain any role in the governance of Hong Kong after 1997. It was an agreement to facilitate a smooth transition to Chinese rule. Britain did register the Joint Declaration with the United Nations, but that did not alter its substance.

In the Joint Declaration, both sides stated what they intended to do before the handover. There were subsequent exchanges of letters to elaborate on the details. Wording was carefully crafted to make clear that each was merely informing the other of what it intended to do. They were not enforceable agreements or commitments. In China's view, Britain breached its own undertaking when Chris Patten was Governor, which led China to adjust its own position.

When China introduced the national security law for Hong Kong in June 2020, arguments were made in London and elsewhere that the law went against the Joint Declaration in diminishing Hong Kong's "high degree of autonomy". To begin with, nothing in the Joint Declaration prevented China from introducing such a law for Hong Kong. All countries have national security laws.

Furthermore, the Joint Declaration did not give Britain any say over what China could or could not do in Hong Kong after 1997. Under Article 23 of the Basic Law, Hong Kong is required to legislate a law on national security. The Legislative Council's refusal to do it forced Beijing's hand.

Deng Xiaoping saw the benefits Hong Kong brought to China and introduced the framework of One Country, Two Systems. Under this, Hong Kong would enjoy a high degree of autonomy, with Hong Kongers in charge of administration except in the areas of foreign affairs and defence. There was one further condition: that those in charge of Hong Kong's administration should love China as well as Hong Kong (一国两制，爱国爱港，港人治港).

In accordance with what was stated in the Joint Declaration, China convened a committee to draft Hong Kong's Basic Law, a mini-Constitution, to be issued by China's National People's Congress (NPC). The Basic Law Committee involved leaders from all walks of life in Hong Kong and consulted widely. It did much to assure Hong Kongers that Hong Kong would remain largely unchanged under One Country, Two Systems.

Tiananmen undid all that. Many Hong Kongers decided to leave or considered leaving before 1997, many of whom headed to Canada and Australia. Seeing an opportunity in the crisis, Lee Kuan Yew decided to position Singapore as a backstop to the potential flood of people fleeing. Singapore created a special Approval-in-Principle (AIP) scheme, giving those whose applications were approved the right of abode in Singapore should they need it in a hurry. If not exercised, the AIP would expire after a certain number of years. The scheme helped to stanch the exodus of people leaving Hong Kong.

I remember Lee Kuan Yew publicly saying that Singapore could benefit more by raiding Hong Kong when it was on fire — but that would only work for the short term. Moreover, it would be foolish. Far better for Singapore to seize this opportunity to get closer to Hong Kong at a time when the latter was in need. Hong Kongers who migrated to Singapore would be geographically close enough to maintain family and business links back home. Not only would Singapore benefit from talented Hong Kongers moving here, the networks they would bring would strengthen Singapore's international reach. This extended beyond Hong Kong itself to its global network, which is much more extensive than Singapore's.

Lee Kuan Yew put me in charge of the AIP programme. During those few years, I travelled to Hong Kong many times and got to meet many important people. I felt like a person delivering coal in wintertime who was welcomed everywhere. When I called on Li Ka-Shing, he immediately asked for an AIP for his *ah mah chay* who had helped to raise his sons Victor and Richard, assuring me that she was a person of means and would not be a burden to Singapore. However, his family needed her in Hong Kong, so could we please not require her to come to Singapore?

I also reached out to the Indian community in Hong Kong through Hari Harilela. Many Hong Kong Indians, especially the Sindhis, were worried about their position after 1997. They were used to Hong Kong and did not want to go back to India. Harilela also requested that we extend the AIP to the entire Parsee community. The Hong Kong Parsees are a small, talented, wealthy community and should not be broken up. Knowing a little about the Parsees and how they sweeten the milk everywhere they go, I saw the wisdom of his advice.

We must have issued a few hundred thousand AIPs in all. However, only a few tens of thousands finally came to Singapore, of which a proportion later returned to Hong Kong — albeit as Singapore citizens.

As part of overall efforts to increase our presence in Hong Kong and embed a Singapore community there, I wrote a cabinet memo for the establishment of a Singapore International School (SIS). It started as a primary school in 1991. The Hong Kong government allocated us a piece of land on the south side of Hong Kong Island. In my ignorance, I was dismayed that it was a slope rather than a flat piece of land. It

Hari Harilela helped me reach out to the Hong Kong Indian community

turned out that the most incredible buildings in Hong Kong are built on slopes.

This was followed by a request to establish a secondary school. The Cabinet thought it might not be a good idea to have our kids spend so many years in Hong Kong. Better for them to come back to Singapore and stay in a boarding school if their parents were working there. But most Singapore parents wanted their children with them and chose to send them to other international schools in Hong Kong for secondary education. We finally relented and allowed SIS to conduct secondary education as well. Till today, it is the only Singapore international school supported by the Ministry of Education. SIS naturally gives first preference to Singaporean kids. It has turned out to be popular among Hong Kongers as well.

Hong Kongers are a resilient people. They respond quickly to changes in the environment and adapt well to new situations. After two or three years, the mood turned buoyant in Hong Kong again. Singapore played its cards well.

We now have a vibrant Hong Kong community in Singapore. I got Aline Wong to help set up the Kowloon Club to facilitate their integration into Singapore society. In a piece I wrote for a book commemorating the 180th anniversary of the founding of modern Singapore, I expressed the hope that Singapore and Hong Kong could become twin cities, one serving the Chinese Mainland, the other serving Southeast Asia. I never expected that one day, my wife and I would set up a second home in Hong Kong and shuttle back and forth every month ourselves.

Q: You were in Hong Kong at the handover on the eve of 1 July 1997. Was it a smooth handover? What were the implications for Singapore?

I was in Hong Kong during the handover, not in an official capacity, but to speak at a conference. Lee Kuan Yew was there too for another conference. Unfortunately, my wife could not accompany me because our youngest son had been diagnosed with leukaemia a couple of weeks before. Lee Kuan Yew heard about it and expressed his sympathy to me.

Robert Kuok hosted a dinner on the eve of the handover. I still have the menu card which all of us around the table autographed to mark a moment in history. When I started work in Hong Kong in 2012, I brought with me from Singapore a picture of Deng Xiaoping superimposed on a Hong Kong which was returned to China. It was created by Yang Shangkun's son, Yang Shaoming, to mark a joyous occasion.

The British delegation led by Tony Blair at the handover ceremony looked downcast and sombre. A few months earlier, I had written a piece saying that it could have ended better for the British, for they did leave much behind. That was indeed what the Joint Declaration envisaged. As an expression of confidence in Hong Kong's future, Governor David Wilson unveiled the plan to build a new airport on reclaimed land in Lantau with highways and bridges linking it to Kowloon and Hong Kong Island. Many commentators, including some in Singapore, were sceptical and cynical, wondering whether this was a scheme for British companies

Portrait of Deng superimposed on Hong Kong by Yang Shaoming, Yang Shangkun's son. I paid $50 plus 3% GST on it, which can still be seen on the tag in the top right hand corner of the frame.

Robert Kuok's dinner menu card, on the eve of the handover

to rake in big money one last time while Britain was still the colonial master. I did not take such a view.

Chief Secretary Anson Chan asked for my help with studying Changi Airport. I gladly made the arrangements, telling her that we had always learned from each other. Singapore's Mass Rapid Transport (MRT) system had benefited much from observing the experience of Hong Kong's Mass Transit Railway (MTR). Later, I led a delegation to study Hong Kong's performing spaces when we were planning for our own Esplanade. On one visit to Hong Kong, Anson arranged a helicopter ride for me to see the construction work being carried out. The scale of the development was huge: in a 360-degree panorama, I could see the reclamation at Chek Lap Kok, the highways and bridges to Tsing Yi Island and Kowloon, and the two ends of the tunnel to Hong Kong Island. The airport project gave confidence to Hong Kongers and foreigners alike that Hong Kong would have a bright future under One Country, Two Systems.

Under David Wilson, the British Administration in Hong Kong was faithful to the letter and spirit of the Joint Declaration. I called on Finance Secretary Piers Jacob when I was Senior Minister of State for Finance under Dr Richard Hu. Dr Hu asked me to check with Piers regarding when Hong Kong would be introducing goods and services tax (GST). Both of them saw the move as a necessity and both cities were considering it. Each, of course, preferred the other to move first.

A few years later, I called on Jacob again and asked the same question. This time, he said that the idea had been abandoned after Christopher Patten took over as Governor. I could understand why Patten was not willing to take on the political burden. In fact, he did the opposite: he reduced medical charges and increased doctors' salaries, causing a reverse flow of doctors from the private sector into government hospitals. When I visited Hong Kong as Health Minister, Peter Woo was the Chairman of the Hong Kong Hospital Authority. He was concerned about the financial sustainability of the changes Patten made.

At the United Kingdom General Election in 1992, Patten, as Chairman of the Conservative Party, played a key role in its victory. John

Major became Prime Minister (PM) but Patten lost his constituency seat in Bath. Major's reward to Patten was to appoint him as Britain's last Governor of Hong Kong.

In 1997, Labour won and Tony Blair became PM. As Governor, Patten took a political approach and decided that too smooth a transition to One Country, Two Systems would be bad for Britain's sense of self in the eyes of the world. He decided to change the course set by the previous governor David Wilson. In the last chapter of British rule in Hong Kong, Patten started introducing democratic reforms. China saw it as Britain walking back from the position under the Joint Declaration. In response, Deng Xiaoping issued instructions that China should prepare a "second stove". There would no longer be a through-train.

Lee Kuan Yew sensed Patten's intentions when the latter called on him in Singapore before taking up his post in Hong Kong in 1992. I remember him telling us about his suspicions in Cabinet. Lee Kuan Yew did not want to be associated with whatever Patten was going to do, which he knew would be disruptive. He decided to issue a statement of what he had told Patten so that he could not be susbsequently accused of giving Patten bad advice.

Later that year, Lee Kuan Yew openly criticised Patten's policy in a speech he gave at the University of Hong Kong. Patten, who was seated next to him, took it all with a stiff upper lip, but he was livid inside and took pot-shots at Singapore after he stepped down as Governor. I kept my links with Patten even though we held different views regarding One Country, Two Systems. Years later, I was a member of a Vatican Commission he chaired to recommend improvements to church communications.

Lee Kuan Yew took a deep interest in Hong Kong. He always found reasons to visit Hong Kong and must have done so every year. He would call on the Governor and got business leaders like Run Run Shaw, Li Ka-shing, Robert Kuok and Robert Ng to host dinners so that he could meet prominent Hong Kong personalities and get a feel of what was happening in both Hong Kong and China.

Lee Kuan Yew criticising Chris Patten at the University of Hong Kong in December 1992

Point of handover at the stroke of midnight on 31 June 1997

Singapore has much to gain by learning from Hong Kong's experiences. Hong Kong has a much thicker layer of entrepreneurs and its people are more resilient. The colonial government took a laissez-faire approach to economic management and very much left Hong

Kongers to fend for themselves. Compared to Singapore, Hong Kong is untidy, but that is also its strength and charm. In Singapore, you can't carve out space for economic activity anywhere, even to mend shoes, without permission. In Hong Kong, there are such nooks and crannies everywhere, some in dark alleyways.

When I was Minister for Trade and Industry, I proposed an a free trade arrangement (FTA) between Hong Kong and Singapore. I thought each had its own strengths and an FTA between us would be mutually beneficial. Among other things, it could include an air shuttle to facilitate travel between the two cities. Through Hong Kong, we gain better access to China. Through Singapore, Hong Kong gains better access to Southeast and South Asia.

I have always remembered a remark that David Wilson made to me: that the rivalry between Hong Kong and Singapore is like the one between Cambridge and Oxford. It is a healthy rivalry. Each has a strategic interest in the other's well-being. However, at that time, Hong Kong was wedded to the multilateral idea and took a dogmatic position against FTAs. My counterpart for trade in culture in Hong Kong of many years, Brian Chau, was a delightful person to work with. Later, Hong

Brian Chau, a colleague of many years in trade and culture

Kong changed its position and requested an FTA with Singapore. My successor in the Ministry of Trade and Industry was less enthusiastic and thought that Hong Kong was better off working on an FTA with the Association of Southeast Asian Nations (ASEAN) instead.

Q: What was it like to work in Hong Kong?

My wife and I could never have imagined that we would one day become residents of Hong Kong ourselves, not even in our wildest dreams.

After I lost the election in 2011, I was in an awkward position. Twice, Lee Kuan Yew asked me whether I needed help with Temasek or GIC, but he made no specific offer. During the election campaign, Lee Hsien Loong had categorically stated that there would be no safety net for PAP candidates who lost. I replied to Lee Kuan Yew that I would try my luck in the private sector, but as a result of my long years as Minister for Trade & Industry and Foreign Affairs, I knew most of the top businessmen in Singapore. If I took a job with any of them, it would seem as if I was being returned a favour.

Two close business friends did offer to take me on as Vice Chairman of their companies. I declined their kind offers. Separately, Kishore Mahbubani at the Lee Kuan Yew School of Public Policy (LKYSPP) and K. Kesavapany at the Institute of Southeast Asian Studies invited me to become a Senior Fellow at their institutes. They said that my network would be useful to them. I decided to take a break instead and spent four months in Peking University. However, I did make an arrangement with Kishore to be a Visiting Scholar at LKYSPP in an unpaid role. In return for an office and secretarial support, I made myself available to faculty and staff but set my own priorities. I wanted my time to be my own. This arrangement continues till today.

During this period, out of the blue, Robert Kuok asked me to join his group in Hong Kong through his son Ean. The idea was put to him by an old Singaporean friend of his, Albert Hong. Robert Kuok had hosted my wife and me for dinner at the Shangri-La around 1989, not

Exhibition of Robert Kuok's collection of Xu Beihong's paintings in Singapore in 1998

Robert Kuok introducing me to a family friend during the Xu Beihong Exhibition
Photo credit: Ministry of Information, Communications and the Arts Collection,
courtesy of National Archives of Singapore.

long after I entered politics. He wanted to meet budding political leaders in Singapore and Albert had mentioned me. I was flattered and found him charming and interesting.

Over the years, I had sought opportunities to meet him in Hong Kong or Singapore in order to learn from him. He had a remarkable memory for personalities and events and told me things about Southeast Asia and China which I was not aware of. When his collection of Xu Beihong's paintings was exhibited in Singapore in 1998, as Minister for Information and the Arts, I opened the exhibition and gave a short speech. When his mother died in Johor Bahru in 1995, my wife and I crossed the Causeway to pay our respects. I knew how much he adored his mother. I was also fascinated by his long association with Lee Kuan Yew, who was just 20 days his senior.

Just before the 2011 General Election, Robert Kuok invited me to another dinner at the Shangri-La. Some friends must have told him my position was shaky. I mulled over his offer for a few months before deciding to take it up. I had done him no favours before and working outside Singapore would be less awkward for me. It would also open up new windows for my wife and me in both Hong Kong and China.

"Round pegs will find round holes." That was Robert Kuok's reply to me when I asked what he wanted me to do. After a few months, he asked me to take on the chairmanship of Kerry Logistics. The following year, we prepared the company for its initial public offering (IPO). In December 2013, we went on our roadshow to Singapore, London, Boston and New York. I quickly learned to be a salesman, making the case for investors who had so many IPOs to choose from. William Ma, the CEO, Ellis Cheng, the CFO, and other key officers of the company were my tutors.

A few months before I joined the company, Xi Jinping had launched the Belt and Road Initiative, first in Astana and a month later in Jakarta. That became the theme of my presentations. Kerry Logistics would become the most important logistics company for the Belt and Road. Since then, my key message in every annual report of the company has been on this subject. I believe Kerry Logistics is well on its way towards

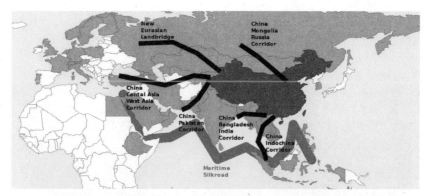

Kerry Logistics riding on the Belt and Road. Russia's invasion of Ukraine has affected one part of it.

achieving this goal and is the reason for its recent acquisition by Shunfeng.

After my wife's brush with death in 2017–8, I informed Robert Kuok of my intention to retire after a year. He asked me to stay on for two years as a Senior Advisor. His youngest son, Hua, took over as Chairman. In all, I spent 10 years with the Kuok Group. I learned much about working in the private sector and its pressures. I also acquired a deeper insight into the difference between companies which are run by professional managers and those run by families. For companies run by professional managers, the perspective is never truly long. Long-term incentives for the great majority of companies do not cover more than three years. Family-controlled companies, in contrast, take a multi-generational view of their possessions.

Robert Kuok was a mentor to me in many ways. Not only is he a shrewd businessman with a nose for opportunity, he understands human beings and their motivations. He is also a sharp observer of politics and politicians. Hua told me that on immigration forms, Robert Kuok puts himself down as a 'merchant'. He believes that a businessman should wrestle with his conscience every day. But, like all great men, he has a complex personality. Although only 20 days younger than Lee Kuan Yew, Robert Kuok was a year behind him in Raffles College. The year was spent learning Mandarin in a Chinese primary school. He told me that both he and Lee Kuan Yew were pigs: one was greedy for power,

IPO of Kerry Logistics in December 2013

Sounding the gong at the Stock Exchange of Hong Kong Limited

With Kerry Logistics colleagues and friends in Hong Kong, China, Taiwan, Thailand and India

Midnight delivery run to Hong Kong Disneyland

the other for money. Over the years, we talked about Lee Kuan Yew a lot. While in government, I had a sense of how Lee Kuan Yew saw him. Theirs was a complex relationship with each having his critique of the other but marked by considerable mutual affection. When Lee Kuan Yew died, Robert Kuok flew down immediately to pay his respects.

One of the first things I did after becoming Chairman of Kerry Logistics was to hop onto a truck late one night for its delivery run to Hong Kong Disneyland. My colleagues thought I might have difficulty climbing onto it but I told them I had trained in the Singapore army. It was a pleasant surprise for me to discover that Kerry Logistics ran a trucking service all the way from China to Singapore through Indochina and Myanmar. For many years, I had worked with ASEAN colleagues to improve internal connectivity within the bloc as well as ASEAN's connectivity with its major partners. This involved both physical connectivity and policies to facilitate trade, including the easy passage of goods in transit. I similarly wanted to board a truck when I crossed from Vietnam to Guangxi through the Friendship Pass but was told that it could not be done. I was required instead to call on the local custom chiefs and pay my respects to them, which I dutifully did.

My office was at the top of a 16-storey warehouse complex in Kwai Chung. Nowhere else in the world is it economically justified to stack so many floors in a warehouse, but then nowhere else in the world is land as expensive as in Hong Kong. Apart from domestic help, Hong Kong brings in relatively few foreign workers. In the warehouses, in the canteens, among the drivers, the language of communication is Cantonese. That homogeneity creates a strong workplace solidarity.

Kerry Logistics recruits its management trainees both from Hong Kong and abroad. It was a pleasure for me to lunch with groups of them and not talk only about work.

My 10 years with the Kuok Group and Kerry Logistics made me lifelong friends in Hong Kong. We were warmly received when we arrived in January 2012. On my first day at Kerry Centre in North Point, I was touched when Robert Kuok's eldest son, Beau, received me at the entrance to the building. Later that year, Hong Kong Polytechnic University gave me an Honorary Doctorate. The Chairman of the University Council, Marjorie Yang, who had been a classmate of Philip Yeo's at Harvard Business School, conferred the award.

In 2013, Hong Kong Chief Executive Leung Chun-ying appointed me to the Economic Development Commission, which prompted a question in Singapore's Parliament. Many people thought that I had left Singapore. In actual fact, I never really left Singapore because my wife and I made it a point to return to Singapore every month and spend at least a week here.

We tried to immerse ourselves in Hong Kong society as best we could. It was easier for my wife, who speaks Cantonese and enjoys the banter in shops and restaurants. My wife established a separate foundation in Hong Kong to serve China, called VIVA China Children's Cancer Foundation. Led by Dr Pui Ching-Hon from St Jude Children's Research Hospital in Memphis, Tennessee, the VIVA programme in China includes over 25 major hospitals and tracks the treatment of thousands of children suffering from acute lymphoblastic leukemia, the most common form of childhood cancer. She also managed to find many willing benefactors in Hong Kong without too much difficulty. Now in its eighth year, the five-year survival rate of its beneficiaries has shot up from 70% to 91%. She also helps out at the Missionaries of Charity Home in Sham Shui Po, a shelter for the homeless. I go down occasionally to help serve food at the shelter and to see a different side of Hong Kong society for myself.

Since the Covid-19 pandemic, our domestic helper has been looking

Honorary Doctorate at the Hong Kong Polytechnic University with Chairperson Marjorie Yang and President Timothy Tong in 2012

after our empty apartment near the University of Hong Kong. Her principal responsibility is to cook two dishes of meat and eggs for a hundred people at the shelter, twice a month. My wife has a reliable food supplier in Kennedy Town who, after learning what the food was being cooked for, made sure to send us fresh meat and fish and good-quality condiments and spices.

Knowing my background, a number of young Hong Kongers interested in politics have sought me out for advice. Singapore is an obvious model for them to study. I am happy to spend time with them, meeting over meals and hiking Hong Kong's many beautiful mountain trails. I grew to understand them socially and politically, and to slowly see Hong Kong through their eyes. People living in Hong Kong are constantly on edge because of uncertainty over the future. The political economy favours big business. During colonial rule, there was uncertainty about the return to China. After the return to China, there was uncertainty over the development of One Country, Two Systems, which was guaranteed by China for 50 years. But what happens after 2047?

Housing is a glaring problem which could not be solved for many years because of land and housing policy. This has always seemed absurd to me. Hong Kong's total land area is 1,100 square kilometres. Of this, some 800 square kilometres — which is larger than the whole of

VIVA China established as a foundation in Hong Kong

Singapore — are zoned green and reserved for either parks or agricultural areas. Unlike Singapore, Hong Kong has no need for air and naval bases, power stations or large water reservoirs. The land shortage in Hong Kong is thus completely artificial, partly created to keep the value of land high. The government itself depends heavily on land revenue. The unfortunate result is that many Hong Kongers have no hope of being able to own a decent roof over their head after working their entire lives.

Young Hong Kong friends

For One Country, Two Systems to work, Hong Kongers must not only love Hong Kong, they must also love China. Many Hong Kongers are either refugees from China or the children of refugees, whether having fled from Communism or from turmoil and hunger. For years, they looked down on the Chinese across the border. Older Singaporeans remember Chow Yun-fat in the series *Men in the Net*, which depicted how bad conditions in China were then. British policy was to keep Hong Kong society separate from the mainland. The mediums of instruction were English and Cantonese and the simplified Chinese script used on the Mainland was not taught to Hong Kong students. Most teachers were anti-mainland and passed this sentiment on to their charges. Thus, when Hong Kong returned to China, the majority of Hong Kongers had no love for the mainland and viewed it as a threat to their way of life.

Under the first two Chief Executives, the policy, sanctioned by Beijing, was to leave things be. The education system was modified to give more emphasis to Cantonese over English, which I remember Lee Kuan Yew saying was a big mistake. He thought much more emphasis should have been placed on Mandarin. A crude attempt to introduce national education in 2012 was met with strong resistance from high school students. Around 1997, Lee Kuan Yew advised the first Chief Executive, Tung Chee-hwa, to take a firm grip of the Hong Kong media. Tung shook his head with a smile and said that it could not be done. The thinking then, both in Beijing and in Hong Kong, was that minimal changes should be made after handover.

Without firm direction from Beijing, Hong Kong's leaders steadily lost control. The Legislative Council was almost in permanent opposition until 2021. Influenced by the media, a younger generation built their hopes on an illusion. It led to tragedy.

With Hong Kong Chief Executive Tung Chee-hwa in Mexico in 2002

❖

CHAPTER 17

Wukong and the Monk

George Yeo recalls his experience with the unrest in Hong Kong in 2019 and reflects on the introduction of the National Security Law and its implications for Hong Kong's future.

Q: What led to the unrest in 2019? What was your experience of it?

Under Article 23 of the Basic Law, Hong Kong legislators were required to enact a National Security Law through local legislation. An attempt in 2003 failed because of mass demonstrations. Regina Ip, the Secretary for Security, resigned, which contributed to Tung Chee-hwa's resignation in 2005.

In 2012, an attempt to introduce National Education also failed because of mass demonstrations, mostly by secondary school students. It was announced by Chief Executive Donald Tsang but left to his successor, Leung Chun-ying, to implement. I was working in Hong Kong then and asked my driver to pass by the student demonstrators. I wanted to take a close look at them. The kids were dressed in black, looking serious. There was no play or laughter, only grim determination. I thought to myself that this did not portend well for the future.

In 2014, university students led the Occupy Central movement, using yellow umbrellas as a colour symbol. The demonstrations completely disrupted the delivery of goods. At Kerry Logistics, we set up an emergency service centre for our customers. In the logistics industry, one has to be resourceful and prepared to improvise. One day, a friend told me how impressed he was to see a Kerry Logistics driver pushing a trolley up a steep road because vehicles could not get through. I remember telling my staff

THE BASIC LAW
OF THE HONG KONG
SPECIAL ADMINISTRATIVE REGION
OF THE PEOPLE'S REPUBLIC OF CHINA

Article 23

The Hong Kong Special Administrative Region shall enact laws on its own to prohibit any act of treason, secession, sedition, subversion against the Central People's Government, or theft of state secrets, to prohibit foreign political organizations or bodies from conducting political activities in the Region, and to prohibit political organizations or bodies of the Region from establishing ties with foreign political organizations or bodies.

Attempt to enact the National Security Law in 2003, required by Article 23 of the Basic Law, failed as a result of mass protest

Hong Kong second Chief Executive Donald Tsang

Hong Kong third Chief Executive Leung Chun-ying

Attempt to introduce National Education in 2012 failed because of mass protest by high school students

that this was the time for us to show how good we were. Our drivers often had to open their trucks for inspection, first by the police, then by the students. We kept good relations with everyone. It reminded me how, during the mass demonstrations in Bangkok a year earlier, our delivery riders wore T-shirts of different colours to get through different parts of the city.

Putting on my political hat, however, I was worried. On the night after police fired tear gas at demonstrators, there was a DBS event at the Island Shangri-La hotel. The guest of honour was a Hong Kong minister. Before he left, he asked me what the government should do. There was no easy answer I could give him. All I said was that our own children could be among the demonstrators.

There were few casualties during Occupy Central. In fact, I was impressed by how civil both sides were. One night, after a dinner at the Island Shangri-La with two Indonesian partners, I asked them whether they would like to take a look at the student encampment, which was nearby. I knew both had been student activists in their youth. They said yes, but only if it was not unsafe. We had to climb a road divider which had been built up into a barricade, about 1.5 metres high. A young girl sat atop it. She held my hand to help me maintain my balance when I stepped across, like crossing the top of Jacob's Ladder in the Singapore Armed Forces.

When it came to one of my Indonesian partners' turn, he did not know how to react when the girl held her hand out to him. He looked at me quizzically. I shouted at him to hold her hand, which he then did. He later told me that he thought the girl wanted money from him. That afternoon, I had withdrawn a wad of cash which was in my side pocket. For a moment, I thought I ought to be more careful about being pickpocketed, but quickly realised that I could not have been in a safer place. The students were well-organised. Their backpacks were neatly stacked in one corner and water was available. In some places, they even provided chargers for those whose mobile phones had gone dry.

Occupy Central failed because the government decided to wait out the demonstrators. I was amazed how patient Hong Kongers were. Every day, my driver had to take long detours to and from my apartment at Mid-Levels, but he didn't complain. Few people did at first. But as it dragged on week after week, people got tired and the students lost support.

However, the underlying social tensions did not go away; in fact, they got worse. In 2019, over proposed amendments to the extradition law, Hong Kong society split into two and plunged into chaos. Despite repeated acts of violence, support for the demonstrators remained high.

Occupy Central in 2014 was largely peaceful

In Kerry Logistics, we had a policy that there would be no discussion on politics in the workplace. In my meetings with young colleagues, and from looking at their postings on social media, I knew that many supported the yellow faction. One evening, a young man committed suicide by jumping from a high floor in one of our warehouses. Our CEO, William Ma, reacted immediately: in the middle of the night, he played back the security camera footage, made it available for anyone to view, and put out all the information we had. Rumours were already flying and our business could have been affected.

As the situation went from bad to worse, my wife and I felt increasingly unsafe. We did not go out at night. Friends who came to our apartment for dinner left early. One evening, we were invited to dinner at Central. We were hurried out before 9:00PM. Shutters were noisily coming down everywhere and first aid units would already be in position, expecting possible injuries when the demonstrations began. At train stations and the airport, my driver would always advise me to go straight in and not dawdle. Whenever we returned to Singapore, we felt a great sense of relief and freedom. We take our sense of safety for granted until we lose it.

I was sickened by widespread support for the violence. Even when someone was burned alive, excuses were made for the perpetrator. The media added fuel to the fire by lionising the demonstrators and demonising the police. Among my close friends, we were convinced that there was foreign involvement. We kept hearing stories of money being paid out, of expensive protective equipment being freely provided and of foreign non-governmental organisations providing training and advice.

The role of American social media was insidious and decisive. One week, American social media platforms blocked pro-government news articles which they claimed had been orchestrated by China. I happened to be visiting Facebook that week and asked how that decision had been made. The local manager had invited me to speak to his staff, which I happily did, and received from them warm applause. When he looked sheepish and did not answer my question, I knew the decision was not taken in Hong Kong.

The unrest in 1998 got very violent. Foreign hands were involved.

The manipulation of social media played a big role in destabilising Hong Kong society. This was the subject I talked about when Singapore's Home Team invited me to address them in April 2020. I titled my speech: *First, Demonise the Police…*

On the night of 18 November 2019, Hong Kong Polytechnic University (PolyU), where a few hundred remaining diehard protesters were gathered, came under siege by the police. It was the demonstrators' last stand and the tense standoff was covered live on television. Many people expected the police to storm the barricades and subdue the holdouts. Many would be injured. There could be deaths.

That same evening, I had invited a group of young Hong Kongers over to my apartment for dinner. The conversation was all about PolyU, which had conferred on me a Honorary Doctorate in 2012. After dinner, one of the youths, Raymond Mak, left to join Gary Wong, Jasper Tsang (the former President of the Legislative Council) and a few others outside PolyU to see how they could help. Gary and Raymond had received a heartrending plea for help over WhatsApp from a young girl holed up in the university. They asked the police for permission to enter the campus and talk to the protesters. After consulting government leaders, the police agreed, but on the understanding that they could not ensure their safety. The campus was a war zone.

As the group crossed the barricades, arrows on the draw were pointed at them. They were shocked to find that, among the protesters, many were well-educated and a few came from well-off families. Some were girls, one only 12 years old. Eventually, they succeeded in persuading 70 of them to leave. Those below 18 were allowed to go home after registering their names. The rest were arrested. When they came out, the crowds cheered, not only those who were physically there, but all over Hong Kong by people watching the events unfolding on television.

The biggest beneficiary of the Hong Kong demonstrations was Tsai Ing-wen. Without Hong Kong, she would have lost to Han Kuo-Yu in January 2020. Meanwhile, the biggest losers were the people of Hong Kong themselves. In the short term, many Yellow and pro-Yellow Hong Kongers

First, demonise the Police...

The final stand at PolyU. Jasper Tsang and a group of young Hong Kongers took personal risk to enter the campus and persuade a number of the protesters to surrender themselves.

are leaving or will leave Hong Kong. Among young people, there is sullenness in the face of China's forceful actions to introduce and implement the National Security Law, followed by the reform of the election system upon the principle of having patriots govern Hong Kong.

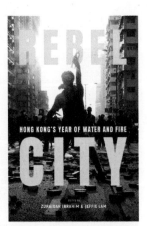

China is now 'cleaning up' Hong Kong, one institution after another — schools, political parties, newspapers, television, the universities, the legislature and the judiciary — but force cannot win China Hong Kongers' love. You cannot demand love. And without love for China, One Country, Two Systems cannot work

SCMP produced a book on its reporting during the demonstrations. I thought it lionised the demonstrators.

well. Without love for China, Hong Kongers will not be allowed to govern by themselves.

In 2020, I was invited by the South China Morning Post (SCMP) to provide an endorsement for a collection of newspaper stories written during that period. It was titled *Rebel City: Hong Kong's Year of Water and Fire*. On the cover is the silhouette of a demonstrator looking like a hero from a Marvel comic. I had to give my honest view and told the editor that what I wrote might not be appropriate for their purposes. As I half-expected, SCMP did not use it, but the editor incorporated my views into her conclusion in the book. I reproduce my comments here:

> *This collection of news articles and analytical pieces carried by SCMP from March to December 2019 records a tumultuous period in Hong Kong's history. Hong Kong society is broken with the majority of people divided into yellow and blue camps. Unlike the experience of SARS in 2003, which created a certain sense of solidarity among Hong Kong people, the current challenge of COVID-19 sees a people polarized and sullen. Even though Hong Kong people have risen well to this challenge, they attribute their*

success not to a government-led effort but to themselves. The extradition bill was not the cause of what happened last year. What the bill did was to unleash forces in Hong Kong society which had been building up over many years. One country, two systems was the brainchild of Deng Xiaoping. Under it, Hong Kong should be governed by Hong Kongers with the precondition that they must love both China and Hong Kong. During British colonial rule, it was deliberate policy not to engender love for China. Hong Kong was therefore handed over to China with a crack that ran through its entire crystal. Engendering love for China should have been a key mission after 1997. It was not. Love for China requires that its national security concerns should be addressed, that the education system should instill patriotism in the young and that glaring inequities in Hong Kong society should be overcome. Stunned by what happened in Hong Kong last year, Beijing is now determined to put right what has been neglected for over twenty years. The journalists and editors of SCMP were not detached observers of the events of 2019. They love Hong Kong but a significant number do not love China which is not surprising since many of them are permanent residents of Hong Kong but not citizens of China. Like the rest of Hong Kong, there are two camps in SCMP. What makes this book eminently readable and historically interesting is the way the romance and disappointment, the hopes and fears, and the laughters and tears of 7 million people were reported, analyzed and reflected upon through their divided lenses.

Q: Having introduced the National Security Law and 'cleaned up' Hong Kong's institutions, what will China do now?

I see China progressively introducing soft measures to win over the hearts of Hong Kongers. This will take time. China is careful that what it does should not be interpreted as weakness. They will take a hard approach initially to establish who's boss. Comprehensive measures to improve the livelihood of Hong Kongers will be taken, especially in housing, education and healthcare.

With the authority of the Chief Executive greatly strengthened by the introduction of the National Security Law and a reformed electoral system, the governance of Hong Kong is already improving. Unlike the past, ordinary Hong Kongers' concerns about welfare are coming to the fore. The big property companies and the big tycoons are seeing their influence diminish. More land is being made available for housing. China can easily transfer shallow water sea space south of Lantau to the Hong Kong Special Administrative Region (SAR), which can then be reclaimed to provide more land for housing and other amenities.

Economically, despite sanctions by the United States (US) and its allies, China can do a lot to boost Hong Kong's economy. I believe China will move into this next phase fairly quickly after the Covid-19 pandemic. There is much which needs to be done. Gradually, a healthier, more hopeful political culture in Hong Kong will come about. A sense of hope for the future is extremely important.

The question mark over One Country, Two Systems beyond 2047 has been removed. There is no longer any reason now for China not to maintain One Country, Two Systems indefinitely. To do so would be completely in China's interests. If Hong Kong becomes just another middle-size city in China, its value to the mainland is small. Hong Kong is much more valuable to China by being located outside the wall, by which I mean the literal and figurative barriers that China has built and rebuilt throughout its history to maintain its own separate identity, as I discussed in the earlier chapter on China's homogeneity.

Xi Jinping decided to impose order on Hong Kong under Chief Executive Carrie Lam in 2021 with the National Security Law

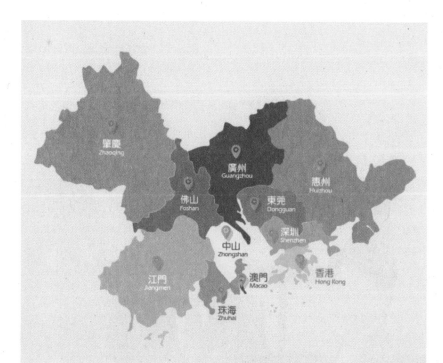

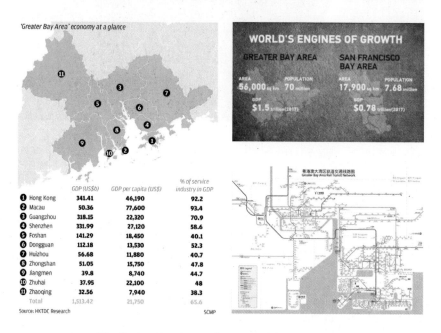

	GDP (US$b)	GDP per capita (US$)	% of service industry in GDP
❶ Hong Kong	341.41	46,190	92.2
❷ Macau	50.36	77,600	93.4
❸ Guangzhou	318.15	22,320	70.9
❹ Shenzhen	331.99	27,120	58.6
❺ Foshan	141.29	18,450	40.1
❻ Dongguan	112.18	13,530	52.3
❼ Huizhou	56.68	11,880	40.7
❽ Zhongshan	51.05	15,750	47.8
❾ Jiangmen	39.8	8,740	44.7
❿ Zhuhai	37.95	22,100	48
⓫ Zhaoqing	32.56	7,940	38.3
Total	1,513.42	21,750	65.6

Source: HKTDC Research

SCMP

The Greater Bay Area and its promise for Hong Kong

China's interactions with the outside world have always been controlled through gates, whether physically, culturally, financially or in cyberspace. In threatening times, controls are tightened. At critical moments, the gates are slammed shut. When that happens, Shanghai is inside the wall; Hong Kong is outside. In the Chinese mind, the region beyond the Great Wall, known as *saiwai* (塞外), conjures images of opportunity and instability; a region to be managed with artful diplomacy and episodic military expeditions, but never fully tamed and occasionally presenting mortal threats. This remains the way China looks at the world.

The idea of the dual circulation economy is not new. China always had a dual circulation economy with complex valves connecting the two economies. Hong Kong is one such valve. Its role in mediating the mainland's interactions with the rest of the world is a most important one. Singapore should try to play a secondary role and can best do this through twinning with Hong Kong. Hong Kong can also help Singapore gain better access to the Greater Bay Area (GBA), which is a major economic pole both for China and the rest of the world.

The GBA consists of nine cities in the Pearl River Delta (Shenzhen, Dongguan, Huizhou, Guangzhou, Foshan, Jiangmen, Zhaoxing, Zhongshan and Zhuhai) and the SARs of Hong Kong and Macao, with a combined population of over 80 million people. At 56,000 square kilometres, it is only slightly less than half the size of Peninsular Malaysia. Its combined gross domestic product was over US$1.6 trillion in 2020, about the same as Korea's.

The GBA is one of the fastest growing economic regions in the world. As the international business and financial hub for the GBA, Hong Kong will prosper with it. The Hong Kong Stock Exchange is one of the largest in the world and still growing strongly. As Chinese companies face increasing difficulties listing on the New Year Stock Exchange, more of them will do so in Hong Kong.

In 2021, China's exports grew 30%. As China's economy was the least affected by the Covid-19 pandemic globally, it produced a large part of the world's demand for manufactured goods. Ships continue to leave China full and return empty, causing international freight rates to jump manyfold.

The GBA accounts for over a third of China's exports. In 2022, both Hong Kong and China faced difficulty handling the Omicron variant of Covid-19. Hong Kong saw many fatalities. Shanghai was not prepared for it and Shanghainese were traumatized by the draconian lockdown. China's lockdown strategy is not just for Covid-19 but for possible future worse epidemics.

Hong Kong has to be dual-facing, looking inwards into China while also looking outwards to the world beyond. The Covid-19 pandemic has created an acute dilemma for Hong Kong. If its front gate is open to the world, its back gate to China will have to be tightly controlled because of China's 'dynamic zero' Covid policy. Conversely, if Hong Kong opens its back gate fully to China, its front gate will have to be tightly controlled. Hong Kong can be like Singapore or it can be like Guangzhou. There is no middle position.

China's wish is for the back gate to be fully open. I think this is for political reasons. After the troubles in 2019, China wants Hong Kongers to know which side of their bread is buttered. Despite some opposition, Chief Executive Carrie Lam was initially determined to impose 'dynamic zero' on Hong Kong too. However, this would have come at the cost of Hong Kong's links to the rest of the world. Economically, it would not be good for Hong Kong to keep the front gate closed too long. Those who needed to travel in the region increasingly found it more convenient to operate out of Singapore instead. However, no pandemic lasts forever. With the more infectious but milder Omicron variant, the end may be in sight, leaving Hong Kong to breathe easier again.

Singapore is a beneficiary of the National Security Law. Some companies have relocated to Singapore and much money has moved here. Like the period after the Tiananmen Incident, Singapore should adopt a similar approach of providing a backstop to the current outflow of talent and capital. When calm returns, there will be a returning flow to Hong Kong which will bring Singapore along with it. We remain twin cities.

Q: With the growth of Shanghai, will Hong Kong become less important to China?

They play different roles. China protects its homogeneity by building walls of all kinds to control external influences and ward off threats. The walls, in turn, have many gates. In times of concern, the gates are carefully controlled. In times of emergency, they are slammed shut. Shanghai is inside the walls while Hong Kong is outside.

China has always had need of settlements under its control outside the walls. It was for this reason that the Ming Dynasty gave Macao to the Portuguese, so that they could trade without their activities interfering with China's internal governance. The Portuguese knew that Macao should never be used as a base to endanger China. After the Ming, the Qing continued with the arrangement.

Q: Is Hong Kong a model for Taiwan?

Only in a very broad sense. One Country, Two Systems has no market in Taiwan. The historical circumstances are also very different. As the Republic of China (ROC) continues in Taiwan, including the Constitution and the symbols of state, China is still divided.

The Constitutions of both the People's Republic of China (PRC) and ROC acknowledge one China, which established the basis of the 1992 Consensus. Despite the party charter of the Democratic Progressive Party (DPP), which contains a clause on Taiwan independence, the DPP (when in power) takes its oath of office on the ROC Constitution. A desire for Taiwan independence among DPP supporters is therefore the reason why Tsai Ing-wen is unwilling to confirm the 1992 Consensus. She has publicly declared that the ROC is already independent.

With the support of all political parties, Taiwan is ending military conscription. It continues for the time being only because there are not enough Taiwanese who want to become professional soldiers. This is telling. It means that without US support, the Taiwanese people are generally not prepared to bear arms and fight reunification by the mainland.

Beijing has repeatedly said that, on the basis of the 1992 Consensus, it is prepared to negotiate on all matters, including Taiwan being allowed to keep its own army. If reunification is achieved by peaceful negotiation, Taiwan could potentially enjoy a much higher degree of autonomy than Hong Kong. Many Taiwanese, however, are unlikely to trust the mainland's promises. Such trust will take time to establish. How China handles One Country, Two Systems in the coming years will be carefully watched in Taiwan.

China is in fact One Country, Many Systems. It has always been so because of the size and diversity of the country. The whole of Hainan Island, for example, has become a free port. By 2025, there will be movement controls across the Hainan Strait to permit a different economic system to operate across the entire province. Tibet and Xinjiang also operate separate systems because of their ethnic minority populations. So long as ultimate political power is not threatened, Beijing takes a permissive approach because it is good for the country. *Tianxia* (天下) is vast. China has always operated on the basis of one *tianxia*, many systems.

Q: Are you optimistic for Hong Kong?

Yes, Hong Kong will rise with the tide in China and the GBA. However, this is provided Hong Kongers are clear about the fundamental situation — which they should have been in 1997. Before the handover, I contributed a piece to a compilation of essays edited by Michael Chugani, titled *Hong Kong 1997: Before, After*. I wrote, rather bluntly:

> *As long as Hong Kong serves the interest of China, it will work and it will be allowed to work. China will leave it as it is. Hong Kong is not and will not be an independent country, so whatever civic participation is allowed in Hong Kong must be within the framework of the Basic Law and within the framework of what China allows. The first thing is to recognise what the necessities are, and to work within those necessities. If this is done, then there is a lot of freedom.*

You can do whatever you want. But if those necessities are not recognised, then your freedom will cause damage to Hong Kong society. One area which is very clear is of course that Hong Kong must not subvert China. Whatever democratic practices you have must be based on that. You cannot cross that boundary. …But if Hong Kong people begin to take up cudgels on behalf of their American friends and start berating China from the SAR, then I find it hard to believe that the Chinese will do nothing about it.

In July 2020, after delivering a speech at Hwa Chong Institution on the occasion of Hwa Chong's 100th anniversary, I was asked about my views on the unrest in Hong Kong. In my answer, I used a metaphor from *Journey to the West*: however much Wukong (the monkey god) tries, he cannot leave the Buddha's palm. To keep Wukong in check, the Monk puts a band around Wukong's head. Whenever he chants a prayer, the band tightens, giving Wukong a terrible headache. In this way, Wukong learns to behave.

Wukong is of course a hero in the quest for the sutras. Without his help, the Monk — Xuanzang, whose exploits in India I described in an earlier chapter — might not be able to accomplish his mission. Meanwhile, the character of Wukong was probably based on Hanuman. My Hong Kong friends were amused by the metaphor I used. Every Chinese child knows of Wukong and wants to be like him. Hong Kongers are resourceful and resilient. These qualities, which gave so much trouble to China, are the same qualities which will help it under One Country, Two Systems.

Once the basis of One Country, Two Systems is firmly embedded in Hong Kong's political culture, a new kind of Hong Kong democracy will gradually emerge. Beijing will not be averse to this. China's objective is for Hong Kongers to govern Hong Kong themselves, on the basis of loving Hong Kong and loving China. A new generation of promising young Hong Kong political leaders are cutting their teeth. During periods of turmoil, there was no middle ground because society was polarised, but this is now wide open. More young Hong Kongers who want to take Hong Kong's future in their own hands should step forward.

Louis Cha. When he died, the entire Chinese nation mourned.

All this will take time, of course. I called on Louis Cha (Jin Yong 金庸) a few times in the early 1990s during my visits to Hong Kong in connection with the Approval-in-Principle (AIP) scheme. He was the editor of *Ming Pao*. When I first went to the *Ming Pao* office, facing me as I walked into the main entrance was a big picture of the man standing in front of a tank at Tiananmen Square. Jin Yong was devastated by the crackdown and subsequently took up French citizenship. The French had honoured him for his writings. All the same, Jin Yong was a profound man and his heart remained deeply Chinese. Beijing never gave up on him.

A few years later, he told me that he was building a house by the West Lake in Hangzhou on land set aside for him by the Chinese government. I visited the house when it was completed. It had separate suites for Jin Yong and his wife. He told me that it would become a museum of his works after his death. After reading the first English translation of his most popular book, *The Legend of the Condor Heroes*, I thought of visiting him again in 2018. Unfortunately, he was too ill and passed away not long afterwards. When he died, China's top leaders wrote touching tributes. No Chinese writer has been so widely read.

I do not believe the wounds in Hong Kong are beyond healing. They will, as they did for Jin Yong. Many Hong Kongers who leave will come back eventually, as they did in earlier times of trouble.

In 1557, Macao was leased to the Portuguese by Ming China as a trading post on payment of an annual rent. The arrangement continued into the Qing Dynasty until 1887, when Portugal wrested perpetual rights in Macao under the Sino-Portuguese Treaty of Peking. After the Carnation Revolution in 1974, Portugal wanted to return Macao to China. Beijing asked Lisbon to wait till the handover of Hong Kong. Macao was therefore an early experiment in One Country, Two Systems. Portugal understood that Macao's status could only be maintained on one key condition: that it did not allow Macao to be a threat to China. Whatever happened on the mainland, Macao must look the other way and not become involved.

The British stuck to the same principle in Hong Kong and never allowed any country to use the city against China. It was only in the last few years before 1997 that that policy was deliberately disregarded. When the British left Hong Kong, they shut down the Special Branch and took the files away with them, leaving the Hong Kong police with no internal security capabilities. This did not happen when the British left Malaya and Singapore.

Under the Portuguese in Macao and the British in Hong Kong, the Catholic Church flourished. Catholic schools played a major role in educating future leaders and Catholic institutions provided a wide array of social services. Catholic religious orders are now pawing the ground looking forward to the day they can return to China. This will not happen so easily. The Vatican takes a prudent approach, never forgetting to give to Caesar what is Caesar's and reserving for itself only the things that belong to God. Only bishops who are not antagonistic towards China can be appointed.

After leaving the Kuok Group, my wife and I bought an apartment near the University of Hong Kong. We attend Sunday Mass at a nearby chapel which serves the community of the university's Ricci Hall, which was established by the Jesuits in 1929. At its entrance are portraits of Matteo Ricci (Li Madou) and Xu Guangqi, the first Chinese minister to be baptised. The complex relationship between the Catholic Church and China from

Calling on China's representative in Macao

The new bridge from Hong Kong to Macao, the longest crossing in the world

the time of Matteo Ricci is a fascinating story and an inspiration for this century. A musical on Matteo Ricci's life was produced in Hong Kong a few years ago. My wife and I were moved by it.

Hong Kong is also playing an interesting role in the current dynamics between China and the Vatican. On 1 October 2021, the China Liaison Office in Hong Kong and China's State Administration for Religious Affairs organised a historic meeting of three leading Catholic bishops and 15 other religious leaders from China, and 15 senior Hong Kong clergymen on Zoom. The private meeting was not publicised, but news of it leaked out a few months later.

In my next series of musings, I will begin with some reflections on the complex but improving relations between China and the Vatican.

Matteo Ricci and Xu Guangqi at the University of Hong Kong Ricci Hall chapel. An excellent musical of his life was recently produced.

Index

I

J

K

Recommended Title

George Yeo on Bonsai, Banyan and the Tao
edited by Asad-ul Iqbal Latif and Huay Leng Lee

ISBN: 978-981-4696-37-1 (box-set)
ISBN: 978-981-4518-69-7
ISBN: 978-981-4520-50-8 (pbk)